Brian Lane came to writing through fine art, experimental music and the theatre. His long-standing preoccupation with the consequences of violent death led to the theatre production of his *Red Roses for Lorca*. After working for the United Nations in Geneva and Vienna, he returned to Britain to found the Murder Club, compiling the eight-volume series 'The Murder Club Regional Guides to Great Britain'. In 1991 he wrote *The Butchers*, also available in the True Crime Series.

D1322410

Also by Brian Lane

The Butchers

THE ENCYCLOPEDIA
OF CRUEL
AND UNUSUAL
PUNISHMENT

Brian Lane

First published in Great Britain in 1993 by
True Crime
an imprint of Virgin Publishing Ltd
332 Ladbroke Grove
London W10 5AH

A catalogue record for this title is available from
the British Library

ISBN 0 86369 670 8

Typeset by Intype, London
Printed and bound in Great Britain by
Cox & Wyman Ltd, Reading, Berks

The Encyclopedia
of Cruel and
Unusual Punishment

INTRODUCTION

This is a study of cruelty; often cruelty of an inconceivable magnitude and wickedness – not simply by one man against another, but by whole nations against their own and other people. It is also an indictment of the single species on the face of this earth that has systematically institutionalised the infliction of pain as a means of punishment and coercion. A succession of oppressors have sought to justify their acts of torture in many different ways – sometimes it is simply revenge; or it may have its goal in trying to force others to change their views on politics or religion. It may be a means of forcing a victim to part with his possessions. Frequently, torture is a device implemented to extract information or force a confession of real or fabricated misdemeanours.

The use of torture has been known in virtually every culture, in every country of the world; it has been described as a 'gangrene' which has eaten away humankind's claim to civilisation. Far from being a comfortably distant relic of the Dark Ages, enshrined in Gothic fantasy, far from being an instrument of fear long since discarded by an increasingly sophisticated society, torture is still regularly used as a tool of legal and political terror in more than sixty countries around the world.

The purpose of a study such as this, distressing as the subject undeniably is, is to provide information. Information of a kind which is vital to an understanding of the social history and development of human nature – for over the years during which I have waded through the most chilling records of inhumanity, I have been uncomfortably aware that punishment, and even torture, is fundamental to the human condition. There will, inevitably, be those who would prefer that these closets remain unopened, the skeletons they contain remain unrattled. There will be those, even, who would seek to deny the right of others to examine, without fear or favour, the darkest corners of their own histories, preferring instead that heads should be firmly buried in the sand. Often these detractors imagine that by turning their backs on the frightful and the obscene they become invested with some moral superiority. In effect the reverse is true, because ignoring this problem not only fails to effect change, but worse still plays into the hands of the torturers by implying approval.

For the benefit of other researchers into this difficult subject, I am sure that Peter Benenson, redoubtable founder of Justice, would not object to my quoting briefly from his introduction to *Gangrene*, a study of the official use of torture in Algeria and Kenya during the late 1950s (John Calder, 1959); 'This book is about the ill-treatment of prisoners. It contains passages which will revolt, nauseate and disgust. It will produce a flare of anger in most of its readers. Some will be angry against the men who allegedly treated fellow human beings with such brutality; others will be angry that allegations of this sort are raised in print against public servants carrying out difficult duties in periods of stress. The greatest display of fury will probably come, as so often happens, from those who have not read the book, but rely on garbled accounts.'

Torture vs Punishment

But the laws are promulgated so that out of fear of them, human wickedness may be held in check, and purity among the upright may be safeguarded, whereas among the wicked, fear of punishment may restrain their disposition to cause harm or injury.

Although these aims were embodied in the Teutonic written legal code, the *Lex Baiuvariorum*, as long ago as the middle of the eighth century, the principles remain both relevant to contemporary views on addressing the problem of crime, and have also become internationally accepted standards. Indeed, it might almost be said that most fields of human endeavour are informed by the twin expectancies of reward and punishment. Just as it is confidently hoped that rewarding the good child and penalising the naughty will engender a growing respect for society's prevailing ethics and codes, so it is believed that this process can continue to be imposed in adult life to ensure social stability. Here, the rewards and punishments are also of a practical and a psychological nature – the good citizen becomes a trusted employee, loving spouse and parent, respected neighbour, and so can expect to reap both financial and spiritual rewards. The miscreant earns the disapprobation of the community, and is penalised by the loss of his money, his liberty or, in some cases, his life.

However, it becomes clear that only if punishment is administered appropriately can it act as a deterrent to further offending. And this is the key to at least one major area of debate over the point at which punishment becomes 'torture' or 'inhuman punishment'. Punishment must always match the severity of the crime tempered with the mitigation of the circumstances. This was highlighted as recently as the beginning of the nineteenth century in England, when 222 offences were punishable by death. Men, women and children, often living in very depressed circumstances, could be executed for the most trivial misdemeanour; and so, on the *literal* principle that it was as well to be hung for a sheep as a lamb, crime escalated. During the days of public executions it was the great irony that the crowds gathered beneath the gallows to witness the event provided excellent prey for the pickpockets who, if they were caught, would likely be the subjects of the next spectacle.

These principles do not, though, take account of either punishment which is so cruel and inhuman as to be excessive for the prevailing legal requirement, or where pain and degradation are imposed for entirely 'non-legal' motives, such as coercing individuals or groups to alter their political or religious beliefs, or as a means of extracting information. Furthermore, the words 'torture' and 'punishment' are both evocative and, to a large extent, subjective. For example what might in less civilised societies be considered appropriate *punishment*, might in others seem unjustifiably cruel; a case in point might be the way in which we of the developed western world view with horror the Muslim religious punishments of *shari'a*, under which thieves can have hands and feet judicially amputated, and those convicted of adultery be subjected to stoning to death. Of course this tends to be less obvious when comparisons are made between ancient and modern civilisations. The early Romans, for instance, were ingenious at devising, and ruthless in inflicting, some of history's most cruel and unusual punishments; however, particularly in the case of non-freemen, suffering, hardship and often ill-treatment were life's expectation, and this brutalising effect was manifest in the great affection in which the citizens of Rome held the worst excesses of the **Roman Circus** and gladiatorial games. In this present century, parts of the Southern states of America are still very depressed and living conditions comparatively harsh, especially in the poor rural areas. Crimes of violence are the highest in the nation, and lynching has still not been entirely eradicated. It is no surprise, then, that Texas, high on the league table of homicide states, is at the top of the statistical graph with far and away the highest number of judicial executions carried out every year – executions which not infrequently result in the most agonising and sordid deaths for the prisoner (see **Electric Chair**, **Gas Chamber** and **Lethal Injection**).

It will be obvious from a moment's reflection that a definition of torture is in many ways a subjective exercise based on individual experience. If torture were a thing of the ancient past, this analysis could be safely left to the historians and academics; but torture is a very real threat in many of the world's *contemporary* societies, and in order to appreciate both the scale of the problem and the way in which it might be tackled, there is a requirement to distinguish what might constitute punishment as a legal instrument of retribution and deterrence and what amounts to torture and cruel and unusual punishment. It was not until 1975 that the United Nations took the initiative in attempting a legal definition of torture, which was embodied in Article 1 of the UN Declaration Against Torture; the relevant clause reads:

> For the purpose of this Declaration, torture means any act by which severe pain or suffering, whether physical or mental, is intentionally inflicted by or at the instigation of a public official on a person for such purposes as obtaining from him or a third person information or confession, punishing him for an act he has committed, or intimidating him or other persons.

This book will indicate just how accurate this definition has been, both historically and in the modern world.

The Psychology of Torture

From the iniquities committed by the emperor Nero against the newly emerging and basically passive Christians, down the ages to the continuing oppression of their peoples by unstable military and civil governments and their agents throughout the modern world, the justification for the use of repressive methods has remained in essence the same – the necessity to protect the security of the state's *status quo*. Although the question of exactly who needs protection from whom is in most cases arguable and purely subjective, this proposes a 'rational' – one could almost say obligatory – function of any government. Where society has a right to express alarm is when the infliction of punishment extends beyond – often far beyond – the requirements of that function, and becomes cruel and inhuman treatment – torture. Where the concept of 'justice' becomes confused with 'revenge', or where legitimate reactions to preserve national security are exchanged for programmes for the suppression of political freedom, or when the evangelical zeal of one religious faith becomes the persecution of another.

We must be particularly cautious of the psychological motives of the 'dictator' (in all senses of that description), for despite protestations that he is adhering to the abstract concepts of freedom and justice, he can invariably be unmasked as one whose view of these two fundamental rights is a very personal and self-seeking one. These men never work alone, and it is plain to see how the regime – whether the result of a modern African military coup or English religious bigotry in the seventeenth century – gives its political, military, security and religious authorities an equally self-seeking motive for the enactment of certain laws and the sanctioning of certain behaviour. For example, it is unlikely that any official executioner has ever entered his 'craft' for the purely altruistic reason of administering 'justice'; rather, he is a paid servant of the state, carrying out that state's *law*, which is too often very different from *justice*.

Although it is written in the language of a former age, George Ryley Scott offers useful analogies in his *History of Corporal Punishment*:

If one wishes to get within measurable distance of the truth, it is well that one should throw overboard the notion that such a thing as pure unalloyed altruism exists. The good which anyone does is almost always incidental and, in a sense, is forced upon one as an inevitable concomitant of what one does for some purpose quite removed from this much-trumpeted but actually subsidiary act of goodness. Birds, by eating up the slugs, give beneficial aid to the farmer, but do not in consequence preen themselves on the good work they are doing on behalf of the Almighty. The farmer chants their praises, but the moment the seeds have been planted he puts up ridiculous images in an effort to scare away his one-time allies; and if he sees a solitary sparrow investigating this sacred territory he curses it to all eternity and reaches for his gun. The cat kills mice, and there are those who hold that the good Lord made the animal for this special purpose; but with equal glee it kills, if it gets the chance, the canary and the chicken – pastimes which the birds' owner is inclined to view rather differently. Similarly the basic motive which leads men and women, in the overwhelming main, to do this and to promote that, to combat evils, to institute reforms, have nothing whatever to do with avowed objects. Any success which is achieved is, in reality, subsidiary to a main basic, but hidden or obscured, objective.

History of Torture

In strictly chronological terms, torture does not have a separate history; rather it is an activity inextricable from the social activities of the human race. It has often been claimed that the human is a naturally cruel animal, and both as a historian and as an observer of contemporary life and crime I have little reason to disagree – certainly the research for this book has shown man to pass up few opportunities to inflict discomfort on his fellows.

It began as a pastime of our primitive ancestors when they felt the need to protect their vulnerable social groups from neighbouring, warring tribes by means of fear. The abuse of prisoners taken as a result of inter-tribal battles would serve as a warning to other potential enemies; it would also strengthen *intra*-tribal bonding by giving expression to a commonly shared hatred and resentment. For this reason death was too good for an enemy; first he had to suffer – usually by being *tortured* to death. It is entirely conceivable that those tortures were the direct ancestors of our own – mutilation, burning, beating with sticks and whips, stoning, and so on.

Wrongdoers *within* the social unit were probably treated in much the same manner, as enemies, to be punished in such a way that they would never forget; or, if they were sentenced to lose their lives, to lose them in a way nobody else would forget. These executions would not merely be public, but ceremonial occasions, and the atmosphere of the carnival was passed down until less than two centuries ago. Indeed, in China today public executions are regarded as popular spectator events – in August 1991 thirteen prisoners were put on public trial in the city of Kunming's main sports stadium; they were found guilty and immediately executed before an enthusiastic audience of some 10,000 people. And lest we are tempted to mutter darkly about uncivilised orientals, it should be recalled that in the same year San Francisco television station KQED was fighting a legal battle for the right to broadcast the state of California's next execution – live from the death chamber.

In other words, if the punishment is to have the deterrent effect claimed for it, then it must be carried out in such a way that people might be directly deterred. Ironically, for opposite reasons, many of those who believed in the abolition of capital punishment also thought that executions should be carried out in public, arguing that such a disgraceful spectacle would eventually sicken people and cause them to press for abolition. At street level, sadly, this did not prove the case, and public executions continued to draw large crowds until abolished in their respective countries (see **Execution Diary**).

Apart from revenge and punishment, torture was also extensively used among early peoples in connection with pagan sacrifice, where the most likely way of propitiating a powerful god was thought to be shedding human blood. To offer but one example, it is recorded that sacrifices to the Mexican Aztec god Tezcatepoca were laid face up along the sacrificial altar, and while the victim was pinioned by priests, the high priest quickly slit open his chest and pulled out his still-beating heart.

Although the subject rarely complained, what might be called cruel and unusual treatment was also inflicted on young tribesmen during initiation ceremonies (see **Venomous Gloves**). One of the best known of all rights of initiation was that of the Mandan tribe of North America;

readers may remember it as the ordeal undergone by the young white man (played by Richard Harris) in the film *A Man Called Horse*. The ritual was described by George Catlin in his 1841 study of the customs of native Americans:

> The initiate placed himself on his hands and feet; an inch or more of the flesh of each shoulder or each breast was taken up between the thumb and finger by a man who held in his right hand the knife, which had been ground sharp on both edges, and then hacked and notched with the blade to make it produce as much pain as possible, was forced through the flesh below the fingers, and being withdrawn, was followed with a splint or skewer from another man, who held a bunch of each in his left hand, and was ready to force them through the wound. There were then two cords lowered from the top of the lodge (by men who were placed on the [roof of the] lodge outside for the purpose), which were fastened to these splints or skewers, and they instantly began to haul him up. He was thus raised until his body was suspended from the ground where he rested, until the knife and a splint were passed through the flesh or integuments in a similar manner in each arm below the shoulder, below the elbow, and below the knees. Each one was then raised with the cords until the weight of his body was suspended by them, and then while the blood was streaming down their limbs, the by-standers hung upon the splints each man's appropriate shield, bow, quiver, etc.

Apart from these diversions, the history of torture followed a simple evolutionary pattern whereby motives, methods and justifications remained fairly constant, while 'improvements' and sophistications took place in some of the hardware used. Under the Greeks and the Romans, torture and cruel means of slow execution flourished; in particular, the reader will find frequent references to the ingenuity of the ancient Roman torturers.

The advent of Christianity is mistakenly believed to have heralded a new era of pacifism; in reality the Christians retained the Hebrew doctrine of retribution ('an eye for an eye . . .') and added to that what they had learned from their Roman persecutors. The burning alive of heretics which was to characterise centuries of Christian oppression can be traced back to the Gospel of Saint Matthew (chapter 13; verses 41–2): 'The Son of man shall send forth his angels, and they shall gather out of his kingdom all things that offend, and them which do iniquity; and shall cast them into a furnace of fire: there shall be wailing and gnashing of teeth.'

The iniquitous, of course, soon came to mean anybody not strictly adhering to the doctrines of the Church of Rome, and from these modest beginnings Christianity spread a reign of religious terror and intolerance over a large part of the globe, which has not ended to this day – historically, it included the Crusades (against that other church of intolerance, Islam), the Papal Inquisitions, the Spanish Inquisition, the witch persecutions, the persecution of the Albigenses, the Waldenses, Protestants and Knights Templar. Protestants in their turn persecuted the Roman Catholics and the Quakers; and Protestants and Papists tortured each other to death in Ireland (and still do). References to religious oppression will be found throughout this volume, but to elaborate on just one representative campaign of terror, the history of the witch persecutions follows on page 13.

Judicial and penal torture kept pace with religious oppression, and as the Roman laws codified by the Emperor Justinian were carried throughout Europe and beyond by the spread of the Holy Roman Empire, so did the predeliction for helping the process of judicial inquiry with torture. This trend was enthusiastically maintained until the sixteenth and even seventeenth centuries. It was also customary during the period of the **Inquisitions** for much of the responsibility for capital sentences to be shouldered by the secular authorities. Although the Inquisition, and in particular the Spanish Inquisition, had a deserved reputation for its oppressive search for heretics and sorcerers, in the interest of balance it should be emphasised that few of the basic instruments of torture used during that dark age of persecution were particularly novel, and nor were many custom-built for the Inquisition's purposes. For a start, the religious authorities rarely had their own 'trained' executioners and torturers: they were simply hired from the secular prisons to do ecclesiastical work. It is true that the Inquisition had its own prisons – called 'secret' prisons – where accused heretics could spend years awaiting trial, but the ecclesiastical authorities had no power to execute prisoners who had been found guilty of serious heretical offences. This accorded with the Roman Catholic doctrine of *Ecclesia non novit sanguinem* ('The Church is untainted with blood'). When the Church had, with greater or lesser degrees of torture, secured a prisoner's confession, and when that confession had been accepted by the Inquisitor and the Holy Office, sentence was passed at the *auto-da-fé* and it fell to the lot of the civil authorities to carry out sentence of death by burning; after all, failing to do so would amount to favouring heretics.

Parallel to the spread of torture Roman-style throughout Europe, Asia was developing its own imaginative palette of cruelty.

Although there were some ingenious new forms of torture, most of the Chinese instruments were variations of western devices such as the rack and the **Spanish boot**; the following is a seventeenth-century description of the *kia quen*, an alternative 'boot': 'For the feet there is an instrument called *kia quen*, being three strips of wood put in a traverse block in which the middle strip is fixed; the other two are loose, and between them the feet are put and squeezed against the centre block till the heel bones are forced into the foot.' The cangue was a form of **halter**, or neck **pillory**, and the excruciating form of **flagellation** known as **bastinado** was also known in the west and, under the name *falaka*, is still in use in some countries of the world today. A form of mutilation causing death was the **Death by the Thousand Cuts**, unique to the orient (the similar 'death by the twenty-one cuts' was current in Japan). **Hara-kiri**, execution by suicide, was entirely confined to Japan.

Torture was widespread in India throughout its history, and as in other parts of Asia most of the early forms developed concurrently with similar methods throughout the world – bastinado and other forms of flagellation were common, as were the stocks, water and fire ordeals, branding, and the rack. The frightful *kittee* appears to have been a cross between the Chinese *kia quen* and the European **thumbscrew**: two wooden blocks, placed either side of some sensitive part of the body – ears, fingers, feet, genitals – were squeezed together until the victim passed out through sheer pain; repeated use of this torture resulted in disfigurement and even, in some instances, death. Ryley Scott quotes a passage from a publication of 1813, of which I have been unable to trace the original. In *Oriental Memoirs*, James Forbes relates this curious incident in Tattah:

> The collector of customs was a Hindoo of family, wealth and credit. Lulled into security from his interest at court, and suspecting no evil, he was surprised by a visit from the vizier, with a company of armed men, to demand his money; which being secreted no threatenings could induce him to discover. A variety of tortures were inflicted to extort a confession; one was a sofa with a platform of tight cordage in a network, covered with a chintz palampore, which concealed a bed of thorns placed under it. The collector, a corpulent banian, was then stripped of his jama, or muslin robe, and ordered to lie down on the couch; the cords bending with his weight the man sunk onto the bed of thorns. These long and piercing thorns of the baubul, or

forest acacia, were placed purposely with their points upwards and lacerated the wretched man whether in motion or at rest. For two days and nights he bore the torture without revealing his secret, and his tormentors, fearing he would die before their purpose was effected, had recourse to another mode of compulsion. When life was nearly exhausted, they took their captive from the bed and supported him on the floor while his infant son, an only child, was brought into the room, and with him a bag containing a wild cat. They put the child into the bag with the animal and tied the mouth of the sack. The agents of cruelty stood over it with bamboos, ready at a signal to beat the bag and enrage the animal to destroy the child. This was too much for a father's heart, and he produced his treasure.

The Witch Persecutions

Fear of sorcery, because it is a simple fear of the unknown, is as old as humankind, and there are accounts of malevolent 'witches', supposed to be in league with the 'devil', from the earliest written records. It was necessary for our earliest ancestors to arrive at some understanding of the bewildering universe in which they found themselves, and this resulted in the deification of then inexplicable natural phenomena. Gods and spirits were believed to rule the earth and heavens, and it became essential for society's continued prosperity and safety that rituals of thanksgiving be exercised to propitiate these powerful forces – after all, if the sun was not offered sacrifice it might feel disinclined to rise one morning. So much is primitive logic. It was also inevitable that individuals possessed by greed or malevolence should seek to harness these supernatural powers for themselves with the purpose of influencing human affairs; indeed, one definition of sorcery describes 'an attempt to control nature, to produce good or evil results, generally by the aid of evil spirits'. So rudimentary was this motivation that similar manifestations of 'sorcery' could be found concurrently throughout the inhabited world. But if the desire to tap into unknown worlds in order to gain reward or avenge jealousy was understandable, so was the fear and mistrust of those individuals and groups who sought to harness the dark spirits. There developed a range of punishment appropriate to the various degrees of sorcery, though it must be emphasised that such activities were officially regarded as nuisance rather than crime; only causing death or widespread destruction by magic was punishable by death. And so until the end of the thirteenth century, in Europe at least, fear of sorcery was connected with common folklore and pagan superstition.

It was in the first decade of the fourteenth century that the Church intervened, and set in motion what was to become a continent-wide drive to exterminate sorcery. The Church Council held at Treves in 1310 declared that divination, conjuration and such like were forbidden, and later, power was granted to punish these acts with excommunication – a considerable threat in more orthodoxly Christian times, when Hell was a very real place and strict adherence to the faith was the only salvation from fire and brimstone. As the power of the Church increased so did its proportionate influence on the secular authorities, and statutes began to be enacted giving agencies the power to punish witchcraft. This also coincided with the enlargement of the scope of the Inquisition to weed out not only heretics, but witches. In 1257 Pope Alexander IV had been asked to include sorcery, but he agreed only insofar as that sorcery arose out of heresy. This was confirmed in 1333 by Pope John XXII, but by a Papal Bull of Innocent VIII in 1484, the Inquisition was empowered to suppress witchcraft. Two years later, Innocent's chief Inquisitors, Sprenger and Kramer, published the first edition of their notorious *Malleus Maleficarum*, or 'Hammer of Witches', which for the first time formalised the procedure for hunting, trying, torturing and punishing witches. It was followed by a succession of other, similar tracts as witch mania spread throughout Europe.

In 1532 Emperor Charles V personally directed the

persecution of witches throughout the Holy Roman Empire, and by 1585 the Bull *Coeli et terrae creator* of Pope Sixtus V officially denounced all forms of sorcery – divination, astrology, incantation, summoning demons, etcetera, which had already, in cases where harm resulted, become punishable by burning alive. In Germany, for the easier identification of witches, lists of characteristics were being drawn up, including bleary eyes and red hair, non-observance of holy days, and an aversion to men. In addition, ordeals such as **ducking**, **pricking** and **swimming** were in use to determine the 'truth' of allegations and sorcery.

The English writer William Perkins (*Discourse on the Damned Art of Witchcraft*, 1608) offered these 'certaine signes whereby the partie may be discovered guilty':

1. Notorious defamation is a common report of the greater sort of people with whom the suspect dwelleth, that he or she is a witch. This yieldeth a strong suspicion.
2. If a fellow-witch or magician give testimony of any person to be a witch, either voluntary or at his or her examination, or at his or her death.
3. If after cursing there followeth death, or at least some mischief; for witches are wont to practice their mischievous acts by cursing and banning.
4. If after enmity, quarrelling, or threatening, a present mischief doth follow.
5. If the party suspected be the son or daughter, the manservant or maidservant, the familiar friend, the near neighbour, or old companion of a known and convicted witch.
6. If the party suspected be found to have the devil's mark [see **Pricking**].
7. If the party examined be inconstant or contrary to himself in his deliberate answers.

In 1597, James VI of Scotland (later James I of England), himself possessing an almost paranoid fear of sorcery, published his *Demonologie* to further swell the existing literature on practical witch-hunting. In it, James outlines 'God's' method of discovering witches:

The fearful abounding at this time and in this country of these detestable slaves of the devil, the witches or enchanters, hath moved me, beloved reader, to despatch in post this following treatise of mine, not in any wise, as I protest, to serve for a show of mine own learning and ingenue, but only (moved to conscience) to press thereby, so far as I can, to resolve the doubting hearts of many, both that such assaults of Satan are most certainly pract-ised, and that the instrument thereof merits most severely to be punished, against the damnable opinions of two, principally in our age; whereof the one called Scot, an Englishman, is not ashamed in public print to deny that there can be such a thing as witchcraft, and so maintains the old error of the Sadducees* in denying of spirits. The other called Wierus, a German physician, sets out a public apol-ogy for all these craftsfolk, whereby procuring for them impunity, he plainly betrays himself to be of that same profession. Witches ought to be put to death according to the laws of God, the civil and the imperial law, and the municipal law of all Christian nations: Yea, to spare the life, and not strike whom God bids strike, and so severely punish in so odious a treason against God, is not only unlawful, but doubtless as great a sin in the magistrate as was Saul's sparing Agag.

Two good helps may be used: the one is the find-ing of their mark, and the trying the insensibleness thereof; the other is their floating on the water — for, as in secret murder, if the dead carcass be at

*A Jewish sect who denied the existence of angels and spirits, and also rejected the concept of punishment in an afterlife and the resurrection of the body.

any time thereafter handled by the murderer, it will gush out blood, as if the blood were crying to Heaven for the revenge of the murderer (God having appointed that secret supernatural sign for the trial of that secret unnatural crime), so it appears that God hath appointed (for a supernatural sign of the monstrous impiety of witches) that the water shall refuse to receive them in her bosom that hath shaken off them the sacred water of baptism, and wilfully refused the benefit thereof – no, not so much as their eyes are able to shed tears (threaten and torture them as you might), while first they repent (God not permitting them to dissemble their obstinacy in so horrible a crime); albeit the women-kind especially, be able otherwise to shed tears at every light occasion when they will, yea, although it were dissembling like the crocodiles.

It is worth noting that it was to 'flatter' King James that Shakespeare wrote *Macbeth*, with its brooding backdrop of witchcraft and sorcery.

Ludovicus of Paramo, in his *De Origine et Progressu Officii Sanctae Inquisitionis* of 1598, estimated that between the years 1450 and 1598, at least 30,000 people had been burned as witches by the Inquisition. But by this time the Inquisition, having initiated the suppression of witchcraft as heresy, had lost control of it to a general hysteria for the eradication of all forms of sorcery, real or imagined; it is no coincidence that the activities of this period have been called the 'great witch delusion'.

By the Middle Ages, the suppression of political dissent was also managed by the threat of witch hunts, and then with the decline of feudalism the witch mania reached its height and began to decline with the new spirit of commercial and political enlightenment. As Robbins reasoned (*Encyclopedia of Witchcraft and Demonology*): 'Businessmen could not put up with a world in which commercial agreements could be capriciously nullified at the whisper of heresy.' He also offered a rough guide to

the last dates on which executions were carried out for
the crime of sorcery: Netherlands 1610, England 1684,
America 1692, Scotland 1727, France 1745, Germany
1775, Switzerland 1782, Poland 1793; and Italy commuted
a death sentence in 1791.

That witches were still nevertheless persecuted to death
in England at the beginning of the eighteenth century is
proved by this account of the sad destruction of one Amy
Townsend:

> We are informed from St Albans [Hertfordshire]
> that one Amy Townsend, who lay under the misfor-
> tune of being a reputed witch, about ten days since,
> going by a watchmaker's shop in that town, asked
> the price of a watch. The apprentice caught her up
> short by stating: 'What is it to you? The forty shill-
> ings is more than you are worth.' At which it was
> observed she only pointed at the boy with her finger,
> and went about her business. Her manner struck
> the apprentice with great terror of the hag and her
> reputation, and the next day he fell sick, keeping
> to his bed and accusing that Amy Townsend had
> bewitched him. Further he claimed he should die if
> he did not immediately take blood from her, and
> the wretched woman was brought to the boy's cham-
> ber. He, in some anger, leaped from his bed and
> sank his fingernails into old Amy's face, drawing
> blood. The boy recovered on the instant and the
> unfortunate woman was turned out to tend her
> wounds as best she could.
>
> It became rumoured about the town that Amy
> Townsend had bewitched the apprentice lad, and it
> was decided that she should be punished in like.
> Consequently the old woman was dragged forcibly
> to a river outside the town and, with ropes, dragged
> back and forth through it as they did witches; so
> much that the woman would have surely expired
> had not some more enlightened citizens returned
> her to her cottage and bed.

Some observers of the Swimming declared that they saw Amy float, in short, that she was a witch, and at this an enraged population dragged the crone from her sick-bed and once more to face ordeal, this time before the magistrate who, in order to calm the passions of the mob, confined her in a cell beneath the court where inside two hours she died.

The last news we have is that at the Hertfordshire assizes next, there are several due to appear who may meet a judicial death for their part in the ducking and its awful consequence.

Torture, in one form or another, was always inseparable from the 'discovery' of witches. In order for them to be legally punished the accused had either to be proved guilty by some ordeal such as ducking or pricking, or by confession. Given that most of these hapless women (though there were some men, and children too) were entirely innocent of any dark dabbling, they were hardly likely to confess themselves to the stake without considerable coercion:

Do but imagine a poor old creature, under all the weaknesses and infirmities of old age, set like a fool in the middle of a room, with a rabble of ten towns round about her house, then her legs tied in a cross so that all the weight of her body might rest on her seat. By this means, after some hours the circulation of the blood would become stopped, and her sitting would be as painful as on the Wooden Horse. So she must continue in pain for twenty-four hours with neither sleep nor meat, and since this was their ungodly way of trial what wonder was it that they confessed any tales asked of them, and much beside. (*Essay Concerning Witchcraft*, Francis Hutchinson, 1718)

Further torture might then be used to encourage the suspect to name other people as accomplices, and again many innocent names are sure to have been given in response to the torturer's persuasive questioning, thus ensuring that the process of discovery was endless – a considerable bonus in view of the fact that the Inquisitors and witch-finders were paid by results. The following is a confession accompanied by accusation given by one Joan Willford at Feversham, Kent, in September 1645:

> She confessed that about seven years since the devil appeared to her in the shape of a small dog and bade her forsake her God and turn to him; which she admitted she was loathe to do. She also mentioned to this spirit that she wished to be revenged upon Thomas Letherland and Mary his wife. And she said that the devil promised her she would want for nothing, and sometimes brought her money, sometimes a shilling, sometimes eightpence. She called her devil 'Bunnie'. Further, this Bunnie once carried Thomas Gardler out of a window and he fell into a muck-pool. It had been, she confessed, near twenty years since she had given her soul to the devil, and her time was nearly come. She also saith that her companions in mischief were Jane Holt, Elizabeth Harris and Joan Argoll. She further added that Bunnie told her that Elizabeth Harris, some six or seven years ago, curst the boat of John Woofcott, and it was destroyed. And that the devil promised that she should not sink, and she was thrown safe into the water. She said that Goodwife Argoll cursed Mr Major and also John Mannington, and said he should pass away; and so he did. This devil had, she said, come twice in the form of a mouse to suck her since she came into the prison.

Although America, like England, was physically and emotionally distanced from the excessive cruelty of the mainland European witch persecutions, it is interesting that the one phenomenon above all which represents witchcraft in the popular imagination is American – the

Salem Witch Trials. New England, and Massachusetts in particular, had been the haven for English Puritan settlers in the decade between 1630 and 1640, and as the result of a combination of social and political grievances, the small-town populations became insular to the point of paranoia. Mistrust grew like a cancer and, as one author described it, 'Neighbour observed neighbour, gossip took the place of conversation, and whispered superstition was often a substitute for resolute faith.' In 1692 the powder-keg exploded into the horror that were the Salem Witch Trials. As the result of hysteria, hundreds of people were arrested, denounced by their neighbours and colleagues, and put on their trial. Of these, nineteen – thirteen of them women – were hanged between 10 June and 22 September 1692. The first to die on the gallows was Bridget Bishop. Her death warrant read:

To George Corwin, Gentleman, High Sheriff of the County of Essex. Greeting. Whereas Bridget Bishop (alias Oliver), the wife of Edward Bishop of Salem in the country of Essex, sawyer, at a special court of Oyer and Terminer held at Salem on the second day of this instant month of June for the counties of Essex, Middlesex, and Suffolk, before William Stoughton, Esquire, and his Associate Justices of the said court, was indicted and arraigned upon five several indictments for using, practicing and exercising on the 19th day of April past and divers other days and times before and after, certain acts of witchcraft in and upon the bodies of Abigail Williams, Ann Putnam junior, Mercy Lewis, Mary Walcott, and Elizabeth Hubbard, of Salem Village, single women, whereby their bodies were hurt, afflicted, pined, consumed, wasted and tormented, contrary to the form of the statute in that case made and provided.

To which indictments the said Bridget Bishop pleaded Not Guilty, and for trial thereof put herself upon God and her country; whereupon she was found guilty of the felonies and witchcrafts, whereof she stood indicted, and sentence of death accordingly passed against her as the law directs. Execution whereof yet remains to be done.

These are therefore in the names of their Majesties William and Mary, now King and Queen over England, &c., to will and command you that upon Friday next, being the tenth day of this instant month of June, between the hours of eight and twelve in the afternoon of the same day, you safely conduct the said Bridget Bishop (alias Oliver) from their Majesties' jail in Salem aforesaid to the place of execution, and there cause her to be hanged by the neck until she be dead, and of your doings herein make return to the clerk of the said court and precept. And hereof you are not to fail at your peril.

And this shall be your sufficient warrant. Given under my hand and seal at Boston the eighth day of June in the fourth year of the reign of our sovereign lord and lady, William and Mary, now King and Queen over England &c. Anoque Domini 1692.

William Stoughton

When the hysteria had subsided, and the innocence of the accused and convicted made clear, there was published what was called a 'confession of error' signed by the jurors in the Salem trials, dated four years later, on 14 January 1696:

We whose names are under written, being in the year 1692 called to serve as jurors in Court at Salem, on trial of many who were by some suspected guilty of doing acts of witchcraft upon the bodies of sundry persons.

We confess that we ourselves were not capable to understand, nor able to withstand the mysterious delusions of the Power of Darkness and Prince of the Air; but were, for want of knowledge in ourselves and better information from others, prevailed with to take up such evidence against the accused as on further consideration and better information we justly fear was insufficient for the touching the lives of any (Deut xvii.6).

Whereby we fear we have been instrumental with others, though ignorantly and unwittingly, to bring upon ourselves and this people of the Lord the guilt of innocent blood – which sin the Lord saith in Scripture he would not pardon (II King xxiv.4), that is, we suppose in regard of his temporal judgements.

We do therefore hereby signify to all in general, and to the surviving sufferers in especial, our deep sense of, and sorrow for our errors, in acting on such evidence to the condemnation of any person. And we do hereby declare that we justly fear that we were sadly deluded and mistaken, for which we are much disquieted and distressed in our minds; do humbly beg forgiveness of God, for Christ's sake, for this error, and pray that God would not impute the guilt of it to ourselves nor others. And we also pray that we may be considered candidly and aright by the living sufferers as being then under the power of a strong and general delusion, utterly un-acquainted with, and not experienced in matters of that nature.

We do heartily ask forgiveness of all you whom we have justly offended, and do declare according to our present minds we would none of us do such things again on such grounds for the whole world; praying you to accept of this in a way of satisfaction for our offence; and that you would bless the inheri-tance of the Lord, that he may be entreated for the land.

Thomas Fisk (Foreman)
William Fisk
John Batchelor
Thomas Fisk, junior
John Dane
Joseph Evelith

Thomas Perly, senior
John Pebody
Thomas Perkins
Samuel Sayer
Andrew Elliott
Henry Herrick, senior

Torture in the Modern World

We have examined the ways in which pressures imposed by states of war are conducive to the use of excessive degrees of repression and brutal interrogation, and it should be added that this observation applies equally in the event of unrest arising *within* a single country, and the emergence of terrorist activities in opposition to the State and, often, the remaining civilian population.

This is a situation which arose in Northern Ireland during the 1970s, and provides a well-documented example of the way in which even a notionally 'civilised' nation can be led into the error of using inhuman punishment. It has long been a factor of common law in England (and consequently Northern Ireland as a division of the United Kingdom) that, according to what are called the Judges' Rules and Administrative Directions to the Police, a statement from an accused person can be accepted as evidence only if it has not been 'obtained from him by fear of prejudice or hope of advantage, exercised or held out by a person in authority, or by oppression'. However, in 1973 the Diplock Commission, appointed to recommend the structure of what became the Northern Ireland (Emergency Provisions) Act, decided that this stipulation in Judges' Rules 'hampers the course of justice in the case of terrorist crime'. This resulted in the word 'oppression' being replaced by the phrase 'subjected to torture or to inhuman or degrading treatment'. In other words, 'oppression' was now acceptable as long as it did not reach a level which might be regarded by the international community as 'torture'. It must be emphasised that the difficult situation prevailing in Northern Ireland as far as finding witnesses willing to give evidence against suspected terrorists has meant that at the trials of political offenders more than three-quarters of all convictions are based solely, or in great part, on confessions.

From around 1975, it began to emerge that the pressure of the state of emergency was resulting in techniques of interrogation being used which contravened acceptable levels of 'oppression'. In 1976, the British government and the Northern Ireland law-enforcement agencies were taken before the European Commission of Human Rights in Strasbourg where it was ruled that activities had taken place which were consistent with torture and inhuman treatment of detainees. These consisted of the following interrogation techniques: hooding, wall-standing, subjection to continuous noise, deprivation of sleep, deprivation of food and drink, exposure to heat and cold. Each of these abuses has been documented, and the following brief extracts are based on statements made by the prisoners themselves:

In Northern Ireland, on the day of internment, 342 men were arrested at about 4.30 a.m. They were held for two days in special military holding centres where a softening-up procedure of beatings, exercises, sleeplessness, bad food, verbal abuse, dogs, strippings, intimidation and interrogation were used. A number of these men, initially twelve and then a further two, were transferred to solitary confinement for special physical and mental torture.
Hooding: 'His head was hooded by a member of the RUC in a heavy black denim bag. At times the ends were twisted so that he nearly suffocated. During interrogation when it was removed a bright light was shone into his face. He was made to wear the hood for almost the entire six days of the procedures.'
Search Position: 'He was made to stand, again for almost six days, in the British Army search position; that is, standing against the wall, finger tips touching

the wall, on the toes, back pushed in, head pulled back. If he moved or fell he was beaten.'

Noise: 'He was subjected to a high-pitched noise like escaping steam; again for almost the six days. In the rest period towards the end when he was allowed to lie on a mattress, this was replaced for some of them by a hissing sound or else by a discordant mixture of playing records.'

Sleep: 'The internee was deprived of sleep for six days.'

Deprivation of Food and Drink: 'For six days deprived of food and drink until the last day when he was given an indication that his torture was over. Generally speaking most prisoners only received a few drops of water and a piece of dry bread pushed into the mouth which they could not eat. A few received a small amount of water.'

Temperature: Extremes of heat and cold were used as forms of torture.

[*Physical Brutality*: Twenty-two different kinds were listed.]

Despite the British government's undertaking that the worst excesses would be abolished, there was sufficient evidence from police surgeons in the province, from the so-called Bennett Report (*Report of the Committee of Inquiry into Police Interrogation Procedures in Northern Ireland*, March 1979), and the Amnesty International Mission Report *Northern Ireland*, 1978, that there were still strong allegations of physical and psychological cruelty being practised – beating, prolonged standing, burning with cigarettes, bending limbs, threatening suspects and their families with death.

Significantly, more than a dozen years after the publication of the first Amnesty International report on Northern Ireland, that organisation issued a further 'urgent action' report as recently as August 1991. In it, AI claimed that a seventeen-year-old youth had been subjected to physical abuse and threats during interrogation by Royal Ulster Constabulary detectives at Castle-reagh interrogation centre in Belfast. The boy had been picked up after a rocket attack in which an RUC officer was tragically killed in May 1991. According to his evidence, the youth had been subjected to constant verbal abuse, was slapped and spat on, and burned on the face with a cigarette; his doctor, in a sworn affidavit, confirmed that he had found evidence of severe assault on his patient. From this and other recent complaints, it would seem that the safeguards supposedly introduced via Westminster for the protection of those under interrogation are being ignored.

Of course, the British government's is by no means the only, or the worst, instance of the use of 'coercion' in the treatment of suspected terrorists or political dissidents. Indeed, by comparison with many nations, the methods employed are almost benign. But as a case study, the Northern Ireland situation does underline one of the most difficult obstacles to the eradication of torture in the modern world. Far from being humbled by the ruling of the European Commission of Human Rights, the British government sought to justify its position on 'oppressive' questioning, even to the stage of extending the normal period during which a suspect could be held without charge (24 hours) by a new power, first to keep a prisoner incommunicado for three days, and then, under the Prevention of Terrorism Act, seven days. This was not, however, accompanied by appropriate provisions to safeguard the rights and physical and mental wellbeing of suspects.

This is a feature of custodial policy which is encountered throughout the world in greater or lesser degrees – the use of torture as a direct policy of government or, scarcely better, a means of coercion and punishment that the state tolerates. In its detailed global report *Torture in the Eighties*, Amnesty International presents details of torture in no fewer than 93 countries – more than one-third of all world *governments*. In this fact, of course, the modern world differs little from the ancient world, for nowhere has there been an outbreak of *individual* torturers; torture is always a sanctioned tool of the state. It is this unique characteristic that may offer the one hope for the eventual eradication of torture, for while it is impossible to rid society of cruel individuals, sufficient pressure exercised by multinational organisations such as the United Nations and Amnesty International may yet change the attitudes of governments, creating a more secure world in which suppression by means of violence becomes unnecessary.

This has led, over the past several decades, to international action to secure agreement on the proper treatment of prisoners, in particular the so-called 'prisoners of conscience'*. In August 1955, the United Nations Congress on the Prevention of Crime and the Treatment of Offenders adopted Articles 31–33 relating to 'Standard Minimum Rules for the Treatment of Prisoners':

Article 31. Corporal punishment, punishment by placing in a dark cell, and all cruel, inhuman or degrading punishments shall be completely prohibited as punishments for disciplinary offences.

Article 32. (1) Punishment by close confinement or reduction of diet shall never be inflicted unless the medical officer has examined the prisoner and certified in writing that he is fit to sustain it.

(2) The same shall apply to any other punishment that may be prejudicial to the physical or mental health of a prisoner. In no case may such punishment be contrary to or depart from the principle stated in Article 31.

(3) The medical officer shall visit daily prisoners undergoing such punishments and shall advise the director if he considers the termination or alteration of the punishment necessary on grounds of physical or mental health.

*Described as men and women detained, in no matter what country, for their beliefs, colour, gender, ethnic origin, language or religion, provided they have not used or advocated violence.

Article 33. Instruments of restraint such as handcuffs, chains, irons and strait-jackets, shall never be applied as a punishment. Furthermore, chains or irons shall not be used as restraints. Other instruments of restraint shall not be used except in the following circumstances:

a. As a precaution against escape during a transfer, provided that they shall be removed when a prisoner appears before a judicial or administrative authority;

b. On medical grounds by direction of the medical officer;

c. By order of the director, if other methods of control fail, in order to prevent a prisoner from injuring himself or others or from damaging property; in such instances the director shall at once consult the medical officer and report to the highest administrative authority.

It is shocking to see discussed in the mid-twentieth century means of restraint – irons and chains – which have been in use for more than two millenia and are still in widespread use throughout the world. Further to this declaration, the United Nations General Assembly, in December 1975, adopted the Declaration on the Protection of All Persons from Torture and Other Cruel, Inhuman or Degrading Treatment or Punishment:

Article 1. (1) For the purpose of this Declaration, torture means any act by which severe pain or suffering, whether physical or mental, is intentionally inflicted by or at the instigation of a public official on a person for such purposes as obtaining from him or a third person information or confession, punishing him for an act he has committed or is suspected of having committed, or intimidating him or other persons. It does not include pain or suffering arising only from, inherent in or incidental to, lawful sanctions to the extent consistent with the

Standard Minimum Rules for the Treatment of Prisoners.

(2) Torture constitutes an aggravated and deliberate form of cruel, inhuman and degrading treatment or punishment.

Article 2. Any act of torture or other cruel, inhuman or degrading treatment or punishment is an offence to human dignity and shall be condemned as a denial of the purposes of the Charter of the United Nations and as a violation of human rights and fundamental freedoms proclaimed in the Universal Declaration of Human Rights.

Article 3. No State may permit or tolerate torture or other cruel, inhuman or degrading treatment or punishment. Exceptional circumstances such as state of war or a threat of war, internal political instability or any other public emergency may not be invoked as a justification of torture or other cruel, inhuman or degrading treatment or punishment.

Article 4. Each State shall, in accordance with the provisions of this Declaration, take effective measures to prevent torture and other cruel, inhuman or degrading treatment or punishment from being practised within its jurisdiction.

Article 5. The training of law enforcement personnel and of other public officials who may be responsible for persons deprived of their liberty shall ensure that a full account is taken of the prohibition against torture and other cruel, inhuman or degrading treatment or punishment. This prohibition shall also, where appropriate, be included in such general rules or instructions as are issued in regard to the duties and functions of anyone who may be involved in the custody or treatment of such persons.

Article 6. Each State shall keep under systematic review interrogation methods and practices as well as arrangements for the custody and treatment of persons deprived of their liberty in its territory, with a view to preventing any cases of torture or other cruel, inhuman or degrading treatment or punishment.

Article 7. Each State shall ensure that all acts of torture as defined in Article 1 are offences under its criminal law. The same shall apply in regard to acts which constitute participation in, complicity in, incitement to or an attempt to commit torture.

Article 8. Any person who alleges he has been subjected to torture or other cruel, inhuman or degrading treatment or punishment by or at the instigation of a public official shall have the right to complain to, and to have his case impartially examined by, the competent authorities of the State concerned.

Article 9. Wherever there is reasonable ground to believe that an act of torture as defined in Article 1 has been committed, the competent authorities of the State concerned shall promptly proceed to an impartial investigation even if there has been no formal complaint.

Article 10. If an investigation under Article 8 or Article 9 establishes that an act of torture as defined in Article 1 appears to have been committed, criminal proceedings shall be instituted against the alleged offender or offenders in accordance with national law. If an allegation of other forms of cruel, inhuman or degrading treatment or punishment is considered to be well founded, the alleged offender or offenders shall be subject to criminal, disciplinary or other appropriate proceedings.

Article 11. Where it is proved that an act of torture or other cruel, inhuman or degrading treatment or punishment has been committed by or at the instigation of a public official, the victim shall be afforded redress and compensation in accordance with national law.

Article 12. Any statement which is established to have been made as a result of torture or other cruel, inhuman or degrading treatment may not be invoked as evidence against the person concerned or against any other person in any proceedings.

It will be seen that this Declaration has been made to embody many of the concepts discussed in this brief Intro-duction, such as the unacceptability of states of war or civil unrest as justifications for torture. The almost un-believably cynical aspect of these United Nations declar-ations is that they were ratified by many member states who are known daily to break the international code on torture; worse still, some nations, again including many in which the greatest abuses of human rights occur, went on to issue *unilateral* declarations against torture. This implies that either there are many two-faced governments around the world (which is not difficult to believe, going on previous experience) or a lot of governments who have so justified their ill-treatment of prisoners that they are themselves genuinely deluded that they do not participate in torture.

So who are today's torturers? According to the Amnesty International report *Torture in the Eighties*,* they number 66 countries representing every one of the five major geographical divisions of the modern world:

AFRICA

Angola	Congo	Ghana
Cameroon	Djibouti	Guinea
Chad	Ethiopia	Kenya
Comoros	Gabon	Lesotho

Torture in the Eighties: An Amnesty International Report (1989) Amnesty International, 99 Roseberry Avenue, London EC1R 4RE

Mali	Rwanda	Zaire
Mauritania	Somalia	Zambia
Mozambique	South Africa	Zimbabwe
Namibia	Uganda	

THE AMERICAS

Argentina	El Salvador	Mexico
Bolivia	Guatemala	Paraguay
Brazil	Guyana	Peru
Chile	Haiti	Suriname
Colombia	Honduras	Uruguay

ASIA

Afghanistan	India	Pakistan
Bangladesh	Indonesia	Philippines
China	Korea	Sri Lanka
		Taiwan

EUROPE

Albania	Poland	Turkey
Italy	Romania	USSR
	Spain	Yugoslavia

MIDDLE EAST AND NORTH AFRICA

Bahrain	Iraq	Morocco
Egypt	Israel	Saudi Arabia
Iran	Libya	Tunisia

This Introduction would become unhelpfully bulky if any lengthy evaluation of individual statistics was entered into here, but in deference to the following section, brief notes are given on the *methods* of torture used by the worst offenders:

Afghanistan Systematic beatings; beatings with electric

shock batons and shocks from electrodes wired to a telephone; food and sleep deprivation. Regularly carried out by state information police (*Khad*) against political prisoners.

Albania Beating and kicking; electric shock. Inflicted on political prisoners.

Angola Severe beatings and flagellation administered with fists, sticks, belts and whips; electric shocks to head and genitals. Inflicted on political prisoners.

Argentina Beatings with fists, truncheons, rifle butts and sticks; kicking; electric shock administered with cattle prods; immersion in water with hood over the prisoner's head, when he is taken from the water the wet cloth sticks to the face and he cannot breathe; burning with cigarettes; standing in awkward positions for long periods; plunging into cold baths; deprivation of food and sleep. Inflicted on political and other prisoners.

Bahrain Beatings and burning. Inflicted on political prisoners by Bahrain security forces.

Bangladesh Prolonged beatings resulting in the breaking of limbs; electric shock; burning with cigarettes; deprivation of food; rape. Inflicted by army on political and other prisoners.

Bolivia Regular beating and flagellation with clubs, rifle butts and whips; kicking; electric shock inflicted with cattle prods to the mouth, ears, breasts, genitals and soles of feet – the victim is often tied to a metal bed during electric shock torture, or has his feet immersed in water; suspension by wrists or feet for prolonged periods; a technique called *chanco*, in which prisoners lie between two chairs supported only by the head and the tips of the toes – if they fall they are beaten; rape; threats of mutilation; mock executions. Carried out mainly by unofficial paramilitary groups on political prisoners.

Brazil Beatings; electric shock; the *pau de arara*, 'parrot's perch', where a prisoner is suspended upside down from a bar placed under the knees with the hands bound to the ankles. Inflicted mostly on ordinary criminal suspects for the purpose of securing confessions.

Cameroon Regular beatings, including *falaqa* – beating on the soles of the feet; electric shock.

Chad Severe beatings and public flogging. Inflicted on political prisoners.

Chile Beatings; electric shock to head, mouth and genitals, as well as the joints of the body, while tied to a metal bed (the 'electric grill'); 'parrot's perch' (see Brazil); sleep deprivation; non-therapeutic use of drugs; *el telefono*, 'the telephone', where a prisoner is beaten on both ears simultaneously. Inflicted on political prisoners.

China Beating; enforced wearing of a gas mask to restrict breathing; subjection to cold. The Chinese government also carries out public executions (see above).

Colombia Systematic beatings; electric shock; enforced standing in awkward positions for extended periods; near drowning by plunging head into filthy water; non-therapeutic use of mind-altering drugs; exposure to sun, insects and cold; suspension by the arms with wrists bound behind back (see **Squassation**).

Comoros Political prisoners systematically beaten with fists and sticks.

Congo Severe beatings with sticks, rifle butts and belts; kicking; electric shock to sensitive parts of the body while the prisoner is tied to a metal bed or has feet immersed in water; suspension for prolonged periods. Inflicted on political prisoners.

Djibouti Beatings; 'parrot's perch' (see Brazil) often accompanied by beating; enforced swallowing of soapy water. Inflicted on both political and ordinary prisoners.

Egypt Beating with sticks, whips and lengths of rubber pipe; burning with cigarettes; suspension by hands or feet for long periods; threats of violence and sexual assault against family.

Ethiopia Beatings on soles of the feet while prisoner is tied to the 'parrot's perch' (see Brazil); electric shock; tying weights to testicles; rape; burning with boiling oil or water. Inflicted on political prisoners; during the period 1977–8 it has been estimated that tens of thousands of prisoners were tortured.

El Salvador Beating; burning with sulphuric acid; mock executions; administration of mind-altering drugs; sexual abuse. Inflicted by the various security forces on those opposing the government.

Gabon Severe beating with fists, sticks and other implements; electric shock; hooding; immersion in water. Inflicted on political prisoners.

Ghana Beating of political detainees with fists and rifle butts.

Guatemala Burning with cigarettes; castration and other forms of mutilation; use of the *capucha*, a hood impregnated with noxious chemicals. Inflicted on opponents of the government.

Guinea Severe beatings with rifle butts, truncheons and sticks; electric shocks to head, limbs and genitals. Widely inflicted on both political and ordinary prisoners.

Guyana Both political and ordinary prisoners subjected to beatings and food and sleep deprivation.

Haiti Beating with sticks; use of the 'parrot's perch' (see Brazil), called the 'Jack'.

Honduras Beating; electric shock; 'psychological' torture; confinement in small spaces so that the prisoner cannot stand or sit down.

India Severe beatings often resulting in broken limbs; electric shock; hanging upside down; burning. Widely used on all classes of prisoner.

Indonesia Beatings, particularly on the head; electric shock; confinement without food; matchsticks inserted under prisoners' fingernails and set alight; offences against religious beliefs – such as being confined with members of the opposite sex or not being allowed to pray openly. Inflicted on opponents of government.

Iran Beating and public whipping inflicted on all classes of prisoner, but particularly for alcohol offences. Amputation of fingers and hands for theft; stoning to death, mainly for sexual indiscretions.

Iraq Beating with fists and truncheons; kicking; flogging; sustained beating of soles of feet (*falaqa*); electric shock; mock executions; sexual abuse. Inflicted on political prisoners.

Israel Severe beating; exposure to the sun, sometimes resulting in death; exposure to extreme cold, and cold showers; deprivation of food and sleep. Inflicted on 'security suspects'.

Italy Prolonged beating; electric shock; burning with cigarettes; hooding; hosing with icy water; squeezing genitals. Not widespread, but said to be used occasionally on political prisoners.

Kenya Beating, including the sexual organs; electric shock; confinement naked in a cell flooded with cold water; deprivation of light; threats of death.

Korea Beating; electric shock; suspension from a club pushed behind the knees when a prisoner's hands and feet are tied together (rather similar to the 'parrot's perch', but called the 'roast chicken'); forcing water through the nostrils of a prisoner suspended upside down; twisting limbs with wooden sticks. Inflicted on political and ordinary classes of prisoner.

Libya Beating and kicking; electric shocks to the head and genitals; whipping with cables; *falaqa*; threats of physical and sexual abuse. A torture apparently unique to the region – placing a beetle under an inverted cup on the prisoner's bare stomach. Used against political prisoners.

Lesotho Severe beatings – prisoners have blankets thrown over the upper part of the body followed by a car tyre which pinions the arms while the beating is carried out on a nearly suffocating victim. Inflicted on political prisoners.

Mali Beating with sticks and truncheons, sometimes while the prisoner is suspended upside down; electric shock; burning with cigarettes; whippings; exposure to the sun for prolonged periods. Inflicted on political prisoners by the police, gendarmerie and army.

Mauritania Severe beatings, sometimes inflicted while the prisoner is hung up by the feet; burning with hot coals; under Islamic law of *shari'a*, public amputation of the hands of thieves, and public flogging.

Mexico Severe beating; electric shock; burning with cigarettes; sexual abuse. Inflicted mainly on political prisoners.

Morocco Beating; electric shock; burning with cigarettes; suspension in painful positions for extended periods; *falaqa*. Inflicted on political prisoners.

Mozambique Public flogging – sentences of between three and 90 lashes are permissible, though only 30 lashes can be inflicted at one time, and a week must separate punishments. Inflicted mainly on political prisoners.

Namibia Beating; electric shock; hooding to produce suffocation and sensory deprivation; deprivation of food. Inflicted on political prisoners, mainly by South African security forces.

Pakistan Severe and prolonged beating; electric shock; burning with cigarettes; *falaqa*; deprivation of sleep; death threats; one 'instrument' of torture is a bench to which wooden rollers have been fitted – the prisoner is strapped to the bench and the rollers forced over his upper legs. Applied to both political and ordinary prisoners.

Paraguay Beating; electric shock administered with cattle prods; immersing a prisoner's head in a bucket of water polluted by excrement; *falaqa*; confinement in painful positions – upright in a large box (*guardia*), in a foetal position (*feto*), wrapped in a plastic sheet and placed in a metal cylinder (*secadera*); suspension by the ankles.

Peru Severe beating; electric shock; hooding for prolonged periods; drenching with cold water; deprivation of food; near drowning, either by plunging a prisoner's head into a tank of water or by sewing him up in a sack and throwing it into water; burning with cigarettes; a form of squassation where the prisoner's hands are cuffed behind his back and he is pulled to the ceiling by means of a rope and pulley attached to the handcuffs; near suffocation with wet rags placed over face or with plastic bags. Inflicted on all classes of prisoner.

Philippines Severe beating; electric shock; sexual abuse; burning with cigarettes. Inflicted mainly by military personnel on political suspects.

Poland Beating, including what is called the 'health walk' – walking the gauntlet between two rows of police armed with truncheons. Inflicted mainly on political prisoners and in particular members of the formerly banned trade union Solidarity.

Romania Severe beating with rubber truncheons and kicking of political prisoners.

Rwanda Beating; electric shock administered to the genitals or other sensitive parts by electrodes or special electric belts; needles inserted under prisoners' fingernails; confinement in dark cells (*cachots noirs*). Inflicted on political detainees.

Saudi Arabia Beating, including *falaqa*, while a prisoner's feet are fastened to the back of a chair; electric shock; under the Islamic law of *shari'a*, thieves can be punished by the amputation of the right hand, and many minor offences are punished by public flogging with as many as 300 lashes. Inflicted on all classes of prisoner.

Somalia Beating; electric shock; confinement in dark cells; rape; death threats and mock executions. Inflicted on political prisoners.

South Africa Beating with fists, sticks and other implements; electric shock; suspension by means of a pole inserted between a prisoner's handcuffed hands and ankles; subjection to extreme cold; sleep deprivation; hooding; forced to stand for long periods, often with heavy weights placed on the prisoner's head; threats of violence to prisoners and their families. Inflicted by the security police on political prisoners.

Sri Lanka Beating; inserting needles beneath the finger- and toenails, and chili peppers into sensitive orifices; suspension upside down. Inflicted mainly in order to secure information and confessions about and by the Tamil extremists.

Suriname Severe beating; deprivation of sleep, food and drink; mutilation and threats of death.

Syria Severe beating and whipping; burning with boiling water, chilling with cold water; tearing out fingernails; electric shock, particularly to genitals; forcing bottle necks, sticks and hot metal skewers into the rectum; torture 'machines' include the *Bisat al-Rih* ('flying carpet'), a piece of wood shaped like a human silhouette to which the prisoner is strapped to be subjected to beatings and electric shock torture, and the Black Slave (*al-'Abd al-Aswad*) an apparatus on to which the prisoner is seated and which automatically inserts a heated metal skewer into the anus. Treatment usually carried out by security forces on prisoners opposing the government.

Taiwan Beating; electric shock; prisoners forced to crouch in an uncomfortable position in front of electric fans for long periods; sleep deprivation and threats of death.

Tunisia Severe beatings with sticks, iron bars and lengths of rubber hose; the 'Swing', suspension from an iron bar inserted behind the knees when a prisoner's hands and ankles have been tied together – called the 'parrot's perch' in many South American countries, and the 'Jack' in Haiti; burning with cigarettes. Inflicted on political prisoners.

Turkey Beating, including *falaqa* (a historic Turkish torture); electric shock; suspension by hands or feet. Inflicted mainly on political prisoners.

Uganda Beating with sticks and rifle butts, hammers and iron bars; whipping with cables and barbed wire; burning of sexual organs and rape; bayoneting and shooting in the limbs; deprivation of food and drink. Inflicted mainly on opponents of the government.

Uruguay Severe beating; electric shock; hooding for prolonged periods (up to one month); enforced standing for long periods; immersion of the head in water polluted by excrement; suspension from wrists, knees or ankles; forcing prisoners to straddle sharp iron or wooden bars which cut into the groin. Inflicted on political prisoners.

Zaire Electric shock to limbs and genitals; use of debilitating drugs; insertion of sticks between a prisoner's fingers which are then crushed together; deprivation of food and drink. Inflicted on political prisoners.

Zambia Severe beating; electric shock; one prisoner is reported as having objects forced into his penis and anus. Inflicted on political prisoners.

Zimbabwe Beating and kicking; electric shock; hooding; pencils inserted between fingers and the prisoner's hands squeezed. Inflicted on opponents of government.

Kinds of Torture

We have already observed in the opening to this Introduction that the use of torture for the purpose of punishment or coercion is as old as humankind, and prevalent throughout the millennia across the whole of the inhabited globe. It would also be true to say that the basic methods of inflicting pain have also remained remarkably consistent; of course, the executioner has taken note of progress and adapted accordingly, but this has resulted in greater sophistication rather than increased inventiveness – beheading with a sharpened steel blade instead of a knapped flint, for example.

Some new contrivances – such as electric-shock torture and the electric chair – emerged with the safe harnessing of electricity; and the medical profession's greater understanding of the mind-altering effects of certain drugs increased the possibilities of psychological torture. Other refinements of mental torture have entered the repertoire, but in reality the psychological cruelty of 'sensory deprivation' is little different from solitary incarceration in a black, stinking dungeon.

So, because motivation and method in torture have remained perennially constant, it is possible to make some convenient grouping of types. Again, because most of the methods were basically very simple, it is not practical to identify accurate geographical 'preferences'. Obviously burial up to the neck in sand is more feasible in Morocco than in Manchester, but the use of sticks and cudgels for beating, and the use of whips for flagellation, for example, have been endemic throughout all earth's races.

Conclusion

In the face of overwhelming evidence of the continued widespread use of torture, and the fact that neither motive nor method has changed over the centuries, it is impossible to draw an optimistic conclusion to this study; for it is certain that without the restraining influence of pressure groups such as Amnesty International and the United Nations, the situation would be far worse.

It will become obvious from the contents of this volume that apart from essential updating references to torture in the modern world, the subject has been treated as a manifestation of social and political history, since it is only by taking an overview – for example of the awful effects of the religious persecutions in the Europe of earlier ages – that we can begin to approach an understanding of the intolerance of faith in our own world, a world in which fundamentalist zealots of both the Christian and the Islamic religions keep the fires of hatred burning. We must face the inevitable realisation that the excuse that wars give for the introduction of institutionalised violence and cruelty will end only with the eradication of war; that the use of torture as a function of government will cease only with the spread of international understanding, tolerance and the rule of democracy. Finally we must recognise that national laws empowering the state to take life and, literally in some places, limb are very imperfect tools of justice, and that the institution of capital execution presents a barbaric example that we must no longer tolerate.

This picture which I have unashamedly painted of man's inhumanity does not have the purpose of causing distress and fear, but rather to act as a caution against complacency – the whips and chains, the ordeals by fire and water, the executioner waiting there in the dark, are still with us, and it will require all our courage and vigilance to eradicate cruel and unusual punishment from our planet.

ACKNOWLEDGEMENTS

Encyclopedic works such as this are compiled rather than written; they are a collage of facts, features and anecdote painstakingly researched, analysed and assembled in what, the author hopes, is an informative and interesting new format. Consequently, this book has had many 'contributors', for it is true that scholarship builds upon scholarship. There are obviously far too many sources to name individually in this brief acknowledgement – they will be found credited throughout the text. However, there have been a clutch of works written by early researchers into the subject of judicial punishment which have proved fundamental to the task of assembling the list of entries contained between these two covers; just as important have been their respective authors' bibliographies and references, because although each reference needs to be checked for accuracy and relevance, together they have saved me many hundreds of hours of tedious searching. One of the most interesting studies is Ernest Pettifer's *Punishments of Former Days*; although it relates only to methods employed in Great Britain it is an exhaustive piece of research by a man who was for many years the Chief Clerk to the West Riding Justices. An indispensable 'trilogy' is the *History of Corporal Punishment*, *History of Torture Throughout the Ages*, and *History of Capital Punishment*, by George Ryley Scott, FZS, FRAI, FPhS (Eng). It is enlightening to read on the very first page to these books that their sale was restricted to 'Members of the Medical and Legal Professions, Scientists, Anthropologists, Psychologists, Sociologists, Criminologists and Social Workers', presumably to protect previous generations from a chance encounter with sado-sexual lust. Anecdotally, the present author can remember as a youth seeing these books on subtle display in the dusty windows of those shops where once rupture belts, support stockings and contraceptives were on sale. John Swain's *Pleasures of the Torture Chamber* contains some marvellously obscure references, and tracking them down has been a work of detection in itself; and William Andrews's *Bygone Punishments* is a classic on the subject. These books and many others I have found a vital source of inspiration to my own researches, and I can only hope that this present study might prove as useful to future students of the subject.

Most of the early reference works which I have consulted are long out of print, and once again I must register my gratitude for the unfailing courtesy and expertise of the British Library Reading Room staff. My sincere thanks are due as always to my partner-in-crime Wilfred Gregg, in whose unrivalled private true-crime library I have always been made to feel more than welcome. It will become obvious while reading this book that it has not always been possible to deal with a comfortable past, for torture is still with us in all its horror – though often its techniques have not changed over centuries. For my information on the state of torture and cruel punishment in the world today I am indebted to reports resulting from the tireless efforts of the Amnesty International organisation and the United Nations.

For reasons of taste as well as availability, the scenes of torture and the instruments which inflict it have been derived mainly from the 'gothic' periods of the Inquisition and the Witch Hunts, as well as from the iniquitous practices of the Romans and other early civilisations. Most of this material originated in the author's own archive; however, where suitable reproducible illustrations were unavailable, I have been fortunate in having the enthusiastic help of Mo Tingey, whose imaginative graphic reconstructions say more than any number of words of mine could have done.

Finally, though by no means less importantly, I would

like to express my grateful thanks to Sally Holloway of Virgin Publishing, who shared with me the creation of the original concept for this book, and whose continuing enthusiasm and encouragement has helped turn that concept into a reality.

Brian Lane
London, 1993

A

Abolition of Capital Punishment

> And naked to the hangman's noose
>> The morning clocks will ring
> A neck God made for other use
>> Than strangling in a string.
>
> (Housman, *A Shropshire Lad*, IX)

The Early Years

For all practical purposes, the 'early modern' period of reform towards abolition had its beginning in Italy in 1764 with the publication of Cesare Beccaria's *Essay on Crimes and Punishments*. Here Beccaria expounded his belief that, since man was not his own creator, he did not have the right to destroy human life, either collectively or individually. He did, however, capitulate on two significant points; the first, to allow an execution if it would prevent a popularly elected government being toppled by revolution; the second, to accept execution if it was the only way to deter others from committing a crime – effectively the claim of retentionists both before and after Beccaria.

These radical ideas found their way into English debate through Jeremy Bentham and Sir Samuel Romilly. Bentham (1748–1832) embraced abolition on purely political reasoning as part of his precocious theories of 'free-thinking'; however, he was constrained to admit that the death penalty produced a far stronger impression on the public mind than any other form of punishment, and maintained that it could be justified for the crime of murder. Bentham is quick, though, to add this warning: judges and witnesses are fallible. Yet once a victim is executed there is no remedy for the punishment of death.

All chance of reform or of gain from productive labour by the convicted person ends on the scaffold.

The movement for the widespread elimination of capital punishment – or at least of its wholesale application – can properly be said to have begun in 1808, when Sir Samuel Romilly petitioned Parliament to remove some of the more than 200 capital offences on the statute (see **Capital Offences**). The retention of these petty crimes as capital charges was, even ignoring the humanitarian argument, a great disadvantage to the proper and effective conduct of law enforcement. It was not unnoticed that people from whom, say, a sheep had been stolen would prefer not to bring charges if it meant that the miscreant's death on the scaffold would be on their conscience. Juries too were refusing to bring in positive verdicts for the same reason, and magistrates and judges were increasingly liberal with their reprieves. It was even suggested by some cynical old lags that they would *rather* be indicted on a capital charge because the chances of getting off scot-free were greater.

This reduction in the draconian list of capital crimes became a particularly popular preliminary target for the repealers; and some enlightened men and societies were prepared to go as far as to bring into question the use of capital punishment in any form, for any crime.

Prominent among these was William Allen, a chemist, member of the Royal Society and fellow of the Linnean Society. Any instinctive feelings of justice would have been greatly reinforced by his adherence to the Quaker faith, and as early as 1809 he founded the first society with a specific mandate to campaign against capital punishment – the Society for the Diffusion of Knowledge Respecting the Punishment of Death and the Improvement of Prison Discipline. In this work he was helped by fellow Quaker Peter Bedford and by Basil Montagu, a friend of Bentham and Romilly. An interesting byproduct of Montagu's commitment was his publication, in 1809, of *Opinions of Different Authors Upon the Punish-*

ment of Death, an anthology of historic and contemporary thoughts on the subject.

A new, more ambitious society was founded in 1828 – the Society for the Diffusion of Information on the Subject of Capital Punishment. William Allen was its London chairman, and its members included the prison reformer Sir Thomas Fowell Buxton, who was also instrumental in the ending of slavery in the British colonies, the Reverend Daniel Wilson (later Bishop of Calcutta) and Lord Suffield. The Society promoted its cause in part by the publication of five pamphlets under the title *The Punishment of Death*, and achieved some modest success as a Parliamentary pressure group.

The Society for Promoting the Abolition of Capital Punishment succeeded this latter group in 1846, and benefited from the infusion of new radical blood in the persons of Thomas Beggs and Alfred Dymond, Secretary of the Society and another Quaker. The lobbying of Parliament, and in particular of the Home Secretary, on matters relating to abolitionist policy was relentless. In 1865 Dymond himself published an important and influential book of anecdotes under the title *The Law on its Trial: or, Personal Recollections of the Death Penalty and its Opponents*. On the approaches to the Home Secretary, Dymond recalled, 'The London deputations hunt him down like a deer; they watch the private entrance to the Home Office like revenue officers snaring a false coiner. They sight his exit as he escapes by the front staircase; raise the hue and cry down Parliament Street; circumvent him as he darts through the Members' entrance and buttonhole him in the lobby.'

But the anti-hanging crusade was beginning to touch the hearts of the people as well, and public sympathy was being gradually mobilised 'to agitate Parliamentary inquiry for the abolition of capital punishment' (*The Times*, 22 November 1856).

The movement was no longer a London-based intellectual talking shop, but had become an evangelical machine

JACK KETCH'S LEVEE

OR, THE

GREAT SENSATION SCENE AT NEWGATE.

BY AN EX OFFICIAL.

CONTAINING AN ACCOUNT OF

THE BARBAROUS CUSTOMS OF THE OLDEN TIMES:

TRIALS BY BATTLE; DEATH PUNISHMENT OF THE INNOCENT;

200 Crimes Punishable by Death reduced to 1

Showing also that the Gallows is no Corrective but a fearful Promoter of Crime.

PRICE 1d.]   PUBLISHED BY C. ELLIOT, SHOE LANE.   [PRICE 1d.

of the reformists: 'Educate, proselytise, and agitate' became the key to the campaign strategy.

Among these new evangelists were Alfred Dymond (Secretary of the Society for the Abolition of Capital Punishment from 1854 to 1857). The great orator and statesman John Bright spoke for the Society, as did Charles Gilpin, who in 1849 had also persuaded Charles

Dickens to speak out against public executions. (Dickens did not think that it was realistic to expect total abolition.)

In 1866 a group of London Quakers set up the Howard Association – its name and aims rooted in the work of the highly respected eighteenth-century philanthropist and prison reformer John Howard. This Association assumed the responsibilities of the Society for the Abolition of Capital Punishment under that Society's former leader, William Tallack. The Howard Association also extended its brief to embrace the wider problems of the rehabilitation of prisoners and reform of the penal system. The SACP struggled on for but a short time under the leadership of Thomas Beggs. But even in modified form, the strict abolitionists had already lost, if not the war, then at least the present battle. In 1866 a Royal Commission on Capital Punishment went only as far as the abolition of *public* executions. With this blow the Society finally disbanded, leaving the Howard Association to incorporate the abolitionist views within its broader mandate.

During the nineteenth century there was an abundance of printed propaganda – particularly of broadsheets and pamphlets, many of which dealt with such moral issues as the abolition of the death penalty. The styles varied in direction, many following the tradition of satire characteristic of the previous two centuries – Charles Gilpin's *Grand Moral Spectacle* of 1847, for example.

Edward Gibbon Wakefield, a colonial statesman, was imprisoned himself for three years in 1826 for abducting and marrying an heiress. This gave him valuable first-hand knowledge of criminals and the state of prison life that was to prove so valuable a background to his subsequent reformist campaigning. Wakefield was a vociferous critic of the penal code, and through a series of savage satirical pamphlets was a great influence on later reformers. Before his vitriolic pen few were safe, he treated with equal contempt the lawyers, the judges, the clergymen, and executioners; he included the 'comfortable' classes who bought special seats at public executions,

GRAND MORAL SPECTACLE!

Under the Authority of the Secretary of State for the Home Department.

THIS DAY, SATURDAY, APRIL 17, 1847,

A YOUNG GIRL

SEVENTEEN YEARS OF AGE

IS TO BE

PUBLICLY STRANGLED

IN FRONT OF THE

County Jail, Bury St. Edmonds.

SHE WILL APPEAR

Attended by a Minister of the Church of England,

Clad in his Robes Canonical;

ALSO BY THE HANGMAN

The Great Moral Teacher,

Who after fastening her arms to her side, and putting a rope round her neck, will strike the scaffold from under her; and if the neck of the wretched victim be not by this shock broken, the said MORAL TEACHER will pull the legs of the miserable girl until by his weight and strength united he

Strangles Her.

This Exhibition, (the admission to which is free,) is provided by a "*Christian* Legislature," for the instruction of "A *Christian* People;" and is intended to impress upon the minds of the multitude an abhorrence of all cruelty, a love of mercy and kindness, and a reverence for human life ! ! ! !

London:—C. GILPIN, 5, Bishopsgate Street Without.

and digested the Gallows Reports the next morning along with their breakfast.

A contemporary of Wakefield was George Jacob Holyoake, whose *Public Lessons of the Hangman* (1864) was directly prompted by his witnessing the execution of Franz Muller. Although it was an exaggeration to suggest (as he did on the title page of the pamphlet) that *The Times* newspaper, or even the Grand Jury at Manchester, was directly influenced by his words, it is certain that Holyoake was a very popular pamphleteer and polemicist, and one who was at his most sensational when dealing with the iniquity of public executions.

Of the very few middle-class publications that espoused the cause of abolition, *Punch* was perhaps the most consistent. Indeed, its first issue made clear its opposition to 'that accursed tree which has its roots in injuries'. Douglas Jerrold, the author and actor, contributed many fine reformist pieces to *Punch*, as predictably did one of the paper's founders, Henry Mayhew, who was already celebrated for his mammoth study *London Labour and the London Poor*, and was an active member of the Committee for the Abolition of Capital Punishment. On 13 November 1849 *Punch* published John Leach's cartoon on the public execution of the Mannings, 'The Great Moral Lesson at Horsemonger Lane Gaol', beneath which appeared a poem – 'The Lesson of the Scaffold; or, the Ruffian's Holiday':

> Each public-house was all alight, the place just like a fair;
> Ranting, roaring, rollicking, larking everywhere,
> Boozing and carousing we passed the night away,
> And ho! to hear us curse and swear, waiting for the day.

But by 1850 even *Punch*'s crusading spirit flagged with the decline in editorial influence of men like Jerrold and Mayhew.

The Eclectic Review was another respectable journal which often published the written views of members of the Society for the Abolition of Capital Punishment. It was this magazine that had strong words to say over the defection of Charles Dickens from the abolitionist camp; strong words that resulted in an acrimonious exchange between the novelist and the magazine over the benefits to be derived from 'private' executions. *The Eclectic Review* believed that behind the closed doors of prisons, all manner of abuses of power might take place in the name of justice.

On Public Executions

It was often the very fact of public executions that excited demands for their abolition; vociferous demands from such eloquent sources as the essayist and novelist William Makepeace Thackeray who in August 1840 was so appalled by his viewing of the execution of Francois Benjamin Courvoisier that he wrote the lengthy essay 'Going to See a Man Hanged' for *Frazer's Magazine* – at that time a platform for the abolitionists. But *Frazer's* too succumbed to the growing tide of conservatism, and in 1864 it was printing hard-line retentionist articles by the noted jurist James Fitzjames Stephens. Of the others, the *Spectator* maintained a consistent, though cautious, policy of attacking the barbarity of public executions, but remained uncommitted to the total abolitionist cause. Until 1864 – just two years before 'private' hangings were recommended by the Royal Commission – the *Spectator* was still hesitant, opting in the end for a kind of semi-private ceremony carried out in a specially built hall at Newgate and attended not only by the usual gamut of clergy and physicians but also by a 'body of witnesses specially admitted to testify to the identity and to the fact of death, and the absence of all cruelty' (*Spectator*, 27 February 1864).

In *Good Words* (April 1865), Henry Rogers, in an article headed 'On Public Executions', made it clear that his reasons for supporting private executions were that their effect would be beneficial to potential criminals – the principle being that a man killed in secret could not be turned into a martyred hero on the public platform.

The air of mystery about a secret hanging would, Rogers reasoned, still ensure that the concept of retribution would deter the ambitions of potential malefactors, without the unseemly spectacle of the public execution. In short, Rogers felt happy enough with capital punishment as a penalty, at least for murder, that he was unprepared to have its retention jeopardised by the outcry at public executions. 'The hour is surely at hand,' he argued, 'when England must abolish either public executions or capital punishments.'

We have seen how attendance at the public hanging of Courvoisier prompted Thackeray to speak out against such spectacles. In the same crowd on that July day in 1840 was another of the country's great writers. The scene that he witnessed caused Charles Dickens to pen several lengthy 'letters' to his own newspaper, the *Daily News*:

> I was present myself at the execution of Courvoisier. I was purposely on the spot from midnight of the night before, and was near witness to the whole process of the building of the scaffold, the gathering of the crowd, the gradual swelling of the concourse with the coming of day, the hanging of the man, the cutting of the body down, and the removal of it into Prison. From the moment of my arrival when there were but a few score boys in the street, and all those young thieves, and all clustered together behind the barrier nearest the drop – down to the time when I saw the body with its dangling head being carried on a wooden bier into the gaol – I did not see one token in all the immense crowd of any emotion suitable to the occasion. No sorrow, no salutary terror, no abhorrence, no seriousness, nothing but ribaldry, debauchery, levity, drunkenness and flaunting of vice in fifty other shapes. I should have deemed it impossible that I could ever have felt any large assemblage of my fellow-creatures to be so odious.

(*Daily News*, 28 February 1846)

Thus did the great social commentator apply himself to one of the great debates of his day. But it was not to be a comfortable dialogue. Dickens made it quite plain that, though he abhorred the practice of capital punishment, he equally abhorred the crime of murder and those who perpetrate it. By the time of the trial of the Mannings in 1849, three years after Courvoisier, Dickens had made an uneasy peace with his conscience and concentrated his efforts on the *reform* of capital punishment – which in effect meant simply the abolition of public executions. On 15 November he expressed to Charles Gilpin the opinion that abolition would never be accepted in England, and that its supporters would be well advised to concentrate on the immediate evil of public hangings. A letter to *The Times* of 19 November 1849 puts Dickens's own model for the procedure into the public arena:

> From the moment of a murderer being sentenced to death, I would dismiss him to the dread obscurity . . . I would allow no curious visitors to hold any communication with him; I would place every obstacle in the way of his sayings and doings being served up in print on a Sunday for the perusal of families. His execution within the walls of the prison should be conducted with every terrible solemnity that careful consideration could devise. Mr Calcraft the hangman [see **Calcraft, William**] – of whom I have some information in reference to this last occasion – should be restrained in his unseemly briskness, in his jokes, his oaths, and his brandy. To attend the execution I would summon a jury of 24, to be called the Witness Jury, eight to be summoned on a low qualification, eight on a higher; and eight on a higher still; so that it might fairly represent all classes of society. There should be present likewise the governor of the gaol, the chaplain, the surgeon and other officers. All these should sign a grave and solemn form of certificate (the same in every case) on such a day on such an hour, in such a gaol, for

such a crime, such a murderer was hanged in their sight. There should be another certificate from the officers of the prison that the person hanged was that person and no other; a third that the person was buried.

Such open apostasy earned Dickens the public vilification of the hard-line abolitionists, and at a meeting he was accused of 'possessing a homicidal disposition'. True or not, it was only another ten years before Dickens went full circle and allied himself with the retentionist lobby.

In 1854 the French writer and revolutionary Victor Hugo, motivated by the execution of the murderer Tapner on the island of Guernsey, added his criticism of barbaric English justice; the climate of feeling against the French being what it was, he was ignored.

Two years later arch-abolitionist William Ewart failed to get the House of Commons to inquire into the question of capital punishment. The Lords, however, had already appointed a Select Committee on Capital Punishment, the report of which strongly recommended that executions should take place 'within the precincts of a prison, or in some place securing similar comparative privacy'. The fact that almost everybody else disagreed weighed heavily against any such recommendation being implemented.

On 3 May 1864 Ewart again pressed the government to inquire into capital punishment; surprisingly, they responded by setting up a Royal Commission, whose brief was to examine the whole question, and in particular public executions. It became clear that a new feeling of moderation was pervading informed opinion.

In the following year John Hibbert's Capital Punishment Within Gaols Bill received its first reading; it turned out to have been premature, as it was necessary to withdraw the draft Bill until the House had received the report of the Royal Commission. This eagerly awaited Report was finally released in January 1866, and eight weeks later Hibbert reintroduced his Bill. Ironically, it was from the staunch abolitionists that much of the opposition to private executions came. They reasoned – perhaps with justification – that the hiding away of the execution would have the effect of obscuring the main issue of total abolition; that it was the gross nature of the public spectacle that would eventually turn public opinion against it. Once again John Hibbert was obliged to withdraw his Bill.

A new Bill embodying the main recommendations of the Royal Commission on Capital Punishment surfaced in March 1866, and wound its weary course through both Houses until, after its third reading, the Law of Capital Punishment Amendment Bill, as it was named, was scrapped by the Home Secretary, Spencer Walpole, at the end of July.

The following year saw another attempt made with the Capital Punishment Within Prisons Bill and predictably the diehard abolitionists proved its worst enemy. In what was becoming a tiresome regularity, the Bill was withdrawn.

When Gathorne Hardy, a dedicated 'privatiser' and active member of the former Royal Commission, assumed the post of Home Secretary on Walpole's resignation in May 1867, it was a clear signal for the reintroduction of the ill-fated 'Within Prisons' Bill. While Hardy was most enthusiastic in his support of the Bill, he made it quite clear that for the foreseeable future there was no possibility of abolition – particularly in the contentious debate on murder, and the recently abandoned Murder Law Amendment Bill. Again it was the abolitionists who presented the most consolidated opposition. Stephen Gaselee, Sergeant-at-law and a radical, observed that executioner Calcraft was bungler enough with his public duties; what carelessness might he not be capable of secure behind walls? Another suggestion (not perhaps as fatuous as it might sound) was that if there were no public scrutiny of the dispatch it would be possible for a wealthy felon to procure a substitute. This was countered by Sir George Bowyer, the Bill's seconder, who claimed that for £1,000 one could already escape hanging – public or not.

Much discussion centred on Charles Gilpin's claim in

opposition that 'if hanging be acknowledged to be so unclean a thing that it is no longer to be tolerated in the broad sunlight, the English people will have none of it'. Charles Newdigate, in his attack both on abolitionists and on private executions, presented a 3,000-signature petition from the residents of Birmingham, who thought the Home Secretary far too generous with his remissions already! Gilpin proposed an amendment to the Bill 'that in the opinion of this House it is expedient, instead of carrying out the punishment of death within prisons, that Capital Punishment be abolished'.

Breakthrough
The philosopher and founder of the Utilitarian Society, John Stuart Mill (in the 1840s an outspoken abolitionist), then rose to add his dissent from the amendment, and with that ungentlemanly babble and turmoil still characteristic of Parliamentary divisions, Gilpin's clause was voted; thus was total abolition once again defeated – by 127 votes to 23. It was significant, however, that the main argument of the Bill – the abolition of public execution – met with success.

Three days before the Capital Punishment Within Prisons Bill received Royal Assent (on 29 May 1868), Michael Barrett, the Fenian who had conspired to cause the Clerkenwell explosion, was hanged. As it turned out, it was to be the last public execution to take place in England. Calcraft's characteristic clumsiness earned him the customary spite of the mob, and he was jeered with cries of 'Come on, body-snatcher! Take away the man you killed!'

The provisions of the new Act dictated that future executions would be carried out inside the prison in which the condemned was held at the time of sentencing. The responsibility for the practical aspects of the hanging lay in the hands of the Sheriff, and the statutory presence was required of the gaoler, the prison surgeon, and the chaplain. The right to attend executions was extended to local and visiting justices and, at the discretion of the

sheriff, to relatives of the prisoner and 'other persons'.
That these other persons included newspaper reporters
was a source of intense irritation to the still vociferous
abolitionists. One reformer, Frederick Hill, spoke for
them all when he said '. . . but the brutalising effect of
an execution is but diminished not banished. The cheap
newspapers carry the account of the final scene of disgrace
and pain far and wide, and it is eagerly read by all who
are eagerly attracted by baneful excitement.' (*An Autobiography of Fifty Years: Times of Reform*, 1894)

Further safeguards to the proper conduct of an
execution were made in the requirement for a surgeon's
examination following death, and a coroner's inquiry to
be carried out within 24 hours.

On the morning of 13 August 1868 Thomas Wells step-
ped on to the scaffold. The scene of young Wells's last
convulsions was spared the roar of the spectators. This
was a small victory in what was to be another 100 years'
struggle against capital punishment. Writing of the Wells
execution, the *Morning Advertiser* warned:

> When we turn . . . to the account of the calm and
> apparently satisfactory manner in which the culprit
> met his doom, we cannot think . . . the system
> yesterday is an act of mercy to the man who is the
> wretched hero of the day . . . We are not reconciled
> to capital punishment by the fact that it was yester-
> day carried out in the least offensive manner of
> which it is capable.

Abolition

Despite the growing demands of a more enlightened
society it was to be almost another hundred years before
the dream of the abolitionists would be realised, when,
in 1965 Parliament passed the Murder (Abolition of the
Death Penalty) Act. This effectively outlawed capital punishment for all of what are classified as 'ordinary' crimes.
However the sentence remains on the statute for treason,
piracy, and some military offences.

Animal Trials and Executions

The extraordinary practice of placing animals on trial, often dressed in human clothes, has been widespread and subjected to considerable serious study.* The concept is of great antiquity and originated in the logical 'revenge' of punishment by destruction of an animal which had caused death or damage.

In the Old Testament, the 21st chapter of Exodus, verses 28–29 insists: 'If an ox gore a man or woman that they die, then the ox shall be surely stoned, and his flesh shall not be eaten; but the owner of the ox shall be quit. But if the ox were wont to push with his horn in time past, and it hath been testified to his owner, and he hath not kept him in, but that he hath killed a man or woman, the ox shall be stoned and the owner shall also be put to death.'

It is this act of **stoning to death**, the common form of judicial execution among the Jews, plus the fact that the animal's meat was to be destroyed, that elevated the acceptable concept of putting down a dangerous beast to an act almost of magic, where the animal is so possessed of 'evil' that its flesh becomes forbidden.

This practice was later ritualised to a sometimes farcical degree. In 1685, for example, in the town of Ansbach, a wolf which had been terrorising the neighbourhood and attacking residents was taken and killed and afterwards publicly hanged on the local gallows wearing human clothes and sporting a mask and powdered wig.

In the Middle Ages animals which had been accused of crimes were not only tried in open court in human dress, but were offered the services of a legal representative. If the animal 'lost' its case, then it could expect no mercy and was frequently subjected to considerable brutality by way of punishment.

In cases where both man and beast were involved in a crime together – as with the ox and its owner above – both man and beast were executed together:

Criminal Prosecution of Animals, E. P. Evans, 1987.

The usual type of crime was bestiality – the sexual abuse of animals – and during the Middle Ages the crimes of bestiality and sodomy were classified as heresy and punished as offences against God. This originated in the book of Leviticus (chapter 20; verses 15–16): 'And if a man lie with a beast he shall surely be put to death, and ye shall slay the beast. And if a woman approach unto any beast, and lie down thereto, thou shalt take the woman and the beast, and they shall surely be put to death; their blood shall be upon them.' In Old Testament times both human and animal would probably have been stoned to death, though later punishment for sexual deviance was burning which, in Germany at least, survived into the nineteenth century; more latterly the burning was preceded by beheading.

A curious incident occurred in Cheapside in the City of London during the Protestant/Catholic persecutions, when a cat dressed as a priest and holding a communion wafer was found hanging from a triple-tree gallows.

Lest it be imagined that the risible sight of the full majesty of the law being assembled and invoked against an animal is a fanciful piece of medieval history, the present author was sent a cutting from an English newspaper dated 25 April 1992, reading: 'An elephant which trampled a drunken attacker to death in Delhi, India, was arrested and put on trial in chains.'

B

Ball Whip
(see **Flagellation**)

Bastinado

In the Orient, particularly in China but to a lesser extent in Japan, a form of flagellation called Bastinado is carried out. The punishment is delivered with a light stick or split bamboo, usually on the buttocks but occasionally (and in Turkey, always) on the soles of the bare feet. It was not the severity of the individual blows which caused the agony, but their number – hundreds of light taps over the course, sometimes, of hours – and the punishment has been known to kill a prisoner.

The following is a first-hand eye-witness account of Bastinado, the origin of which I have been unable to trace and attribute, but which appears to date from the second half of the last century:

> The crowd fell back, and one of the little group in front of the magistrate's chair wrung his hands and heaved a theatrical sigh. Before we could realise what had happened, several pairs of very willing hands were helping him to let down his trousers, and when this was accomplished to the satisfaction of everybody he laid himself face downwards on the floor. Then one of the magistrate's 'runners' stepped forward with the bamboo, a strip of this toughest of plants, three feet long, two inches wide and half an inch thick. Squatting by the side of the victim and holding the bamboo perfectly horizontal close to the flesh, he began to rain light blows on the man's buttocks. At first the performance looked like a

farce, the blows were so light and the receiver of them so indifferent. But as the shower of taps continued with monotonous persistence I bethought me of the old torture of driving a man mad by letting a drop of water fall every minute on his shaved head.

A fanciful depiction of the water torture

After a few more minutes of the dactylic rap-tap-tap, rap-tap-tap, a deep groan broke from the prisoner's lips. I walked over to look at him and saw

that his flesh was blue under the flogging. Then it
became congested with blood, and whereas at first
he had lain quiet of his own accord, now a dozen
men were holding him tight. The crowd gazed at
him with broad grins on their faces, breaking out
from time to time into a surprised 'Hi-yah', as he
writhed in special pain or cried out in agony. And
all the time the ceaseless shower of blows continued,
the man who wielded the bamboo putting not a
particle more or less force into the last stroke than
into the first. At length the magistrate dropped
another word and the torture stopped as suddenly
as it had begun, the prisoner was lifted to his feet
and led across the court to lean against a wall. For
obvious reasons he could not be accommodated with
a chair.

Beheading

Decapitation, in one form or another, has an exceedingly
ancient history, both as a means of judicial execution and
as a punishment – for example, prisoners of war. A wall
relief in the British Museum depicts the mass decapitation
of prisoners by the Assyrians after their defeat of the
Chaldean marsh dwellers. Among the writings of the
Greeks and the Romans, for whom it represented the
most honourable form of death, there are many references to execution by beheading. The Roman technique
of what, in Latin, was called *decollatio* or *capitis amputatio*
began with the prisoner being tied to a post and whipped
with rods. He was then led to the place of execution and
his head placed over a block set in a specially dug pit. If
the prisoner was a military man the *decollatio* would take
place outside the camp perimeter, if he was a civilian then
he was executed outside the city walls. In the early years
of the Empire decapitation was by axe, but this was gradually superseded by the sword – presumably because the
sword was seen as an honourable weapon appropriate to
a noble death.

During their intensive persecution of the Christians in the first few centuries AD, the Romans put to the sword many converts from the nobility. Among the best known of these first holy martyrs was Cecilia, a patrician girl from Rome who had been brought up in the Christian faith. After her marriage to Valerian, another young noble, Cecilia successfully persuaded him not only to forgo consummating the marriage, but also to become a Christian himself. In fact Valerian in his turn converted his brother Tiburtius and between them they became such zealous Christians that they attracted the attention of the Prefect Almachius, who had them scourged and beheaded by the sword (a mark of respect for their rank). Next Cecilia was paraded before the Prefect and openly laughed in his face; for this she was condemned to be suffocated in her own hot-air bathroom. However, despite the furnace being fed with seven times its normal amount of fuel, Cecilia survived. A soldier was sent to dispatch her, and with trembling hands struck the three sword blows which the law permitted, but left her still living, her head almost severed, on the floor of the bath. Here

The martyrdom of Saint Cecilia

she remained for three days, during which Christians
flocked from miles around to the house. Finally she succumbed and was buried in the catacomb of St Callistus.
As St Cecilia she is widely venerated as the patron saint
of music and musicians.

Beheading as a means of execution was also widespread
in Asia, and particularly favoured in China where the
double-handed sword had a short blade widening towards
the point, in some cases almost resembling an axe – in
which manner it was wielded. The English hangman
James Berry (active 1884–92) had nothing but praise for
the method: 'In China decapitation has been reduced
almost to a science, and the Chinese executioners are
probably the most skilful headsmen in the world. I have
in my possession a Chinese executioner's knife with which
the heads of nine pirates were severed in nine successive
blows, and a terrible knife it is, and well fitted for the
purpose.'

Beheading is all but unknown in the history of the
United States, a single instance being recorded in Massachusetts in 1644. In a statute of 1852, the then 'territory'
of Utah gave courts and convicted individuals the choice
of execution by shooting, hanging or beheading. The last
option was never selected and was dropped from the
statute in 1888. Frederick Drimmer, in his excellent study
of the death sentence in America (*Until You Are Dead*),
explains: 'Both beheading and shooting were originally
chosen because the territory's legislators were mostly
Mormons, and Mormons believe in the biblical doctrine
of blood atonement.' This doctrine is firmly based on a
literal interpretation of the sixth verse of the ninth chapter
of the Book of Genesis: 'Whosoever sheddeth man's
blood, by man shall his blood be shed.'

The only official survival of execution by beheading is
confined to some Arab states and the Congo (which still
uses the **guillotine**). The prescribed method in Qatar,
Yemen, the United Arab Emirates, and Saudia Arabia is
decapitation by the sword. In 1989 one British tabloid
newspaper led with an 'exclusive' – 'I Have Chopped Off

600 Heads' screamed the headline – and went on to describe the life and work of the Saudi official executioner Saeed Al Sayaf. Describing the tools of his trade, the 60-year-old public servant said: 'To chop off the heads of men I use a special sword, following the writings of the prophet Mohammed, while I use a gun to execute women . . . When the job is done I get a sense of delight, and thank God for giving me this power.'

England's Axe

Beheading as a means of execution entered England via the Norman conquest, and was carried out with an axe. The first recorded instance of decapitation is that of Waltheof, earl of Northumberland, in 1076. Although in the centuries closely following the Conquest, beheading was not infrequently the punishment for common thieves, later, like its Roman ancestor, beheading was reserved for prisoners of high rank. Between 1388 and 1747, 91 people were publicly executed on Tower Hill, outside the walls of the Tower of London where a permanent scaffold stood during the fifteenth and sixteenth centuries.

Meanwhile the block and axe *within* the Tower was reserved exclusively for the private executions of seven of the highest prisoners of state in the land, among them Lady Jane Grey, Robert Devereux the second Earl of Essex, Catherine Howard and Anne Boleyn, second wife of King Henry VIII. Having failed to present Henry with a son and heir, Anne was arrested on 2 May 1536 on unsupported charges of adultery with four separate men, including her own brother. Two weeks later, on 19 May, she was executed at the Tower. Anne elected to die by the sword rather than the axe, and as no executioner competent with the sword could be found in England a headsman had to be imported from St Omer in France. It seems that Anne Boleyn had an incipient sixth finger on her left hand, and as this was generally taken to be the sign of a witch it is interesting to speculate whether, had she been of lowly birth, she would have suffered an entirely different kind of execution.

Although there was a pool of axes stored at the Tower to be selected for use as necessary, it was customary for a new block to be fashioned for each execution (or series of executions) and the one now on show in the Bowyer Tower was custom-made for the public decapitation on Tower Hill of Simon Fraser, eleventh Baron Lovat, in 1747. Lovat was one of the last Jacobite leaders to be sentenced to death for their part in Bonnie Prince Charlie's rebellion of 1745 – he was also the last person to die by block and axe in England. The eleventh Baron was a thorough scoundrel who was thought to deserve death not so much for his support of the Pretender's cause as for his lifelong double-dealing; activities which, by the time of his trial for treason on 17 March 1747, had earned him the contempt of the English and Scottish nations alike. One particularly cynical crime was the taking of his wife by force in order to strengthen his title to the estate. For this both he and his father had been sentenced to death, but they managed to escape capture. The trial was a minor *cause célèbre*, with Fraser roundly abusing both the officers of the court and the witnesses, and then pleading his own patriotism in mitigation. Lord Lovat was returned to the Tower where a warrant for his execution arrived on Friday 3 April, sentence to be carried out on the 9th. During the intervening days, Fraser's brash humour never failed him – even at the foot of the scaffold he gazed out at the immense crowd gathered for the occasion and exclaimed: 'God save us, why should there be such a bustle about taking off an old grey head that cannot get up three steps without two men to support it.' On the scaffold itself, Fraser presented the executioner with the customary purse, saying: 'Here Sir, is ten guineas for you. Pray do your work well, for if you should cut and hack my shoulders, and I should be able to rise again, I shall be very angry with you.' So saying he asked to inspect the axe, and running his finger along the blade muttered that he supposed it would have to do. In the event it did, and as John Millbank reported: '. . . he laid down his head on the block, which was struck off at one blow.' In fact the oak block bears *two* deep axe cuts, and it has been suggested that the second indicates an earlier 'practice' stroke.

Less than a year earlier two more of the 'Rebel Lords' – Kilmarnock and Balmerino – had been similarly executed on Tower Hill. Both by all accounts behaved with exemplary dignity and calm on the scaffold, the former after 'dropping his handkerchief, the executioner at once severed his head from his body, except only a small part of the skin, which was immediately divided by a gentle stroke'. It was customary for the prisoner to pre-arrange a signal, such as dropping a kerchief, to make sure that both parties were ready. Lord Balmerino was not quite so fortunate. A contemporary report from the *Newgate Calendar* states: 'Immediately, without trembling or changing countenance, he knelt at the block, and having his arms stretched out, said "Oh Lord reward my friends, forgive my enemies, and receive my soul", he gave the signal by letting his arms fall; but his uncommon firmness and intrepidity, and the unexpected suddenness of the signal so surprised the executioner, that although he struck the part directed, the blow was not given with strength enough to wound him very deep. Upon which it seemed as if he made an effort to turn his head towards the executioner, and the under-jaw fell and returned very quick, like anger and gnashing the teeth . . . A second blow immediately succeeding the first rendered him quite insensible, and a third finished the work.'

The most famous beheading carried in England was the execution of King Charles I in 1649. England had begun to reject the total power exercised by the monarchy under the so-called 'divine right of kings'. When James I ascended the throne in 1603 he reigned as absolute monarch; but when his son, Charles I, took power, he dissolved Parliament and proceeded to rule without it. The effect was to divide the country between the Parliamentarians, under the Puritan Oliver Cromwell, and the King's army and his supporters. During the bloody Civil War which followed, Charles's Cavalier army was defeated, and the king captured and charged with being a 'Tyrant, traitor, murderer and public enemy'. Charles was tried by a special court of 67 judges (called the 'regicides') and executed on a scaffold constructed outside Whitehall Palace, London. Although Richard Brandon was the public executioner at the time, there remains some doubt as to whether he was responsible for beheading the king, because in order to protect the headsman's identity two executioners, both masked, stood on the scaffold. Brandon died six months later, and some time after, his gravestone was given the inscription: 'This R. Brandon is supposed to have cut off the head of Charles I.' According to some authorities, and certainly as depicted in some contemporary illustrations, the block on which Charles was executed was the comparatively rarer 'low' block, obliging the prisoner to lie almost prone on

Contemporary cut of the execution of Charles I

the ground. The more familiar form was the 'high' block such as that used at the Tower, where the victim knelt with his head in the shaped groove. Also preserved at the Tower of London is the 'processional' axe. The head is

20 inches high and 10 wide, set in a 5ft 4in wooden handle decorated with four rows of burnished brass studs. The axe was paraded before state prisoners as they left the Tower to attend their trial, and as they returned there. There is a legend that on the outward journey the blade of the axe was turned away from the prisoner, but on the way back, if he had been sentenced to death, it would be symbolically turned towards him.

It was sometimes the case that decapitation formed just one part of a more elaborate sequence of execution, such as hanging, drawing and quartering. This occurred as recently as 1820 after the execution of the Cato Street conspirators. Arthur Thistlewood and his associates planned to murder the Cabinet while they dined with the Earl of Harrowby at Grosvenor House on 23 February 1820. The conspirators met in an attic room in Cato Street where, before they could carry out their plan, some were arrested; Thistlewood and the others escaped but were arrested on the following day. Five, including their leader, were executed by hanging and their heads were removed by a masked executioner; five others were sentenced to transportation.

[*Note*: In some parts of England decapitation was by an early type of mechanical 'guillotine' called the **Halifax Gibbet**, and in Scotland by a similar machine called the **Maiden**.]

Germany's Sword

Like much of the rest of Europe, Germany consistently employed decapitation as a means of executing capital offenders; although latterly and more rarely the axe and block were used, Germany historically favoured the sword.

Under the medieval Saxon statutes known as the Sachsenspiegel (enacted 1220–35) beheading with the sword was prescribed for arson, and as recently as 1855 the arsonist J. Kilchenmann was thus executed.

Under Article 119 of the 1532 'Carolina', the first authoritative criminal code set for the whole of Germany, the rape of a wife, widow or virgin was punished, like theft and infanticide, with decapitation, and among other sexual crimes, sodomy was also a capital offence punishable by beheading; in fact this remained the case until the middle of the eighteenth century. Decapitation was the penalty for a variety of religious transgressions such as blasphemy, and political crimes headed by treason.

Descriptions and illustrations of early German decapitations show the prisoner either kneeling or sitting in a chair, usually bound (though the older prints sometimes depict the man simply kneeling at prayer). Standing behind the prisoner, the executioner sought, with a single swing, to bring the edge of the sword between two vertebrae and thus ensure a clean cut. The operation required considerable skill, and bungled executions were commonplace, with the headsman needing to hack at the victim's neck several times. Far from enjoying this spectacle of depravity, the crowds frequently attacked an incompetent executioner, and there is one record of a

German headsman of the sixteenth century

botched beheading at Prague Castle in 1509 resulting in the executioner being stoned to death.

There were sometimes permanent execution scaffolds

situated in market places in front of the town hall. The platform of wood or stone was approached by a flight of steps, and in cases where the prisoner was from the nobility, or was a particularly despised criminal, the scaffold would be ringed with armed guards to prevent the onlookers from crowding the executioner.

Most of the surviving headsmen's swords originate in German workshops, and follow a fairly standard pattern. The chief characteristic is the straight blade with its almost parallel sharp edges and curved 'point'; the blade is usually 80–85 cm long and about five cm broad. The double-handed grip enabled the executioner to maximise the power of delivery of his stroke. The decoration was also suitably standardised with scenes of executions being most common, sometimes with moralising texts, such as 'When I raise this sword I wish the sinner everlasting life; the Lords judge evil and I execute their judgement'. Three swords preserved in the Tower of London date from the seventeenth century, and the engravings of the executioner's wheel and the gibbet are finely and elaborately drawn; a later sword in the Prague Military History Museum shows how these images became stylised into

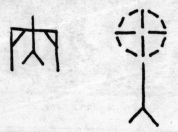

little more than symbols. The scabbard for the executioner's sword was made of wood covered with leather and metal fittings; often he would have lesser scabbards attached to take small knives (rather like the Gurkha 'kukri' or some early hunting swords). The purpose of these knives was to carry out other punishments ordered by the courts, such as cutting out tongues or disembowelling.

Cutting out the tongue, 1590

Beheading with the axe made use of the 'high' block after the English fashion, and executions by beheading were carried out until Germany's rejection of capital punishment after Second World War:

On Thursday morning Hoedel was officially acquainted with the contents of the Crown Prince's order. He remained perfectly quiet, the only sign of inward emotion being the spread of a deadly pallor over his face. Being questioned as to his last wishes, he requested to be executed in public and asked for cigars, some beer and paper to write a letter.

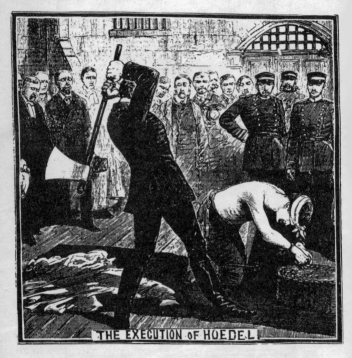

THE EXECUTION OF HOEDEL

Punctually at six o'clock in the morning, Hoedel was led to the scaffold temporarily erected in the prison yard. Hoedel, followed by the warders was dressed in the costume worn by him on the day of the attempted assassination. At the urgent request of the clergyman who was walking by his side, Hoedel on leaving his cell threw away the cigar stump which he had intended to smoke to the very last. At this moment the bell tolled out its dire tones.

The executioner who had been standing quietly holding the axe behind him, then advanced, and with one powerful stroke that cut the air like lightning, severed the head from the body.

It is said that Germany was also home to an instrument of mechanical decapitation of the guillotine type called a **Diele**.

Bell Collar
(see **Collars**)

Benefit of Clergy
This remarkable loophole in the English law originated in the separation, in the Middle Ages, of the ecclesiastical and secular courts, which enabled the clergy to exempt themselves from secular jurisdiction. Thus, persons in Holy Orders accused of a crime were sent before the Bishop's Court, a notable feature of which was its powerlessness to pass sentence of death. (It was to reverse such encroachments by the church courts upon secular law that Henry II appointed Thomas Becket archbishop of Canterbury in 1162. Becket proved less compliant than his former friend had supposed, and the archbishop – as much a victim of his own arrogance as of Henry's displeasure – was assassinated in Canterbury Cathedral in 1170.)

This Benefit of Clergy was subsequently extended to all persons who were eligible for ordination into the Church – effectively anybody who could read. So corrupt, however, were the courts that in order to 'plead' it was necessary only to learn by heart the first verse of Psalm 51, which became known as the 'neck-verse'*: 'Have mercy upon

---

*Other authorities have claimed the fifth verse of Psalm 51 as the 'neck-verse': 'Behold I was shapen in iniquity; and in sin did my mother conceive me.'

me, O God, according to thy loving kindness; according unto the multitude of thy tender mercies blot out my transgressions.'

The judge would ask: 'Legit aut non legit?' ('Can he read or not?'). The chaplain replied: 'Legit ut clericus' ('He reads like a clerk'). Sentence would then be reduced to some other form of physical punishment, such as flogging, or to imprisonment or fining. Nor was it entirely necessary to learn the saving verse by heart; a few coins in the chaplain's hand would ensure a few promptings in the felon's ear.

By a statute of 1490 it became impossible for secular prisoners to plead Benefit of Clergy more than once. To ensure this laymen were marked by branding on the ball of the thumb (colourfully described as 'glymming in the paw', or 'burning in the hand'). There always having been 'one law for the rich and another for the poor', it comes as no surprise that many judges were prepared, either for money or favour, to allow the use of a cold iron.

Benefit of Clergy was abolished in England in 1827, but is said to have been successfully invoked in the state of Carolina, USA, in 1855.

Berry, James

Despite being possessed of a calling which few would envy, executioner Berry was, by all accounts, a kindly and warm-hearted man who, ironically, best displayed these virtues in his professional life. Throughout his career, Berry was at pains to develop his craft so that his executions were carried out with a speed and efficiency that caused the least distress and suffering to his prisoners.

James Berry was born in Heckmondwike, Yorkshire, on 8 February 1852, the son of a wool-stapler. He was educated at Wrea Green School, near Lytham, and was later employed as a lithographic artist. In 1874 Berry joined the Bradford Borough Police Force. It was during this period that he met, quite by chance at a friend's house, the then official hangman William Marwood.

Berry was much impressed by Marwood, and without the least encouragement from the hangman, developed an ambition to enter the 'trade' himself. Subsequently he applied to the Sheriffs of London and Edinburgh, and on 21 March 1884 he received a letter from the magistrates' clerk at Edinburgh inviting him to act as hangman at Calton Gaol where, on the 31st of the month, the double execution of the 'Gorebridge Murderers' was scheduled to take place. Apparently Berry acquitted himself well, and in his own account of 'My First Execution' he concluded: 'The magistrates and doctors, and even the pressmen, admitted that the execution of the two men had been carried out in as humane manner as possibly could be, and that the poor fellows had not suffered the slightest pain in going through the execution; doctors have given me a testimonial as to the skilful way I had carried out the execution.'

James Berry, executioner, was in business! And would remain so until 1892 when, perhaps haunted by the ghosts of his past 'clients', he took up the cause of abolition, and is on record as declaring that 'My experiences have convinced me that we shall never be a civilised nation while executions are carried out in prison.' Nevertheless he did continue to make a satisfactory living out of his past, launching himself as an 'entertainment' with a slide lecture entitled 'Prisons and Prisoners' embodying his experiences and skills as an executioner. Berry made his debut at the Westminster Aquarium on 19 March 1892, sharing the same bill as some American clairvoyants, a team of trick cyclists, and the Sidonia Quartette, singing 'Ta-Ra-Ra-boom-de-ay'. An extra one shilling was charged above the ticket price to 'assist with the expenses of Mr Berry's campaign against capital punishment'. From a rather prim, schoolmasterly start, Berry relaxed into his own inimitable pace as he looked forward to eleven further dates at the Aquarium, followed by a nationwide tour. He also began to be more explicit in his condemnation of the death penalty, with asides such as 'High Sheriff is just a flash name for executioner. Now that I've had the chance of washing my dirty hands of the business for ever, if I had my way I'd make the sheriffs do the job themselves', adding, 'a lot of them still owe me money'. At other times, when he appeared before less 'intellectual' audiences, Berry was not above lightening the programme with a sprinkling of jokes; one of his favourites was: 'Thus we have the body hanging there to dry for an hour while the sheriff's officers go out to wet. After this the body is laid in quicklime to keep it warm until resurrection.' Things came to an abrupt end one evening as Berry was lecturing at the Liverpool Hippodrome and the oxyacetylene cylinder he carried around to provide limelight for his magic lantern exploded. Thankfully nobody was hurt, but it destroyed Berry's slide collection. After this he tried his hand at a number of occupations including that of inn-keeper. James Berry died in 1913. (See also **Hanging**, for a description of James Berry's method of execution.)

James Berry's Business Cards

James Berry,
EXECUTIONER.

8, BILTON PLACE,
BRADFORD, YORKS.

'A little anecdote, which I call the toothache story, happened in 1887; when crossing from Ireland there was one of the passengers who was terribly ill with *mal de mer* and toothache combined. He was rather a bother to several

travellers who were not sick and wished to enjoy the
voyage, and he must have given a lot of trouble to the
stewards. I think that one of the latter must have told
him that I could cure him, for he came and begged me
to tell him what was the best thing for his complaint. I
admitted that I was in the habit of giving drops that would
instantly cure both the toothache and the sea-sickness,
but assured him that he would not be willing to take my
remedy. Still he persisted, so I handed him a card [see
illustration above], and as he was a sensitive man it gave
his nerves a shock that was quite sufficient to relieve him
of the toothache and me of his presence for the rest of
the voyage. The wording was in black with the fern in
green and the border in gold. I now use a perfectly plain
card.

James Berry,
Executioner.

Bradford,
Yorkshire.

'I am not ashamed of my calling because I consider that
if it is right for men to be executed (which I believe it is,
in murder cases) it is right that the office of executioner
should be held respectable. Therefore I look at hanging
from a business point of view. When I first took up the
work I was in the habit of applying to the sheriff of the
county whenever a murderer was sentenced to death. I no
longer consider it necessary to apply for work in England,
because I am now well known, but I still send a simple
address card when an execution in Ireland is announced.'

(Both the above extracts are from James Berry's auto-biography *My Experiences as an Executioner*.)

Black Cap

Thankfully now only a bleak memory, the Black Cap was once Britain's most potent symbol of the ultimate sanction of the law. A piece of black silk about nine inches square, it has been part of a high court judge's dress costume since the time of the Tudor monarchs. As an 'accessory', it is carried, and occasionally worn, on ceremonial occasions such as Lord Mayor's Day and the State Opening of Parliament. It was the placing of the Black Cap atop the judge's wig while he pronounced sentence of death that put this modest square of cloth firmly into folklore, though this use was not obligatory. The Royal Commission on Capital Punishment in its 1953 report recommended that the wearing of the Black Cap during capital sentencing should be left to the discretion of the judges themselves.

It is a popular myth that no judge has ever been photographed wearing the Black Cap – but, considering that photography is forbidden while a court is sitting, it would come as no surprise; in fact there *have* been several occasions on which the event has been surreptitiously snapped. With the abolition of capital punishment in 1965, however, such discussion became purely academic.

Bloody Assizes
(see **Jeffreys, Judge George**)

Boiling to Death

Boiling to death is commonly reported in ancient literature, and predictably the Romans included this punishment in their extensive and imaginative catalogue of persecutions against the early Christians. One of the best known examples of this kind of death is that suffered in the year 303 by the young Sicilian boy who became Saint Vitus. Vitus (sometimes called Guy or Guido) was the son of a noble, though 'unenlightened', father, and became converted to Christianity through the good teachings of his old nurse Crescentia. Nothing, however, escaped the eagle eye of the parent, and as soon as he learned Vitus's secret, his father had the boy scourged and thrown into prison. It was while he was here that a band of angels came and danced for Vitus, radiating a light so bright that his father was blinded. Mindful of his filial duties, even *in extremis*, Vitus prayed for the return of his father's sight, and his entreaty was granted. If the lad had expected gratitude he was to be sadly disappointed, and so severe were his father's renewed persecutions that Vitus decamped with his nurse and old Moderatus, his tutor, and fled into Italy. It was a bad move, and the three were at once taken up as Christians and hurled into a cauldron of boiling oil. It is said that after their gruesome death a wolf stood guard over the three bodies until they could be buried by fellow Christians.

In Germany in the Middle Ages boiling alive was the usual punishment under the Schwabenspiegel (Swabian tribal law) for forgery, as it was under the Carolina for counterfeiting coins. Boiling was in water, oil or wine – water always being used for the execution of heretics.

Boiling entered the English statute in 1530–31 via an Act of Henry VIII. The law seems to have been enacted in response to a specific instance of poisoning: 'On the 18th day of February, 1531, one Richard Roose, of Rochester, a cook, did cast poison into a vessel full of yeast, or baum, standing in the kitchens of the Bishop of Rochester's Palace at Lambeth March, by means of which seventeen of the household were poisoned and two of the persons who happened to eat the pottage died . . . The said poisoning be adjudged high treason, and that the said Richard Roose, for the said murder and poisoning of the said two persons, shall stand, and be attainted of high treason and the offender be deprived of his [right to

Benefit of] Clergy and boiled to death.' Quite why a poisoning of this nature, which posed no threat to the safety of the state or monarch, should have been considered grave enough to rank as high treason is a mystery.

The infernal punishment of the seven deadly sins – the greedy were boiled alive in cauldrons of oil (a woodcut published in 1496)

It could have been covered by petty (or petit) treason, which punished with death the murder (or sometimes attempted murder) of a husband by his wife, a master by his servant, or an ecclesiastic by an inferior. As it happened, Roose was pipped to the post by another poisoner, a young female servant who was publicly executed by boiling alive in the market place at King's Lynn in 1532. Richard Roose met his end at **Smithfield**, a popular place of execution in London, on 15 April 1532.

Boiling to death remained a useful political tool in Henry VIII's persecution of the Carthusians during the dissolution of the monasteries, but in March 1542, the Act was once again invoked against a poisoning maidservant. Mary Davy (or Dawe) was boiled alive at Smithfield after being convicted of the murder of members of the household in which she served. This barbaric law was repealed by Henry's son, Edward VI, when he acceded to the throne in 1547; however it survived in Europe as a periodic feature of religious persecutions.

Branding

Since at least 4000 BC, when the Babylonians decreed that to speak ill of a married woman or a priestess should be punished by branding, this form of mutilation has been used variously as a punishment and as a mark of identification; indeed, cattle are still marked in this way.

The ancient Greeks branded their slaves as proof of ownership, as did the Romans, who also used branding on the forehead as a punishment for slaves who tried unsuccessfully to escape.

Subsequently branding spread throughout the world and reached England even before the Anglo-Saxons ratified its use in law; and it remained a punishment in one form or another until the early years of the nineteenth century. What is less widely known is that branding was also employed as a means of identifying *English* slaves. By an Act of Edward VI, dated 1547, any vagrant or beggar could be taken before a Justice of the Peace and ordered to be branded on the chest with a letter V (Vagrant or Vagabond); the unfortunate man then became the property of the person presenting him to the Justice for a period of two years, 'and fed on bread and water and set to work, no matter how vile that work may be, and if necessary be chained and beaten'. Should the 'slave' escape and be recaptured, a Justice would cause him to be further branded – this time with an S (Slave) on the forehead or cheek – and become his 'owner's' property till the end of his days. Attempting to escape for a second time was punishable by death. This Act was not repealed until 1636.

Under the laws governing those entitled to **Benefit of Clergy** it was enacted during the reign of Henry VII that non-clerical felons could plead Clergy only once, and to ensure this they were branded on the ball of the thumb with an M (Malefactor). This mark was made in open court before the judge, and to this day in the old Assize Court at Lancaster Castle the metal bands, or 'hold-fast', into which the prisoner's hand was secured, and the branding iron with which he was marked, can be seen. Like much legal procedure of earlier centuries, this 'burning in the hand' was open to abuse, and a modest bribe usually ensured that the warder responsible for branding would use a cold iron. Some crimes were punishable by burning in the face – usually the forehead or the cheek just below the eye – and a common variant was burning a hole with a red-hot skewer through the flesh of the ear or through the tongue.

The following list, compiled from several sources, gives the abbreviations used for offences punishable by branding:

B – Blasphemer
F – Fray-maker/Felon
FA – False Accuser
M – Malefactor/Murderer
P – Perjuror
R – Robber/Rogue
S – Slave
SL – Seditious Libeller

T – Thief
V – Vagrant/Vagabond

In France, where branding was a common punishment for many less serious misdemeanours, the brand was usually in the pattern of the fleur-de-lys. One notable exception concerned the Countess de la Motte who, for stealing a diamond necklace, was whipped naked through the streets at the cart's tail (see **Flagellation**) and then branded on the shoulder with a letter V (presumably *Voleuse*, or 'thief').

Brank
(see **Scold's Bridle**)

Brazen Bull

Perilaus, roasted in the bull he made,
Gave the first proof of his own cruel trade.
                            (Ovid)

Of this ingenious device we have only a classical description from the Greek satirical writer Lucian (c. AD 120-c. 190). Unfortunately as both Ovid and Lucian wrote 'imaginary' stories, and Lucian's report of the Brazen Bull comes from *True History*, his parody of travellers' tales, one might be tempted to doubt its authenticity. That said, as an instrument of torture it is certainly believable, and far less fantastic than many for which we have solid proof.

The evil genius behind the design of the Brazen Bull was a man named Perilaus. The machine itself was cast in metal as a life-size effigy of a real bull, with a hollow interior and a trap-door in its back leading into the cavity. The victim was locked inside the Bull and a fire kindled beneath it, the searing heat causing him to scream in pain and terror of an excruciating death. And now Perilaus's cruel ingenuity was best displayed, for inside the creature's nostrils was an arrangement of pipes which transformed the agonised wretch's death cries into melodious lowing sounds. The inventor was so pleased with his work that he transported the Brazen Bull to the temple of the only man he knew who was as wicked as himself – the tyrant Phalaris. For reasons known only to himself, Phalaris took strong exception to both Perilaus and his infernal beast, and decided to indulge his own sadistic taste in entertainment at his guest's expense. Lucian takes up the story:

The Brazen Bull of Perilaus

'Well now, Perilaus,' the tyrant said, 'if you are so sure of your creation give proof of it; mount up and get inside and imitate the groans of a man tortured in it, that we will hear the music that you tell us will issue from it.' Perilaus obeyed his master's instruction, but as soon as he was in the belly of the beast

Phalaris closed the door after him and ordered a fire built. 'Take this as the only reward such a piece of art is worth, and chant for us the charming notes of which you are the creator.' And so the cruel wretch suffered. Nevertheless, so that the fine craftsmanship should not be sullied, Phalaris ordered his prisoner to be taken alive from the Bull, cast from a high rock and his corpse left unburied.

Breaking on the Cross

A variation of breaking on the wheel in which two crossed wooden beams in the figure of a St Andrew's cross are substituted for the wheel. Although this was a method of execution widely used in Europe, it is interesting to read in Stedman's *Narrative** that breaking on the cross was practised in the late eighteenth century by the natives of Suriname – mainly as a means of executing slaves. Once the victim had been securely tied to the cross, the executioner approached and hacked off the man's hand with a chopper. He then proceeded with an iron bar to systematically 'Break his bones to shivers, till marrow, blood and splinters flew about the field'. The helpless prisoner was then cut from the cross, still alive, to endure six more hours of agony. Although his plea for the *coup de grâce* was constantly refused this hapless man was eventually put out of his misery when a 'compassionate' guard stoved in his head with a rifle-butt. It ought to be added that it was the European practice to end the prisoner's suffering quickly with a lethal blow to the stomach.

THE MARTYRDOM OF SIEUR BOETON

The executioner advanced in his turn, holding in his hand a square bar of iron, an inch and a half wide, three feet long and rounded at one end. At the sight

**Narrative of a Five Years' Expedition Against the Revolted Negroes of Surinam . . . From the Year 1772–1777*, J. G. Stedman, London, 1796.

Martyrdom of Sieur Boeton, broken on the cross

of him, Boeton began to chant a psalm, which he interrupted by a slight cry; the executioner had broken the bone of his right leg . . .

Breaking on the Wheel
(see **Wheels**)

Bridle
(see **Scold's Bridle**)

Brodequins
(see **Spanish Boot**)

Brownrigg, Elizabeth

After living seven years in Greenwich, James Brownrigg, whose occupation is variously recorded as plumber and house-painter, came to London and took a house in Flower-de-Luce (Fleur de Lys) Court, Fleet Street, where he carried on the greater part of his business; he also had a small dwelling at Islington used as an occasional retreat. His wife Elizabeth was the mother of sixteen children, and having practised midwifery, helped feed the many hungry mouths by virtue of this skill. The fact that she was held in some respect is indicated by her appointment by the overseers of the poor of St Dunstan's parish to the post of midwife to the poor women in the workhouse, which duty she appeared to perform to the entire satisfaction of her employers and, it is said, with great care and tenderness.

Mary Mitchell, a poor girl in the care of the precinct of Whitefriars, was put out as an apprentice to Mrs Brownrigg in the year 1765; and at about the same time, Mary Jones, one of the children of the Foundling Hospital, was likewise placed with her in the same capacity; and she also had other apprentices. Lest it be thought that Brownrigg was charity personified, it must be remembered that anybody willing to take on an 'apprentice' from the workhouse was given five pounds towards expenses (as any reader of Dickens's *Oliver Twist* will remember). As Mrs Brownrigg also received pregnant women to lie-in privately at her home, these girls were taken with a view of saving the expense of women-servants. At first the workhouse orphans were treated with some degree of civility; but this soon gave way to the most savage barbarity. Once, having laid Mary Jones across two chairs in the kitchen, Mary Brownrigg whipped her with such wanton cruelty that she was occasionally obliged to rest through sheer fatigue; this treatment was frequently repeated. The punishment was sometimes concluded by Mrs Brownrigg throwing water on the child when she had done whipping her; sometimes she would dip the girl's head into a pail of water. The room appointed for the girl to sleep in adjoined a passage leading to the street door, and, smarting under the many wounds on her head, shoulders and various parts of her body, she determined not to bear such treatment any longer if she could escape.

Observing that the key was left in the street door when the family went to bed, Mary Jones opened the door cautiously one early morning and escaped into the street. Thus freed from her wretched confinement, she repeatedly enquired her way to the Foundling Hospital till she found it, and was admitted after describing the manner in which she had been treated, and showing the bruises she had received. The child was examined by a surgeon, who found her wounds to be of a most alarming nature. The Governors of the Hospital therefore instructed Mr Plumbtree, their solicitor, to write to James Brownrigg, threatening a prosecution if he did not give a proper reason for the severities exercised on the child.

Seeing no notice of this letter being taken, and the Governors of the Hospital thinking it imprudent to indict at common law, the girl was discharged in consequence of an application to the Chamberlain of London. The other girl, Mary Mitchell, continued with her mistress for the space of a year, during which she was treated with equal cruelty, and she also resolved to quit her service. Having escaped from the house, she was met in the street by the Brownriggs' younger son, who forced her to return home, where her sufferings were greatly aggravated on account of her vain bid for freedom. In the interim the overseers of the precinct of Whitefriars bound Mary Clifford apprentice to Brownrigg, and it was not long before she too experienced cruelties similar to those inflicted on the other poor girls, and possibly even more severe. She was frequently tied up naked and beaten with a hearthbroom, a horsewhip or a cane till she completely lost the power of speech. This unfortunate girl having a natural infirmity, the mistress would not permit her to lie in a bed, but placed her on a mat in a coal-hole that was remarkably cold; however, after some time, Mrs Brownrigg must have had a change of heart, and a sack and a quantity of straw was given to form her bed, in place of the mat. During Mary Clifford's confinement in this wretched situation she had nothing to subsist on but bread

and water; and her covering, during the night, consisted only of her own clothes, so that she sometimes lay and almost perished with the cold.

On one particular occasion, when she was almost starving with hunger, she broke open a cupboard in search of food, but found it empty; and on another occasion she broke down some boards in order to procure a draught of water. Though the child was thus pressed for the humblest necessaries of life, Mrs Brownrigg determined to punish her rigorously for her audacity in taking steps to supply herself with them. She caused the girl to strip to the skin, and during the course of a whole day, while she remained naked, Brownrigg repeatedly beat her with the butt-end of a whip.

After whipping her till the blood streamed down her body, Brownrigg let the girl down, and made her wash herself in a tub of icy water. Mary Mitchell, the other orphan apprentice, was forced to be present during this chastisement. While Clifford was washing herself, Mrs Brownrigg repeatedly struck her shoulders, already sore with former bruises, with the butt-end of a whip; and she treated the child in this manner five more times that same day.

In the course of this most inhuman treatment a collar and chain was fixed round the girl's neck, and its end was fastened to the yard door and pulled as tight as possible without strangling her. A day being suffered of this savage treatment, the girl was remanded to the coal-hole at night, her hands tied behind her, and the chain still about her neck.

Through the intervention of young Mary Clifford's aunt – who had been refused permission by the Brownriggs to see her niece – and through reports given by neighbours of the screaming of the children, the parish authorities were at length persuaded to take action – action resulting in swift retribution in the person of Mr Grundy, overseer of St Dunstan's, who caused James Brownrigg to be conveyed to the Wood Street Compter. His wife and son had already beaten a hasty retreat, taking with them a gold watch and some money. Mr Brownrigg was taken before Alderman Crossby, who committed him for trial, and ordered the girls to be taken to St Bartholomew's Hospital, where Mary Clifford died within a few days. A coroner's inquest was summoned, and a verdict of wilful murder against James and Elizabeth Brownrigg, and John Brownrigg, their son, was found.

In the meantime Mrs Brownrigg and the boy shifted from place to place in London, buying clothes in a ragshop to disguise themselves and going finally to Wandsworth, where they took lodgings in the house of Mr Dunbar, keeper of a chandler's shop.

The chandler, by chance reading a newspaper on 15 August, saw an advertisement which so clearly described his lodgers that he had no doubt but that they were the murderers. A constable was called to the house, and the mother and son were quickly conveyed to London. On 2 September 1767, during the ensuing Sessions at the Old Bailey, father, mother and son were indicted. Elizabeth Brownrigg, after a trial of eleven hours, was found guilty of murder, and ordered for execution, to the unrestrained delight of the large crowd that had gathered outside the court. The man and his son, being acquitted of the higher charge, were detained to take their trials for a misdemeanour, of which they both were convicted and imprisoned for the space of six months.

After sentence of death was passed on Mrs Brownrigg she was attended by a clergyman, to whom she confessed the enormity of her crime, and acknowledged the justice of the sentence by which she had been condemned. The parting between her and her family, on the morning of her execution, was said to be very moving. The son fell on his knees, and she bent over him and embraced him, while the husband knelt on the other side.

Along her route to the fatal tree the people gave expression to their abhorrence of her crime in terms which testified to their detestation of her barbaric cruelty.

After execution her body was put into a hackney-coach, and in accordance with the law conveyed to Surgeons'

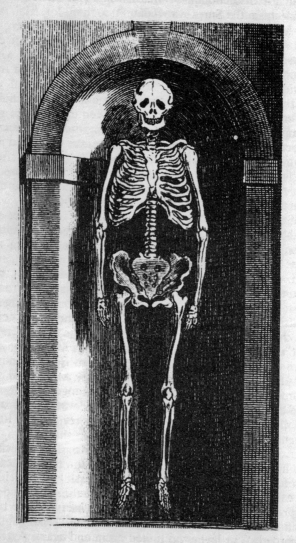

Elizabeth Brownrigg's anatomised skeleton at Surgeons' Hall

Hall for dissection and anatomising. Her skeleton was hung up in the **Surgeons' Hall**.

Bungled Executions

Along with stories of people being hanged in error – of which, due mainly to the unsound foundations of the law-enforcement system and the huge number of capital offences on the statute in former centuries, there are many – are a host of cases of people who were hanged several times, hanged and then revived, or reprieved just as they had been 'launched into eternity'. In fact, there are a number of reliably recorded cases where, for reasons generally connected with the crudeness of the method of execution, the prisoner simply would not hang.

The most celebrated case was that of John Lee, the Babbacombe Murderer, who, in 1884, at the age of nineteen years, was convicted of the brutal murder of the elderly spinster for whom he served as footman.

Lee was to have been executed by **James Berry** then the official hangman, whose competence had never been held in doubt. The prisoner was in position beneath the gallows, a hood over his head and a rope round his neck. Berry pulled the lever. The trap remained stuck fast, with John Lee standing on it. The hangman pulled again; and again; still the prisoner could not drop. Berry stamped several times on the doors of the trap, and so did the warders; still the doors remained firmly together.

With Lee removed, the 'machine' was tested and checked, and worked perfectly – until they tried to hang John Lee for the second time.

A much embarrassed James Berry once again checked his apparatus, and once again completed a successful test drop. And once again he was unsuccessful in launching Lee, as they say, 'into Eternity'. To the dismay, and by now more than a little disgust, of the observers, the trap then refused to open for a third time. The chaplain recorded: 'The lever was pulled again and again. A great noise was heard, which sounded like the falling of the drop. But to my horror, when I turned my eyes to the scaffold, I saw the poor convict standing upon the drop as I had seen him twice before. I refused to stay any longer.'

The only person not surprised by the strange occurrence was Lee himself, for he had dreamed that he would not hang; 'The Lord will never permit me to be executed,' he said. And, indeed, John Lee's sentence was commuted to imprisonment, and he was released in 1907.

Of the subsequent explanations (including many involving divine intervention), the most likely seems to be that the flaps of the trap had become swollen as a result of soaking up the recent heavy rain, and when a weight was put directly on them the edges bound.

But the case of John Lee is a rare one, for though a large number of early executions failed the first time, in most cases this was due to the incompetence – often through drink – of the executioner. The two major causes of error were misjudging the length of drop, so that when

One of the problems of early hanging techniques

the prisoner fell he landed on his feet; and failing to secure the rope to the gallows properly so that man tumbled to the ground, followed by the rope. Not infrequently the rope itself would break, and in one such instance the prisoner had to be carried back up to the scaffold and held under the beam because he had broken his leg in the fall. It can only be said that in the vast majority of cases the operation worked successfully the second time, as in the case of Benjamin Renshaw, immortalised in the *Newgate Calendar*. '. . . After he was turned off, the noose of the rope moved under his chin, and it was deemed proper to put him back in the cart, that the rope might be adjusted afresh, after which he was turned off again. This circumstance occasioned a considerable sensation among the spectators, who generally expressed their abhorrence of the executioner, to whose carelessness they attributed the accident.'

One of the most ghastly cases of bungling took place at the execution of soldier Private Hales, at Jersey: 'He was accompanied to the place of execution [by the Revd G. Du Heaume]. He joined him in prayer, and ascended the scaffold with coolness and composure. At length he was turned off; and, when he had hung about a minute and a half, the executioner, taking hold of his convulsed body, suspended himself on it, and by this additional weight, the rope gave way, in such a manner that the miserable sufferer's feet touched the ground. The executioner then pulled him sideways, with a view to strangling him, and being unable to effect it in this way got upon his shoulders. To the great surprise of all who witnessed this dreadful scene, the poor criminal rose straight up on his feet, with the hangman on his shoulders, and immediately loosened the rope from his throat with his fingers. No language can describe the sensations which were excited among the bystanders by this shocking scene. The sheriff ordered another rope to be prepared; but the spectators interfered, and the sheriff agreed that, before proceeding with the execution of the sentence, he would wait till the will of the magistracy should be known . . .

Petitions were prepared by the inhabitants and forwarded to His Majesty, and he was pardoned accordingly.'

A further complication that arose in consequence of the crude early method of hanging – which amounted to little more than slow strangling at the end of a rope – was that the time of fatality differed from one person to another. There are more than a few reports from anatomists (to whom the bodies of executed criminals were consigned for the purpose of medical dissection and teaching) of 'corpses' maintaining a heartbeat several hours after being cut down from the gallows. One or two even made a complete recovery, such a one being resuscitated by Sir William Petty, Professor of Anatomy at Oxford University in 1650. After hanging for half an hour, the woman concerned recovered to live, it is said, a further nine years, during which she married and gave birth to two children (see **Revivals After Execution**).

A less happy conclusion attended the execution in 1885 of Robert Goodale, condemned to death for the murder of his wife; it was the duty of the aforementioned James Berry to carry out the sentence of the law at Norwich. Berry recorded the incident in his autobiography: 'At that time I was working with my original table of lengths of drop, which I had based on Mr Marwood's system. Goodale weighted fifteen stones, and the calculated drop for a man of that weight, according to the old table, was seven feet eight inches. As the prisoner did not seem very muscular I reduced the drop by about two feet – in fact as closely as I could measure it, to five feet nine inches. The rope that I used was one made and supplied by the Government and I had used it seven days previously for the execution of John Williams at Hereford. The drop was built on a plan supplied by the Government, and had been used before. In fact everything was in perfect working order. The Governor of the jail had been specially anxious that everything should be right, and had taken all possible precautions to avoid a hitch. He had personally tested the drop on the Thursday morning before, and on the Saturday had again tested it, in company with an engineer. The whole of the arrangements were carried out in the usual manner, and when I pulled the lever the drop fell properly, and the prisoner dropped out of sight. We were horrified, however, to see that the rope jerked upwards, and for an instant I thought the noose had slipped from around the culprit's head, or that

the rope had broken. But it was worse than that, for the jerk had severed the head entirely from the body, and both had fallen together to the bottom of the pit. Of course, death was instantaneous, so that the poor fellow had not suffered in any way; but it was terrible to think that such a revolting thing should have occurred. We were all unnerved and shocked.' Berry added with some satisfaction that the inquest on the incident had completely exonerated him and that 'the Governor and the Gaol Surgeon both gave evidence as to the care with which every detail had been carried out'.

It should not be thought, however, that such appalling scenes attend only historic executions, or that they are confined to Britain. On 22 April 1983, John Louis Evans, who had been convicted in 1977 of killing a store owner during an armed robbery, was finally led into the death chamber at Alabama state prison. Evans's head had been shaved and, as he was strapped into the electric chair, conducting gel was applied to his scalp and the electrodes attached to his head and left leg. As the first 1,900-volt shock surged through his body, what was later described as 'a fiery arc' shot from beneath the mask covering his face and smoke began to pour from the electrode on his leg before the strap burned through. Witnesses claimed they could see Evans struggling for breath, and doctors pronounced him still alive. The burned straps were replaced and, four and half minutes after the first, a second surge of current was passed through the prisoner's body. But John Evans was still alive, and appeals were immediately made to the state governor – George Wallace – to stop the execution on the grounds that it had become 'intolerably cruel and unusual' and was therefore in contravention of the Constitution. Wallace refused, and Evans was given a third, and this time fatal, surge of electricity. It had, in all, taken fourteen agonising minutes to kill him. The autopsy on Evans's body revealed that while alive he suffered two fourth-degree burns on the temple and second-degree burns on the leg.

Burial Alive

It might be thought that so obviously terrifying a cause of death as burial alive* would have a lengthy pedigree: however, there are tantalisingly few references in either anthropological or criminological literature. One usually reliable source claims that 'apart from savage races, burying alive as a specific method of execution seems to have been infrequently practised' (Scott, *History of Torture*), and another: 'exactly how this punishment was carried out cannot be definitely established from the available sources'.

Some help is provided by the Mittelalterliches Kriminal-museum treatise *Criminal Justice through the Ages*, which suggests that, in Germany at least, the punishment was reserved for men and women who had been found guilty of some sexual transgression. 'The offender was laid, alive and bound, in a pit dug near the gallows and the removed earth thrown back over him. To make any return of the condemned person more difficult, he was laid face down like a suicide and tangled thorny bushes were placed over the grave. If the delinquent was placed on his back, a tube was put in his mouth, not to enable him to breathe, but to give the soul a chance to leave the body (called a 'soul-hole'). **Impaling** was closely related to burial alive – after burial a stake was driven into the pit and through the condemned person.'

There is some evidence for the occasional use of burial alive in France, and in his *Manners, Customs and Dress during the Middle Ages*, Paul Lacroix records that in 1460 a convicted female thief called Perette was condemned

*'. . . It may be asserted, without hesitation, that *no* event is so terribly well adapted to inspire the supremeness of bodily and of mental distress, as is burial before death. The unendurable oppression of the lungs – the stifling fumes of the damp earth – the clinging of the death garments – the rigid embrace of the narrow house – the blackness of the absolute Night – the silence like a sea that overwhelms – the unseen but palpable presence of the Conquerer Worm . . .'

(Edgar Allan Poe, 'The Premature Burial', 1844)

by the Provost of Paris to be buried alive beside the
gallows; earlier, in the thirteenth century, Aymeric, sister
of the Governor of Le Voeur, is said to have been ordered
to be thrown alive into a pit and covered with rocks.

Burning Alive

So obvious is the use of the all-consuming flame as a
means of causing death that it is no surprise to find the
use of fire as a means of torture mentioned in the earliest
written history. However, it is more practical to open this
brief study of execution through burning alive with two
biblical references, from the Old and New Testaments
respectively. The first is taken from the book of Joshua
(chapter 7; verse 25): 'And all Israel stoned him with
stones, and burned them with fire, after they had stoned
them with stones'. The second comes from chapter 15 of
the book of St John: 'If a man abideth not in me, he is
cast forth as a branch, and is withered: and men gather
them into the fire and they are burned.' The 'cleansing'
qualities of fire continued to put burning to death in the
forefront of punishments for heresy throughout Europe,
and from at least the twelfth century onwards it was highly
favoured by both the Papal and Spanish Inquisitions (see
Inquisition).

Isolated examples of burning at the stake for heresy
can been found in English records as early as the first
years of the thirteenth century. One case occurred in
1222, when a young deacon was tried before an ecclesiastical court and later burned on the order of the Sheriff of
Oxford. The man's 'crime' had been to fall in love with
a Jewish girl and take up her religion in preference to his
own. However, by the Statute of Heresy passed in 1401
under Henry IV, power was given to the clergy to arrest
all those accused of spreading heresy, whether by the
written or the spoken word. Those who recanted were
imprisoned anyway, and those who did not were publicly
burned at the stake. The first victim of the statute was
William Sautre, a priest, who was burnt at St Paul's Cross,

Public notice announcing the burning of heretics in Germany, 1555

Lynn, in March 1402. Although the Act was repealed in 1533, Henry VIII reintroduced burning at the stake for those who denied the doctrine of transubstantiation (a belief that the whole substance of the bread and the wine change into the substance of the body and blood of Christ when they are consecrated during the Eucharist); in effect this included all Protestants, but Henry, without fear or favour, had Roman Catholics burnt as well.

It was during the reign of Henry VIII's daughter Mary (1553–58) that the most notorious persecution of the English Protestants took place, and at least 274 men, women and some children were consigned to the flames; such was the backlog that at times it was necessary to execute the 'heretics' in groups. Most of those burnt met their martyrdom in London's **Smithfield**, a traditional place of execution. It happened that the cruelty and unreason of Mary's attempt to impose the Church of Rome on the English proved counter productive, and weakened the cause of Catholicism. The public view of Mary as tyrannical was reinforced by John Fox's celebrated chronicle of the persecutions which he had witnessed at first hand and published as the *Book of Martyrs;* it was said that for a century following, this was the only book, apart from the Bible, read by poor people.

On 9 February 1555, John Hooper, Bishop of Gloucester and Worcester, was burned in his own diocese before an estimated crowd of 7,000 people:

The place of execution was near a giant elm tree, over against the college of priests, where he was used to preach; the spot round about and the boughs of the tree were filled with spectators. Bishop Hooper then knelt down and prayed. Having closed his devotional exercises the Bishop prepared himself for the stake. He took off his gown and delivered it to the sheriff; he then took off his doublet, hose, and waistcoat. Being now in his shirt he trussed it between his legs, where he had a pound of gunpowder in a bladder, and under each arm the same quantity. He now went up to the stake where three iron hoops were brought, one to fasten him round the waist, another round the neck and another round his legs; but he refused to be bound with them saying: 'You have no need to trouble yourselves; I doubt not God will give me sufficient strength to abide the extremity of the fire without bands; notwithstanding, suspecting the frailty and weakness of the flesh, but having assured confidence in God's strength, I am content you do as you think good.' The iron hoop was then put round his waist, which being made too short, he shrank and put in his belly with his hand; but when they offered to bind his neck and legs he refused them, saying: 'I am well assured I shall not trouble you.' Being affixed to the stake he lifted up his eyes and hands to heaven, and prayed in silence. The man appointed to kindle the fire then came to him and requested his forgiveness, of whom he asked why he should forgive him, since he knew of no offence he had committed against him. 'Oh, sir,' said the man, 'I am appointed to make the fire.' 'Therein,' said Bishop Hooper, 'thou dost nothing to offend me: God forgive thee thy sins, and do thy office I pray thee.'

Then the reeds were thrown up, and he received two bundles of them in his own hands, and put one under each arm. Command was now given that the fire should be kindled, but owing to the number of green faggots, it was some time before the flames set fire to the reeds. The wind being averse, and the morning very cold, the flames blew from him, so that he was scarcely touched by the fire. Another fire was soon kindled of a more vehement nature: it was now the bladders of gunpowder exploded, but they proved of no service to the suffering prelate. He now prayed with a loud voice: 'Lord Jesus, have mercy upon me; Lord Jesus have mercy upon me; Lord Jesus receive my spirit'; and these are the last words he was heard to utter. But even when his face was completely black with the flames, and his tongue swelled so that he could not speak, yet his lips went till they were shrunk to the gums. And he knocked his breast with his hands until one of his arms fell off, and then continued knocking with the other

while the fat, water and blood dripped out of his
finger ends. At length, by renewing of the fire, his
strength was gone and his hand fastened in the iron
which was round him. Soon after, the whole lower
part of his body being consumed, he fell over the
iron that bound him into the fire, amidst the horrible
yells and acclamations of the bloody crew that surrounded him. This holy martyr was more than three
quarters of an hour consuming; the inexpressible
anguish of which he endured as a lamb, moving
neither forwards, backwards, nor to any side; his
nether parts were consumed and his bowels fell out
some time before he expired. Thus John Hooper
perished, in a manner the most horrible that the
rage of hell itself could devise.

(*Complete Protestant Martyrology*,
Henry Moore, 1809)

But it was not only the English 'orthodox' religions that
were cursing each other for heretics; throughout Europe,
from the start of the thirteenth century the Inquisition
tortured and burned its way through centuries of persecution. The subject of the Inquisition has been treated
as a separate entry, but in the interests of continuity it
should be mentioned here that the death penalty that
awaited those found guilty by the Inquisitors of heresy
was burning at the stake. These executions took place at
the end of the *auto-da-fé* (Portuguese, 'act of faith'), a
procession at the end of which the condemned were
handed over to the secular authorities for punishment (the
Church itself could not take life – it could only torture,
sometimes to death). The reason for burning being the
prescribed punishment was bound up in the Roman Catholic doctrine *Ecclesia non novit sanquinem* ('the Church
is untainted with blood').

Closely associated with the activities of the Inquisition
were the witch trials. Witches, of course, were heretics
of a sort and always popular targets for orthodox religion.
Almost everywhere on mainland Europe the death sen-

tence on a witch, following conviction either by a secular or ecclesiastical court, was burning at the stake.

It was during the sixteenth century that the most concentrated persecution of witches took place, although one authority (Rossell Hope Robbins) claims that what he calls 'the witchcraft delusion' extended from 1450–1750. In his *Encyclopedia of Witchcraft and Demonology*, Robbins attempts to assemble some statistics for the rate of execution of witches in some German districts: in Osnabrück, 121 witches were burned in 1583, and in 1589 around 133; at Ellwangen in 1612, 167 were burned; and 'in the five years from 1631 to 1636, the records of three villages in the jurisdiction of the Archbishop of Cologne – Rheinbach, Meckenheim and Fierzheim – show that from 300 households between 125 and 150 persons were executed as witches'. The last witch-burning in Germany was at Kempten in 1775. Quite how many so-called witches were burned during the centuries of the Inquisition will never, even roughly, be known for certain, but one contemporary account (Ludovicus A Paramo's *De Origine et Progressu Officii Sanctae Inquisitionis*, 1598) claims that within the space of 150 years, 30,000 witches had been burned. There was one exception – England. For although neighbouring Scotland followed the European pattern and put their witches to the stake, England hanged hers – a reliably estimated one thousand of them.

However, this is not to say that the English eschewed the horrors of burning alive, or that the punishment was uniquely reserved for heretics. The criminal laws of England – and indeed other parts of Europe – had already extended the punishment of burning to death to cover various secular as well as ecclesiastical crimes. John Scott, for example, was burned to death in 1605 for the unseemly crime of bestiality with a horse – the unfortunate and innocent mare was also roasted at the stake beside him. This punishment was also current for the same crime in Germany some centuries earlier.

Germany also shared with England the distinction of executing coiners and counterfeiters by burning at the stake, and various editions of the *Newgate Calendar* document the fates of such miscreants. Of Barbara Spencer, found guilty of counterfeiting and burned at Tyburn on 5 July 1721, one early version records:

> When she stood at the stake she seemed to have less fear of death than on the preceding day. She was very desirous of praying, and complained of the dirt and stones thrown by the mob behind her, which prevented her thinking sedately on futurity. One time she was quite beat down by them. She declared that she had been taught to coin by a man and a woman who had now left it off, and lived reputably, though when they first began that trade, they were in very poor circumstances; but she would not discover who they were, it being, in her opinion, a pity that a family should be ruined who had given over that practice, and so many hundreds live secure in London who still continue the same; and added that, though she saw the faggots lie ready to burn her, she would never take away the life of another by making herself an evidence, even if a magistrate was to come in person and offer her a pardon to do it. And therefore she found it difficult to forgive Miles, her old companion and accuser. But, however, just before the fire was kindled she said she forgave not only her, but all the world, and died in perfect charity; that she suffered justly, and hoped others would take warning by her unhappy exit.

The last recorded instance of burning at the stake in England was in 1788, when the coiner Phoebe Harris was executed at Newgate:

> She is described as a well-made little woman, something more than thirty years of age, of a pale complexion and not disagreeable features. When she came out of prison she appeared languid and terrified, and trembled greatly as she advanced to the

stake, where the apparatus for the punishment she was about to experience seemed to strike her mind with horror and consternation, to the exclusion of all power of recollectedness in preparation for the approaching awful moment. She walked from the debtors' door to the stake fixed in the ground about half-way between the scaffold and Newgate Street. She was immediately tied by the neck to an iron bolt fixed near the top of the stake, and after praying fervently for a few minutes the steps on which she stood were drawn away and was left suspended. A chain fastened by nails to the stake was then put round her body by the executioner and his assistants. Two cart-loads of faggots were piled about her, and after she had hung for half-an-hour the fire was kindled. The flames presently burned the halter, the body fell a few inches, and hung then by the iron chain. The fire had not quite burnt out at twelve, in nearly four hours that is to say. A great concourse of people attended this melancholy occasion.

(*Chronicles of Newgate*, Arthur Griffiths, 1883)

The procedure of extending some little mercy by strangling the victim before the fire was lit had come into practice some years before, but it was by no means a certainty that the prisoner would be thus spared. The most common means of effecting strangulation was by the executioner pulling on a noose round the woman's neck from outside the perimeter of the fire; if the hangman was negligent in his duty, or if the flames burned through the rope before it had done its job, then the victim would be burned alive. In the case of Catherine Hayes, the fire burned the executioner's hand and he was forced to let go the rope. Hayes had been found guilty of the other crime for which women could be put to the fire – petty treason. By a statute of Edward III in 1351, petty treason was aggravated murder – which could mean a wife killing her husband, an ecclesiastic killing his superior, or a servant killing his master. Mrs Hayes, in a conspiracy with her paramour Thomas Billings and a friend Thomas Wood, bludgeoned her husband to death, dumped his decapitated body in a pond at Marylebone and his head in the Thames. The head was recovered and erected on a pole in St Margaret's Churchyard, Westminster, to be identified. Catherine Hayes was burned at the stake in 1726:

On the day of her death, Hayes received the Sacrament, and was dragged on a sledge to the place appointed for execution. When the wretched woman had finished her devotions, in pursuance of her sentence an iron chain was put round her waist, with which she was attached to the stake. When women were burned for petty treason it was usual to strangle them by means of a rope passed around the neck and pulled by the executioner, so that they were mercifully insensible to the heat of the flames. But this woman was literally burnt alive, for the executioner let go the rope too soon, in consequence of having his hand burnt by the flames. The flames burnt fiercely around her, and the spectators beheld Catherine Hayes pushing away the faggots, while she rent the air with her cries and lamentations. Other faggots were instantly piled on her, but she survived amidst the flames for a considerable time, and her body was not perfectly reduced to ashes until three hours later.

(*The Newgate Calendar*)

C

Calcraft, William

Throughout his long career as official hangman (1829–74), there was much written about William Calcraft, and in keeping with the generally despised view held of the position much of it was scurrilous. However, he was, by one account, said to be 'fond of gardening, children and small animals'; and, in his professional capacity, 'to favour the short drop so that he could leap upon the back of his still conscious victim and thus strangle him', a not inconsiderable act of mercy in the circumstances, which often had the condemned swinging at the end of a rope for some length of time, slowly choking to death.

The following insight into the life and occupation of this remarkable individual is derived from contemporary writings, though it must be added that many of the Calcraft stories are aprocryphal, and should be treated with caution.

Becoming a Hangman

In course of time Calcraft got initiated into the mysteries of the hanging profession; but though there are circumstances connected with his career involved in some obscurity, we can positively assert, that when the common rumour respected his having been convicted of felony, and that he afterwards received a pardon on condition of his becoming a hangman, *is not founded on fact* . . . We have shown that whatever vices have belonged to him, were not originally created by himself; while the fact of his undertaking to learn the trade of a shoemaker and of his own accord endeavouring to shake off his bad companions to get his living by a better manner, proves that he only wanted to be surrounded by favourable circumstances, when without doubt he would have made

THE GROANS

OF THE

GALLOWS,

Or the Past and Present

LIFE OF

WILLIAM CALCRAFT,

THE LIVING

Hangman of Newgate.

" The Cross shall displace the Gibbet,
and all will be accomplished."   Victor Hugo.

ENTERED AT STATIONERS' HALL.

what the world calls a 'bright man'. Messrs Read and Company, the great porter brewers in Liquorpond Street, Grays Inn Lane, about the same period took him into their employ as a private watchman; and he might to this day have continued there or followed some more advantageous employment, had not his unlucky genius still haunted him. Rightfully or wrongfully, our watchman was compelled to leave, and he was led to become our executioner.

(*Groans of the Gallows*, London, 1864)

Official Appointment

While the case of the wretched woman [Esther Hibner, convicted of murder and sentenced to death] was pending, and during the period of its adjournment, the authorities were on the lookout for a good suitable man whom they could appoint as the fully recognised common hangman and general official executioner.

We have already stated that the former celebrated executioner, John Foxton, died on the 14th of February [1829] and that for a little time he was succeeded by his assistant, the notorious Jack Cheshire. This man, however, was also getting advanced in years. He was constantly drinking in the lowest tap-rooms, and associating with the most disreputable characters, or anyone who chose to treat him with drink. The authorities not wishing, therefore, to run the risk of such another disreputable bungle as occurred in the hanging in Birmingham – one of the ring-leaders of the Field-lane gang of thieves – thought it more prudent to endeavour to obtain the services of a more steady and younger man. It was quietly made known, therefore, in certain circles, after the burial of Foxton, that the office of 'Prime Executioner' would be vacant, and that it would be filled up at the earliest opportunity by the election of the most suitable candidate the authorities could get. There were a good many who, no doubt, would have aspired to the office if they thought their claims likely to be worth consideration. Under the circumstances, however, we find there were but two applications – one from a man named Smith, and the other from Calcraft. The merits of the respective candidates will be best judged of by the qualifications they urged, and by a report of the meeting at which the election took place.

The Court of Aldermen
Yesterday a meeting of the Court of Aldermen took place for the purpose of appointing an executioner in the room of J. Foxton who a few weeks ago departed this life a short time after he had given two further awful proofs of his skill . . . The following abstracts of the communications of the respective candidates were then read to the meeting:

Calcraft wrote to the following effect:

Hoxton, March 28th, 1829
To the Hon. Court of Aldermen for City of London. Gentlemen – Having been informed that the office of executioner is vacant I beg very humbly to offer myself as a candidate. I am twenty-nine years of age, strong and robust, and have had some experience in the office. I am familiar with the model of operation, having some months ago been engaged on an emergency to execute two men at Lincoln. I did so, and as the two culprits passed off without a struggle, the execution was performed to the entire satisfaction of the Sheriff of the County.

I am, gentlemen, your very obedient and very humble servant.

The Alderman presiding said the second application was as follows, from a man named Smith:

Westminster, March 27, 1829
Gentlemen – Hearing that you are about to elect another executioner and hangman in the room of John Foxton, deceased, I beg to solicit the appointment. I have been for some years in the army, but am now pensioned off. While I was in the army I

was always selected to shoot those who by court-martial were deemed deserving of death. During the whole time, in the whole number I have shot, I have never missed the front of the forehead of the man I shot at twelve paces distant. Under these circumstances, I feel myself fully qualified for the office of hangman, and I hope, therefore, that you will be pleased to give me immediate opportunities for dispatching after another fashion.

I am, gentlemen, your very humble servant. &c

The presiding Alderman said he thought that the qualifications of the last named candidate were very good, yet as the man Calcraft had already had experience as a hangman, he thought he was the most suitable candidate. It was unanimously resolved that the applicant William Calcraft be appointed the common hangman and executioner for the City of London. Calcraft, who is described in the report as a strong, robust, good-looking and very respectable man, was then called in and informed of his election to the office, and on the following Saturday, April 4th, he was duly sworn in.

(*Life and Recollections of Calcraft the Hangman*)

Personality

At the corner of Devizes Street, Hoxton, is the Tiger public-house, famed for being his [Calcraft's] chief place of resort, for playing at skittles, etc., and meeting a number of associates and rabbit fanciers, among whom he was held in great repute as a famous breeder of the choicest kind. Many violent scenes have there occurred, when amidst their inebriety they have wantonly insulted Calcraft, and jeeringly alluded to his calling. Near to the above house is a shop where he used to purchase oats for his rabbits, the proprietor of which, having for the first time deviated inadvertently from his usual reserve, and in the most gentle manner asked how the last man he hung bore his fate, our ill-starred hero at once flew from his presence, speedily sold off all his fine stock of prize rabbits, and to avoid any more such allusions on a similar errand, never went near the inquisitive tradesman again.

(*Groans of the Gallows*)

The Hangman's Daughter

. . . a young mechanic who courted one of his [Calcraft's] daughters, ignorant of her family at the time, had an invitation to meet her and partake of supper at a friend's house. The appointed night came, and the young woman with a goodly number of friends of both sexes, were assembled, anxiously awaiting the arrival of her lover. At length he was announced, and on entering the room was joyfully saluted by his sweetheart and the rest of the company, who welcomed him to the seat of honour at the supper table . . . Everyone was served and about to eat and drink right merrily; when hark! footsteps are heard on the stairs; the door, already half open, shows approaching from the dark landing the figure of a stout man, of the middle height, with remarkably determined looking features, rather pock-marked, fair hair, and peering, bluish green eyes, who on approaching the light is announced by his name and saluted 'Father!' by the young woman sitting beside the invited stranger, whose features now assumed a corpse-like paleness, as the startling fact suddenly flashed across his dizzy brain, that he has been courting the Hangman's daughter; that he was going to sit at the same table with him, eat off the same joint, drink out of the same glass, and perhaps be asked to shake hands with him! It was a horror to him! He trembled in every limb; was speechless; became seized with sickness and bowel complaint. At last summoning all his rapidly failing strength into one super-human effort, ere he fell, with one sudden bound he ineffectually tried to jump over the table towards the door, and overturning in all directions the dainty repast, escaped down stairs. The force of prejudice had made the sight of the Hangman to this young man like a frightful apparition.

(*Groans from the Gallows*)

*Calcraft officiating at the execution of James Wiggins in October
1967*

Financial Rewards
The reward that he receives for exhibiting his skill in the
art of driving immortal souls into eternity, amounts to 21
shillings weekly, paid by the authorities of the City of
London and Middlesex, and £5 quarterly, contributed by
those of the county of Surrey, for executions done at
Horsemonger Lane Gaol. He also appropriates whatever
property is found on the persons of those he executes,
including the clothes they suffer in, unless when specially
ordered in accordance with the dying wish of a favoured
criminal to be given to surviving friends. He may now
almost be called the Executioner of England, for there is
scarcely an execution in any part but it is not performed
by him; for which he is paid extra, according to the distance; unless his famed rival Nathanial Howard, the

Hangman of York Castle, should get the start of him, and successfully compete for the job. It is his office also to flog with the *blood-red cat* . . . He and his rival Nat have realised many pounds by the sale of criminals' apparel to the exhibitors of wax figures; amongst the most famous of them being Madame Tussaud . . . As profitable have proved the sale of various ropes which strangled the criminals, the hangman's tarrif of prices rising from 5 shillings to £1 per inch, according to the notoriety of the criminal, the circumstances of the purchasers, and the pressure of demand for a piece of the curiosity.

(Groans from the Gallows)

Calcraft's Death
He died peacefully at his residence in Poole-street, Hoxton, on Saturday the 13th of December, 1879, in the eightieth year of his age, having resided in the same house over twenty-five years. He used to be a regular attendant at the Church of England, and prior to his death was constantly visited by the clergyman of Hoxton Church. He was buried at Abney Park Cemetery, and leaves behind him a daughter and two sons.

Calcraft was never known to have committed any crime, and he left the world respected by all his personal friends.

(Life and Recollections of Calcraft the Hangman)

Cangue
(see **Halters**)

Capital Offences
There has always been some controversy regarding the early history of capital punishment in Britain, but it seems reasonable that the first judicial executions were carried out in the middle of the fifth century BC, when it was the custom to throw condemned criminals into bogs and quagmires to die. The general method of the Anglo-

Saxons was hanging, but other methods included stoning, burning, drowning, beheading and throwing from a height. Many authorities believe that capital punishment fell into disuse at the time of the Norman Conquest, and was reintroduced during the reign of Henry I (1100–35). By the end of the fifteenth century English law recognised eight major capital crimes – high treason, petty treason (the killing of a husband by his wife, a master by his servant, an ecclesiastic by his inferior), murder, larceny, robbery, burglary, rape and arson. The number of annual executions seems to have reached a peak under Edward VI when an average of 560 were hanged at Tyburn alone. During Henry VIII's reign the national annual average stood at 2,000, and was slightly less under Elizabeth I. With the increasing emphasis on the value of property the number of capital offences on the statute by the beginning of the nineteenth century had grown to an astonishing 222, including stealing a pocket handkerchief, shooting a rabbit, and adopting a disguise.

The following list was assembled by the abolitionist P. Colquoun, LL.D. and printed in Basil Montagu's *Opinions of Different Authors Upon the Punishment of Death*, dated 1809. They represent the *principal* crimes punishable by the deprivation of life:

Arson, or wilfully and maliciously burning a House, Barns with Corn, etc.

Attempting to kill Privy Councillors, etc.

Bankrupts not surrendering, or concealing their effects.

Being accessories to Felonies deemed capital.

Breaking down the head of a Fish-pond, whereby Fish may be lost (called the Black Act).

Burglary, or House Breaking in the night time.

Challenging Jurors above 20 in capital felonies; or standing mute.

Concealing the death of a Bastard Child.

Cottons, selling with forged Stamps.

Cutting down trees in an Avenue, Garden, etc.

Cutting down River, or Sea Banks.

Cutting Hop Binds.

Destroying Ships, or setting them on Fire.

Destroying Silk or Velvet in the loom; or the tools for manufacturing thereof; or destroying Woollen Goods, Racks or Tools, or entering a house for that purpose.

Deer-stealing, second offence; or even first offence, under the Black Act, not usually enforced.

Destroying Turnpikes or Bridges, Gates, Weighing Engines, Locks, Sluices, Engines for draining Marshes, etc.

Escape by breaking Prison in certain cases.

Forgery of Deeds, Bonds, Bills, Notes, Public Securities, etc. Clerks of the Bank Embezzling Notes, altering Dividend Warrants; Paper Makers, unauthorised, using moulds for Notes, etc.

Government Stores, embezzling, burning or destroying in Dock-Yards; in certain cases.

Highway Robbery.

House Breaking in the day time.

Maiming or Killing Cattle maliciously (see Black Act, 9 Geo. I. cap. 22).

Maliciously maiming or disfiguring any person, etc. or lying in wait for the purpose.

Mutiny, Desertion, etc. by Martial or Statute law.

Murder.

Personating Bail, or acknowledging fines, or judgements in another's name.

Piracy, or robbing ships and vessels at sea; under which is included the offences of sailors forcibly hindering their captains from fighting.

Prisoners under Insolvent Acts, guilty of perjury.

Privately Stealing or Picking Pockets, above one shilling.

Pulling down Houses, Churches, etc.

Rape, or the forcible violation of chastity.

Returning from Transportation; or being at large in the Kingdom after Sentence.

Riots by twelve or more, and not dispersing in an hour after proclamation.

Robbery of the Mail.

Sacrilege.

Setting fire to coal mines.

Servants purloining their Master's Goods, value 40 shillings.

Sending Threatening Letters (Black Act).

Shooting at a Revenue Officer; or at any other person (Black Act).

Shop Lifting above five shillings.

Smuggling by persons armed; or assembling armed for that purpose.

Sodomy, a crime against nature, committed either with man or beast.

Soldiers or Sailors enlisting into Foreign Service.

Stealing an Heiress.

Stealing Bonds, Bills, or Bank Notes.

Stealing Bank Notes or Bills from Letters.

Stealing above 40 shillings in any House.

Stealing above 40 shillings on a River.

Stealing Linen etc. from Bleaching Grounds, etc. or destroying Linen therein.

Stealing Horses, Cattle or Sheep.

Stabbing a person unarmed, or not having a weapon drawn, if he die within six months.

Stealing Woollen Cloths from Tenter Grounds.

Stealing from a Ship in Distress.

Taking a Reward for helping another to Stolen Goods, in certain cases.

Treason and petty treason, etc. Under the former of these is included the offence of counterfeiting gold and silver coin.

Uttering counterfeit Money, third offence.

It is interesting to compare this with a similar list of capital offences in France at around the same time. It was published under the title *Pastoret* in the year 1790:

Behold a list of the crimes punishable by death, and even this does not comprehend the whole.

1. Enormous blasphemy.
2. Composing works against religion.
3. Or causing them to be written.
4. Or printing them.
5. Sacrilege joined to superstition and impiety.
6. Sacrilege with the profanation of sacred things.
7. Pulling down or destroying crosses and images.
8. Every act of scandal and impious sedition.
9. Heretics assembling with arms.
10. Heretical preaching.
11. Witchcraft and magic.
12. Regicide.
13. Outrage against the persons of the king's children.
14. Leagues and associations.
15. Enlisting soldiers unlawfully.
16. Plots.
17. Not disclosing a plot.
18. To parley with an enemy, without the consent of the commanders of the army.
19. Omitting to inform the commanders of a letter or message received from a prince, or nobleman belonging to the enemy.
20. To levy troops without permission from the king.
21. Unlicensed assemblies under any pretence whatever.
22. To wear armour, carry arms, arquebuses, etc. not being ordered into garrison, or on the king's service.
23. Screening or favouring those who have carried arms unlawfully.
24. Desertion.
25. Collecting arms for horse or foot soldiers.
26. Buying without permission, more powder, shot or matches, than is wanted for the necessary defence of one's house.
27. Casting ordnance, or having it in possession without leave.
28. To fortify castles, or to seize on those already fortified.

29. Counterfeiting the current coin.
30. Circulating counterfeit coin, or introducing it into the kingdom.
31. Clipping of coin.
32. Buying the clippings.
33. Coiners delivering Coin below the standard; too light, or imperfect in other respects.
34. Receivers and paymasters, who knowingly distribute counterfeit money.
35. Bankers who fail to cut in the presence of the seller, the pieces of gold and silver coin which they have bought.
36. To carry more gold or silver out of the kingdom, than is necessary for the voyage.
37. Foreigners, or even natives, who deal in coin at a price above its value, if they buy it to export, or for the use of forgers.
38. Locksmiths, blacksmiths and other workers in iron, who shall have made utensils or tools for coining, even when the intention is unknown to them.
39. Those who shall have engraved dies, and other instruments used in the fabrication of specie, without permission of the officers of the mint.
40. Carriers who knowingly convey the instruments used in coining, without informing the solicitors-general or surveyors.
41. Clerks of the general and particular receivers offices, having the management of public affairs, who embezzle more than three thousand livres.
42. Treasurers, receivers and other overseers, embezzling the public money.
43. Extortion, under certain circumstances.
44. To abuse and insult magistrates, officers, door-keepers or bailiffs in the execution of justice.
45. Receiving or concealing a person condemned to death.
46. Breaking prison, in certain cases.
47. Wilful murder.

48. To associate with murderers, under any pretence whatever.
49. The plotting to kill, injure or abuse any one, although it be not carried into effect.
50. Highway robbery.
51. Theft with burglary.
52. House breaking.
53. Theft in the king's palaces, without any regard to the value of the goods stolen.
54. Robbery in the Banks.
55. Robbers of a church and their accomplices, according to the existence of the case.
56. Those who associate with thieves.
57. Those who conceal or receive stolen goods, when the theft deserves death.
58. Nightly robbery with arms.
59. Sometimes nightly robbery with ladders.
60. Robbery by pick-locks.
61. The crime of improperly detaining a person according to circumstances.
62. A galley slave mutilating himself.
63. Taking poison whether it prove mortal or not.
64. To make or distribute poisonous compositions.
65. To know that they have been asked for or given, and not to inform the solicitor general, or his deputy, according to circumstances and the exigences of the case.
66. Duelling.
67. Arson.
68. Parricide.
69. Incest in a direct line.
70. Incest, by ecclesiastical law.
71. Rape.
72. Forcible abduction.
73. Seduction, according to circumstances.
74. Confining young women by means of Lettres de Cachet, in order to marry or cause them to be married without consent.

75. Noblemen who force their subjects, or others, to give their daughters or wards in marriage.
76. Concealment of pregnancy.
77. Procuring abortion.
78. Unnatural crime.
79. A person taking the law into his own hands.
80. Fraudulent bankruptcy.
81. Monopoly of corn.
82. Breach of public trust.
83. Forging letters and seals of chancery.
84. Forging the signature of secretaries of state.
85. Counterfeiting, forging, or altering edicts, royal records, or other royal or public papers.
86. Counterfeiting, or altering papers relating to receivers, treasurers, etc., royal or public.
87. Farmers of the revenue of whatever condition, who forge receipts, discharges, accounts and inventories.
88. Forging a duplicate of a deed.
89. To cast, copy, or counterfeit the marks of the towns, in which there is a magistrate, or of the revenue of farmers.
90. Applying the counter mark in any manner to gold, or silver goods, which have not been taken to be assayed, and marked at the public office.
91. Bearing false witness, which shall endanger the life of the accused.
92. Smuggling tobacco, printed clothes, etc. by five or more armed persons in company.
93. Officers holding correspondence with smugglers.
94. Smugglers forcing doors, and guard houses of revenue officers.
95. Revenue officers convicted of having been unlicensed salt merchants, or having participated in the trade.
96. Dealing in salt by the officers of the warehouses or depots.
97. Smuggling salt by five armed persons in company.
98. To print, sell or circulate books, or new compo-

sitions, without permission granted in the manner prescribed.

99. The master convicted of having delivered up his ship to the enemy.

100. The master convicted of having maliciously wrecked or destroyed his vessel.

101. Mariners or passengers in vessels who cause any difficulty in the exercise of the Catholic religion.

102. A ship writer who makes false entries in his register.

103. A pilot who maliciously causes the destruction of a vessel.

104. A coast pilot guilty of the same crime.

105. Wasting a ship's liquors, or destroying bead by seamen or others.

106. Causing a leak in a ship.

107. To excite sedition, in order to frustrate the voyage.

108. Striking the master under arms.

109. Captains who detain, or suffer any thing to be taken from vessels belonging to the king's subjects, or allies, who lower their sails and produce their charter-parties and policies.

110. Sinking captured vessels.

111. Putting prisoners on shore, in an island, or distant country, to conceal the prize.

112. Robbery of cordage, or shipping utensils, and cutting or stealing cables, if it occasion the loss of the ship, or the death of a man.

113. To place false lights upon the sea shore, and in dangerous places, for the purpose of misleading and wrecking vessels.

114. To attempt the life or goods of persons shipwrecked.

115. Foot or horse soldiers who run after shipwrecks.

Capital Punishment

Some discussion of the early movements to abolish capital punishment as they related to England can be found under

Abolition of Capital Punishment; however, any lengthy debate on the issue would be space-consuming and tend to duplicate much of what can be found in the individual entries throughout this book. Furthermore, the present author's abolitionist views are so well known that even the brief comments which follow may be seen as rhetoric.

The most frequently invoked argument in favour of capital punishment, and really the only one capable of a straight 'scientific' rebuttal, is that the death sentence acts as a deterrent: that is to say, judicially killing one offender dissuades others from committing the same crime. Although this may seem plausible, it can only be relevant if the potential offender *at the time of his offence* makes a calculated decision. In most cases where a crime is committed for which the death penalty is applicable, the offender does not weigh up the possibilities before committing the act, or if he does, and continues, *per se* he must believe that there is a favourable chance that he will escape detection. This is particularly true of homicide, where the majority of incidents are the result of angry exchanges and are committed in 'hot blood'. Thus to remove capital punishment is not necessarily to invite a state of bloodshed and anarchy. In its conclusion to the 1962 report on the state of capital punishment in the world, the United Nations committee studying abolition stated: 'All the information available appears to confirm that such a removal [of the death penalty] has, in fact, never been followed by a notable rise in the incidence of the crime no longer punishable by death.'

Despite this information, it remains a sad indictment of humankind's inability to cope with the problem of the serious offender that some one hundred countries throughout the world retain, in some form or other, an active policy of capital punishment, and still plead deterrence as their justification. Of course, this is not the only reason why the 'the shadow of the gallows' has proved so useful to governments; for some it is a suitable means for 'legally' eliminating political opposition, for others it is an instrument of terror in the battle against dissidence.

The following tables show the way in which the world is currently divided between the retentionists and the various shades of abolition. On the whole the picture holds few surprises, the tendency being for the more advanced industrial nations to have rejected the 'ultimate sanction', and for the developing nations to a great extent to rely upon the death sentence as an observable instrument of state power. The one anachronism remains the United States of America.

Retentionist
Countries which retain the death penalty on their statutes and carry out judicial executions:

Afghanistan
Albania
Algeria
Angola
Antigua and
   Barbuda
Bahamas
Bangladesh
Barbados
Belize
Benin
Botswana
Bulgaria
Burkina Faso
Burma
Burundi
Cameroon
Central African
   Republic
Chad
Chile
China (People's
   Republic)

Congo
Cuba
Czechoslovakia
Dominica
Egypt
Equatorial
   Guinea
Ethiopia
Gabon
Gambia
Ghana
Granada
Guatemala
Guinea
Guinea-Bissau
Guyana
Hungary
India
Indonesia
Iran
Iraq
Jamaica
Japan

Jordan
Kampuchea
Kenya
Korea
   (Democratic
   People's Rep.)
Korea (Republic)
Kuwait
Laos
Lebanon
Lesotho
Liberia
Libya
Malawi
Malaysia
Mali
Mauritania
Mauritius
Mongolia
Morocco
Mozambique
Namibia
Nepal

Nigeria
Oman
Pakistan
Poland
Qatar
Romania
Rwanda
Saint Christopher and Nevis
Saint Lucia
Saint Vincent and the Grenadines
Saudi Arabia
Sierra Leone
Singapore
Somalia
South Africa
Sudan
Suriname
Swaziland
Syria
Taiwan (Republic of China)
Tanzania
Thailand
Tonga
Trinidad and Tobago
Tunisia
Turkey
Uganda
Union of Soviet Socialist Republics*
United Arab Emirates
United States of America
Viet Nam
Yemen (Arab Republic)
Yemen (People's Democratic Republic)
Yugoslavia
Zaire
Zambia
Zimbabwe

Abolitionist for all Crimes

Countries which do not have the death penalty on their statutes:

Australia
Austria
Cape Verde
Colombia
Costa Rica
Denmark
Dominican Republic
Ecuador
Finland
France
Germany
Haiti
Honduras
Iceland
Kiribati
Liechtenstein
Luxembourg
Marshall Islands
Micronesia
Monaco
Netherlands
Nicaragua
Norway
Panama
Philippines
Portugal
San Marino
Solomon Islands
Sweden
Tuvalu
Uruguay
Vanuatu
Vatican City State
Venezuela

*Since the abolition of the Union, all currently autonomous countries retain the death penalty, though this may change with greater internal stability.

Abolitionist for Ordinary Crimes Only

Countries who have abolished the death penalty for all but 'exceptional' crimes – such as are committed under military law or during times of war:

Argentina	Italy	Sao Tome and
Brazil	Malta	Principe
Canada	Mexico	Seychelles
Cyprus	New Zealand	Spain
El Salvador	Papua New	Switzerland
Fiji	Guinea*	United Kingdom
Israel	Peru	

Abolitionist in Practice

Countries which retain the death penalty but have not carried out executions for at least ten years:

Andorra	Cayman Islands	Nauru
Anguilla	Comoros	Niger
Bahrain	Cote d'Ivoire	Paraguay
Belgium	Djibouti	Senegal
Bermuda	Greece	Sri Lanka
Bhutan	Hong Kong**	Togo
Bolivia	Ireland	Turks and Caicos
British Virgin Is.	Madagascar	Is.
Brunei	Maldives	Western Samoa
Darussalam	Monserrat	

Cat-o'-Nine-Tails
(see **Flagellation**)

---

*Papua New Guinea voted to reintroduce the death penalty in August 1991.

**Although Hong Kong has not implemented the death penalty since 1966, there are plans to scrap the legislation for fear that China could use the death penalty for an extensive range of crimes when it takes over the colony from the British in 1997.

Chain Whip
(see **Flagellation**)

Cheater's Chain
(see **Halters**)

Collars

At their simplest, collars, or neckbraces, were just an additional means to restrain and add discomfort to the life of an imprisoned felon or suspect.

However, some were provided with screw devices so that when the band was tightened blood would be forced out of the eyes, nose and ears. Still others show a gratuitously cruel inventiveness.

Bell Collar

Attributed to the Venetians, this deceptively innocuous, almost comic device is reminiscent of **Shame Masks** and **Scold's Bridle** in appearance; in effect it could prove devastating. The collar was originally designed for use in prisons (like the bells round the necks of Alpine cattle) so that the gaolers might keep tabs on their charges. More fiendishly, the device served to prevent the prisoner from sleeping – waking him up by ringing at his every movement. It is reported that a combination of inadequate sleep and the perpetual din of the bell above his head sent many a man quite insane.

Iron Collar

This particular design originated in China where it was used as a punishment until at least the first decade of the twentieth century. The sharp-toothed metal collar is attached to leather side-straps which meet at an iron ring. When the prisoner has been fitted with the collar, a rope is fed through the iron ring and the man suspended from a roof beam so that the serrated collar is digging into his throat and his toes just touching the ground. It is clear that if the victim relaxed for just one moment his neck would be severely lacerated by the collar. The instrument was an inquisitional one – that is, it was used as a torture to extract information or elicit a confession. With quaint old-fashioned chauvinism one account of the Iron Collar concludes: 'Sometimes it happens that the victim dies before this occurs; but that is a detail too trivial for the Oriental mind to bother about.'

Spiked Collar

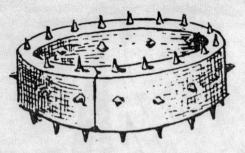

Another Spanish device, this was a collar of thick leather or metal studded on the inside and out (presumably to frustrate removal) with sharp metal spikes. Once the neck is inside the collar it is all but impossible for the captive to move without at least suffering considerable discomfort and being unable to lie down and sleep.

Copper Boot

Into the beaten and welded copper boot a prisoner's foot was thrust – often both feet were treated to the punishment simultaneously. While he was strapped immobile into the chair, boiling water or oil were poured into the top of the boot. The effect was to cook and strip the flesh from the bones and shrivel the sinews; a supremely horrible punishment which always resulted in the maiming of the victim for life, and often caused his death. Sometimes molten lead would be substituted, and this would simply burn the victim's legs and feet to cinders.

Gauntlets

Sometimes similar receptacles were fashioned to take the prisoner's hands, and a variation was to bring the glove itself to red heat before thrusting the victim's hand inside.

Crank

The crank was an English instrument of penal punishment contemporary with the **Treadmill**. The Prison Act of 1865 demanded that a male offender aged sixteen or over should be sentenced to hard labour. This usually meant turning the treadmill, but if the prisoner proved reluctant he could be isolated in a special cell and set to crank-labour – a soul-destroying and completely useless activity used as a punishment rather than as 'labour':

Sometimes a prisoner, tired of working at the tread-mill, or fatigued with the monotony of working at his trade as a tailor, or cobbler, will complain of some ailment such as pains in the back or chest, thereby hoping to achieve some change of labour. In such instances the man is sent to the surgeon to be examined. If he be really ill he is ordered to rest; but if, as often, he is merely shamming, then he is sent back to his former occupation. Should he still continue to complain he is set to crank-labour, and it is said that after a few days at this employment the most stubborn usually ask to return to their previous occupation.

Crank-labour consists in making 10,000 revolutions of a machine resembling in appearance a Kent's Patent Knife-cleaner, for it is a narrow iron drum, placed on legs, with a long handle on one side which, on being turned, causes a series of cups or scoops in the interior to revolve. At the lower part of the interior of the machine is a thick layer of sand which the cups, as they come round, scoop up and carry to the top of the wheel where they throw it out and empty themselves – after the principle of a dredging machine. A dial-plate fixed in front of the iron drum shows how many revolutions the machine has made.

It is usual to shut up in a cell the man sent to crank-labour, so that the exercise is rendered doubly disagreeable by the solitude. Sometimes a man has been known to smash the glass in front of the dial-plate and alter the hands; but such cases are a rare occurrence.

As may be easily conceived, this labour is very distressing and severe; but it is seldom used excepting as a punishment or, rather, as a test of feigned sickness. A man can make, if he works with ordinary speed, about twenty revolutions a minute and this, at 1,200 the hour, would make the task, of 10,000 turns last eight hours and twenty minutes.

(*The Criminal Prisons of London*, Mayhew and Binney, 1862)

It is recorded that at Wandsworth Prison alone there were one hundred cranks, so its deterrent effect on malingerers was clearly limited. For lovers of facts and figures, the machine's resistance was seven pounds, though provision was made for added weights to increase this to ten or twelve pounds.

Like the treadmill, crank-labour fell victim to penal reform during the early years of this century, and of 29 establishments using cranks in 1895, only five persisted in 1901 and within a few years even these became defunct.

Crucifixion

Because of the extensive international publicity given to the incident that took place at Golgotha almost two thousand years ago, it is not fully appreciated how widespread and common torture and execution by crucifixion was in the ancient world. For example, it was widely used by the Assyrians, Carthagenians, Egyptians, Greeks, Persians, Phoenecians, Scythians, and of course the Romans who, at the insistence of the Jewish Sanhedrin, executed Jesus Christ.

The customary form of crucifixion, though there were many variations, was to tie or nail the victim to a stake (with or without a cross-beam), though despite the widespread use of this method of execution and (when the prisoner was dead) display, very few detailed descriptions of crucifixion have survived; in fact the account of Christ's death contained in the Synoptic Gospels represents one of the best existing narratives on the subject.

The prisoner was first scourged (though this was a preliminary to many of the Roman capital punishments) and then, if a cross-beam was to be used, he would be made to carry this heavy wooden member to the place where an upright post was already securely fixed in the ground – usually alongside a main road to ensure maximum exposure of the body after death. The victim was then stripped and forced to lie face up on the ground with his arms outstretched while the executioner nailed or bound his hands to the cross-beam; sometimes both methods were used so that the weight of the body did not cause the flesh of the hands to tear away from the nails. The beam, with its victim suspended from it, was then hauled to the top of the upright. Again to prevent the hands tearing away from the nails, a wooden peg protruding from the upright between the captive's legs gave some measure of support. The preparations were concluded by nailing both feet to the upright. In this position the victim suffered a slow, agonising death, aggravated by whatever supplementary torments the executioner and the mob might indulge in – breaking his legs with clubs, tearing his skin with combs like metal rakes, stoning . . . In the case of the execution of Christ, the executioners had already exhibited uncommon ingenuity in fashioning the crown of thorns.

Other novelties were effected by changing the position in which the victim was attached to the cross – upside down was a popular variant, and Josephus described a Roman mass execution of Jews, where 'They nailed those they caught in different postures to the crosses, by way of jest'.

For the Romans, crucifixion was rated above burning and decapitation as the most common penalty for severe crimes such as treason, desertion from the army, murder, the practice of 'magic' (particularly if it involved making predictions concerning the welfare of the emperor!), and incitement to rebellion. Initially it was a punishment for slaves and foreigners (prisoners of war, etcetera), though later it could be invoked in cases of aggravated crime committed by Romans of the lower class. This is in direct contradiction to the attitudes of the Carthagenians and Persians, for whom crucifixion was a punishment appropriate only for high-ranking officials and military commanders.

Self-Crucifixion

Among the penitents of New Mexico there are incidents recorded of a form of self-crucifixion where the subject is bound by the arms to the cross-member of a huge wooden cross which he is obliged to drag over ground littered with broken glass and sharp stones. A refinement involved the tying of a sharp spear to the body with its point touching the arm, in such a position that should the penitent stumble or fall, the weapon would pierce his flesh.

Crucifixion of Christ

The following account of the crucifixion of Christ is a composite narrative derived from the texts of the Gospels:

Now it was the feast of the Passover. And the chief priests sought how they might kill Jesus, for they feared his popularity. Then entered Satan into Judas, surnamed Iscariot, being one of the twelve disciples; and he went unto the priests and said: 'What will ye give me? and I will deliver him up to you.' And they covenanted with him for thirty pieces of silver.

Now the disciples made ready the Passover, and as they sat and did eat, Jesus said: 'Verily I say unto you, one of you that eateth with me shall betray me.' And they said unto him one by one: 'Is it I?' Then Judas which had betrayed him said: 'Master, is it I?' And Jesus answered unto him: 'Thou hast said.'

And as they did eat, Jesus took bread and gave it unto them, saying: 'Take, eat, this is my body,' and he took the cup and said: 'This is my blood,' and they all drank of it.

And they went out into the Mount of Olives; and Jesus said unto them: 'All ye shall be offended because of me this night,' and Peter answered: 'Though all men be offended, yet will I never be.' And Jesus said unto him: 'This day, before the cock crow twice, thou shalt deny me thrice.'

And they came to the place which is named Gethsemane, and he said unto his disciples: 'Sit here while I shall pray.' And when he rose up from prayer, and was come to his disciples, he found them sleeping and said: 'Rise up; let us go; lo, he that betrayeth me is at hand.' And while yet he spake, lo, Judas came, and with him a great multitude with swords and staves. Now Judas said: 'Whomsoever I shall kiss, that same is he.' And he came to Jesus and said: 'Hail Master.' And he kissed him. But Jesus said unto him: 'Judas, betrayest thou the son of man with a kiss?' Then Simon Peter, having a sword, drew it, and smote the high priest's servant, and cut off his ear. And Jesus touched his ear and healed him, saying to Peter: 'Put up thy sword; for all that take the sword shall perish by the sword.'

Then they took him into the high priest's house. And Peter followed. And when they were set down together, Peter sat among them. And there cometh one of the maids, and she saw Peter and said: 'Thou wast also with Jesus of Nazareth,' but he denied it saying: 'I know not, neither understand I what thou sayest.' And the cock crew. Then they that stood by said to Peter: 'Surely thou art one of them, for thou art a Galilaean.' But he began to curse and swear, saying: 'I know not this man of whom ye speak.' And a second time the cock crew. And Peter remembered the word of the Lord and wept bitterly.

And the men that held Jesus mocked him, and smote him . . . and many other things blasphemously spake against him. And the elders and the chief priests led him into their council, saying: 'Art thou the son of God?' and he replied: 'Ye say that I am.' Then the high priest rent his clothes, saying: 'He hath spoken blasphemy; what think ye?' and they answered: 'He is guilty of death.'

And they bound him and led him to Pontius Pilate, the governor, and accused him, saying: 'This fellow forbids tribute to Caesar, saying that he himself is a king.' And Pilate asked: 'Art thou the King of the Jews?' And Jesus answered: 'Thou sayest it.' Then Pilate said to the chief priests and the people: 'I find no fault in this man; what then shall I do with Jesus, which is called Christ?' And they all say unto him: 'Let him be crucified.' And when Pilate saw that he could prevail nothing, he took water and washed his hands, saying: 'I am innocent of the blood of this just person; see ye to it.'

Then Pilate therefore took Jesus and scourged him, and the soldiers took Jesus, and they stripped him and put on him a scarlet robe, and plaited a crown of thorns and put it on his head. And they bowed the knee before him and mocked him, saying: 'Hail, King of the Jews,' and they spit upon him. And they led him away to crucify him. And there followed a great company of people.

And when they were come unto a place called Golgotha, they gave him wine to drink mixed with gall, and he would not drink. And they crucified Jesus. The soldiers took his coat and cast lots for whose it shall be. And they set up over his head his accusation, written 'This is Jesus, King of the Jews'. Then are there crucified with him two robbers and one of them railed on him saying: 'Art thou not the Christ? Save thyself, and us.' But the other, rebuking him, answered: 'Dost thou not even fear God?' And he said unto Jesus: 'Lord, remember me when thou comest into thy Kingdom.' And Jesus answered: 'Today, thou shalt be with me in Paradise.'

And darkness came over the whole land until the ninth hour, when Jesus cried with a loud voice, saying: 'My God, my God, why hast thou forsaken me?' And there was set there a vessel full of vinegar; so they put a sponge full of vinegar upon a hyssop and brought it to his mouth. And Jesus said: 'It is finished,' and gave up his spirit.

Then came soldiers and broke the legs of the first thief,

and of the other, but when they came to Jesus they saw he was dead already; but one of the soldiers with a spear pierced his side.

Then arrived Joseph of Arimathea, and boldly went unto Pilate and asked for the body of Jesus; and he granted the corpse to Joseph. He came therefore and took away his body; and there came also Nicodemus bringing a mixture of myrrh and aloes. So they took the body of Jesus, and bound it in linen cloths with the spices.

Now in the place where he was crucified there was a garden in which a new tomb had been hewn out of the rock. There they laid Jesus. And Joseph rolled a great stone to the door of the tomb and departed.

Cucking Stool

Although they eventually came to be synonymous, the cucking stool and the **ducking stool** were originally two quite separate and different punishments. Of the two, the cucking stool was probably the earlier in use.

Such a device is mentioned in the Domesday Book as being employed in Chester, and it was later described as 'a seat of infamy where strumpets and scolds, with bare feet and head, were condemned to abide the derision of those that passed by, for such time as the bailiffs of the manors, who had the privilege of such jurisdiction, did approve'. The cucking stool was simply a chair, sometimes elevated, usually portable, but sometimes set up in some prominent place in a village or town, and reserved almost exclusively for the punishment of women. For example, aside from the aforementioned 'strumpets and scolds', William Andrews wrote in *Bygone Punishments* that: 'Ale wives in Scotland who sold bad ale were placed in the cucking-stool', and there was a later Scottish Act which stated that itinerant singing women should be put on the 'cuck stool'. In the reign of Henry VIII, it was used to 'punish those carders and spinners of wool who were convicted of fraudulently defrauding their customers'.

One interesting link with the ducking stool is that while

in Britain the cucking stool was the instrument used to expose brewers and bakers who gave short measure, the same crimes in Germany were punished with the ducking stool – indeed, it was commonly known as the 'Baker's Baptism'.

That the cucking stool was a valued feature of village society is evidenced by a surviving record of the building of the Kingston-upon-Thames stool in 1572 for what, at the time, would have been a small fortune:

	£	s	d
Making of the cucking stool	0	8	0
Iron work for the same	0	3	0
Timber for the same	0	7	6
Three brasses for the same, and three wheels	0	4	10
	1	3	4

D

Death by the Thousand Cuts

One of the notorious cruelties of old China, the punishment of *Ling-chy* is unarguably one of the most barbarous practices ever devised. In English translation *Ling-chy* has been variously described as 'Torture of the Knife', 'The Slicing Process', 'Cutting in Ten Thousand Pieces' and, more usually, 'Death by the Thousand Cuts'. In his *History of Torture Throughout the Ages*, George Ryley Scott quotes two rare eye-witness accounts by Europeans, that of Sir Henry Norman in 1895 and that of T. T. Meadows in 1851:

> There is a basket covered with a cloth in which is a collection of knives. Each of these knives is marked with the name of some portion of the body or some limb. The executioner puts his hand under the cloth into the basket and selects a knife at random; he then proceeds to cut off whatever limb or part of the body is indicated on the knife. However, there seems ground for the belief that the technique described has been largely displaced by a method of execution in which no element of chance is allowed to interfere with the infliction of one of the most frightful forms imaginable of death by torture. A single keen-bladed instrument is used, and the slicings, cuttings, hackings and amputations proceed slowly step by step through the whole ghastly allotted course. According to Sir Henry Norman the condemned man is fastened upon a rough cross and the executioner proceeds first to cut away pieces from the fleshy parts of the body, then the joints and excrescences of the body, proceeding with the excision of the external appendages and pieces from

the limbs, culminating with a stab to the heart . . . T. T. Meadows writes relative to the execution of thirty-four rebels or bandits on 30 July 1851: 'A hole in the ground near to which a rough cross leant against a wall showed me that one man at least was going to suffer the highest legal punishment – cutting up alive, called *Ling-chy*, a disgraceful and lingering death. As soon as the thirty-three were decapitated, the same executioner proceeded, with a single-edged knife, to cut up the man on the cross. His sole clothing consisted of his wide trousers, rolled down to his hips and up to his buttocks. He was a strongly made man, above middle size, and apparently about forty years of age . . . As the man was at the distance of twenty-five yards, with his side towards us, although we observed two cuts across his forehead, the cutting off of his left breast, and the slicing of the flesh from the front of the thighs, we could not see all the horrible operation. From the first stroke of the knife to the moment the body was cut down from the cross and decapitated, about four or five minutes elapsed.' According to J. H. Gray, both the technique and the number of cuts varied depending on the character of the crime, ranging from as few as eight in cases where clemency was indicated, to as many as 120 where the offence was of an exceptionally heinous nature, though in most instances twenty-five appears to have been the prescribed number.

In former times in Japan a similar punishment existed called the 'Execution of the Twenty-one Cuts' where, before delivering the *coup de grâce*, the executioner cut flesh from various parts of the body. Similarly the ancient Peruvians performed a ritual execution involving slicing off parts of an offender's body.

Decapitation
(see **Beheading**)

Dice
(see **Thumbscrew**)

Diele
To this tantalisingly elusive early Teutonic 'guillotine' there are but scant references. Sometimes called the Hobel or the Dolabra, the diele was supposed to have been a mechanical beheading machine in use in Germany during the Middle Ages. There was a report of one having been installed in the old Nuremberg palace, but otherwise the best we have are various artistic representations, and even these are inconsistent in their design and it is possible

Early German semi-automatic guillotine

Execution of Saint Matthias by mechanical decapitation

that there were at least two distinct variations. One, depicted in a print in the collection of the Feldhaus-Archiv at Wilhelmshaven, shows the machine to be only partly automatic, with the executioner required to knock the blade through the victim's neck with a heavy mallet.

The second type shows a more conventional rope-and-pulley mechanism, with the blade falling from a height to cut off the prisoner's head.

This is a puzzling illustration, because although it depicts the execution of Matthias, the apostle chosen to replace Judas, the symbolic attribute of Saint Matthias is a double-bladed axe – his method of execution – and here he is seen suffering on a mechanical decapitator.

Whether the diele ever existed is called into doubt by Alister Kershaw (in *A History of the Guillotine*): 'Almost one begins to doubt whether Germany ever made any contribution to mechanical decapitation, since forthright information in the manner of Camden and Holinshead [see **Halifax Gibbet**] is so conspicuously lacking. The most that one can do is to believe wistfully in the cumulative significance of different scraps of evidence, none of them persuasive in itself.'

Disembowelling

This seems most often to have been an accompaniment to some other execution or sequence of torture – notably hanging, **drawing and quartering**. But there is at least one, albeit uncertain, reference to disembowelling as a form of execution in its own right; it is the description of the death of Saint Erasmus (sometimes called Saint Elmo). Erasmus was Bishop of Formiae in Campania, and in the year 303 suffered the unique martyrdom of being disembowelled and having his entrails wound round a ship's windlass. There is a miniature painting of the scene in a late fifteenth-century Book of Hours preserved in the British Museum.

A similar method of winding out the entrails, this time on a long pole, is shown in an engraved plate in the *Theatrum Crudelitatum Haereticorum* of 1592.

Dissection

As early as 1540, in the reign of Henry VIII, an act was passed by which surgeons were each year granted four bodies of executed offenders to dissect for the purpose of anatomical research and teaching; the privilege was subsequently extended during the reign of Edward VI.

In 1752 a further Act was passed entitled 'An Act for better preventing the horrid Crime of Murder' (popularly known as the Murder Act). The object was to emphasise that 'Whereas the horrid Crime of Murder has of late been more frequently perpetrated than formerly, and particularly in and near the Metropolis of this Kingdom, contrary to the known Humanity and natural Genius of the British Nation: And whereas it is thereby become necessary that some further Terror and peculiar Mark of Infamy be added to the Punishment of Death, now by law inflicted on such as shall be guilty of the said heinous Offence . . .'

The Act, pioneered by, among others, the celebrated novelist and magistrate Henry Fielding, made provision for the dissection of *all* executed criminals which, it was hoped in more orthodoxly religious times, would strike such fear into the hearts of potential offenders that they would resist temptation. That this was not entirely realistic is amply proved by the fact that condemned criminals already frequently sold their bodies in advance to surgeons in order to provide for their families.

The substance of the Act can be summed up in this way:

1. Sentence was to be pronounced in open court immediately after the conviction. Apart from the usual judgement of death, the sentence was to stipulate the time of execution and 'Marks of Infamy directed for such offenders' (i.e. dissection).

2. The execution should take place two days after sentence had been passed, unless that day hap-

pened to be a Sunday, in which case it was to be deferred until the following Monday.

3. During the time between conviction and execution the murderer was to be confined in a separate cell and no person, except the gaoler and his servants was to have access to him without a licence issued by the judge or sheriff. During this period he was to be kept on a diet of bread and water only, except for the sacrament, or medicines if administered by a physician.

4. *The body of the murderer shall be delivered to surgeons for dissection.*

5. The judge was empowered to direct that after the execution the murderer's body should be hung in chains. But while this was left to the discretion of the court, the Act laid down that in no case whatever should the body of any murderer be buried until it had been dissected. Gaolers who failed to obey this rule would forfeit their office and face a fine of £20; anybody attempting to rescue a murderer while in prison, on the way to execution or during the execution, were to be guilty of a felony and suffer death without benefit of clergy; and those rescuing a body after execution were to be transported for seven years. As an additional punishment, the convicted murderer would forfeit all his goods and land.

It was recorded in the *London Magazine* that the first offender to be sentenced in accordance with the new Act, Thomas Wilford, 'was taken from the bar weeping and in great agonies, lamenting his sad fate'.

This dissection was carried out for Newgate prisoners in Surgeons' Hall, adjoining Newgate, the site of the present Sessions House of the Old Bailey, and the operation was witnessed by students and a

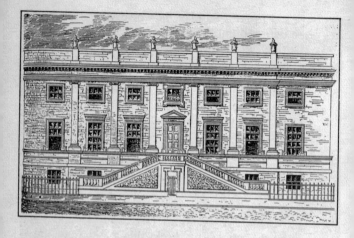

Surgeons' Hall

number of curious spectators. Lord Ferrers' body was brought to Surgeons' Hall after execution in his own carriage and six; after the post-mortem had been carried out, the corpse was exposed to view in a first-floor room. Pennant, in his *London*, speaks of Surgeons' Hall as a handsome building, ornamented with Ionic pilasters, and with a double flight of steps to the first floor. Beneath is a door for the admission of the bodies of murderers and other felons. There were other public dissecting rooms for criminals; one was attached to Hicks' Hall, the Clerkenwell Sessions House. Persons were still living in 1855 who had witnessed dissections at Hicks' Hall, and 'whom the horrid scene, with the additional effect of some noted criminals hanging on the walls, drove out again sick and faint, as we have heard some relate, and with pale and terrified features, to get a breath of air.

(*Chronicles of Newgate*, Arthur Griffiths, 1883)

One of the celebrated skeletons that adorned the niches

Lord Ferrers' body on display at Surgeons' Hall

around the Surgeons' Hall dissecting room was that of the torturer and murderess **Elizabeth Brownrigg**.

The Murder Act was not abolished until 1832.

'Resurrection'

So unreliable was the method of hanging (see **Bungled Executions**), that it was not unknown for the apparently dead to revive on the dissecting table. There is a special entry on **Revivals After Execution**, but the case of William Duell deserves mention here, because it was at Surgeons' Hall that he made his remarkable recovery under the scalpel:

> William Duell was convicted of occasioning the death of Sarah Griffin, at Acton, by robbing and ill-treating her. Having suffered, 24th of November, 1740, at Tyburn, his body was brought to Surgeons' Hall to be anatomised; but after it was stripped and laid on the board, and one of the servants was washing it in order to be cut, he perceived life in him, and found his breath to come quicker and quicker, on which a surgeon took some ounces of blood from him. In two hours he was able to sit up in his chair, and in the evening was again committed to Newgate, and his sentence, which could again have been inflicted, was changed to transportation.
>
> (*Newgate Calendar*)

Draco (or Drakon)

Drakon's legislation, in which the first 'code', or laws, of Athens were written is reliably given as 'during the thirty-ninth Olympiad' (624–621 BC), but more specifically 621–620. It is thought that Drakon's support for such far-reaching and severe laws was in part due to the tense political situation pervading Athenian life, and the recognition that now was the time to write down a set of laws. Although there is still considerable controversy over the original 'Draconian' laws and the severity of their punishments, it is certain that *all* forms of theft were punishable by death, and that this excessive penalty also applied to offences as modest as laziness and vagrancy has also been recorded. However, the laws were so radically revised by Dracon's successor, the archon Solon, in 594–593 that we cannot be certain of the original texts save for the highly regarded 'Law on Homicide', which remained intact until the fourth century.

Drawing and Quartering

As a punishment, the dread excesses of drawing and quartering were not to be wasted on common ruffians and delinquents, but reserved as a punishment for that most heinous of crimes – high treason. The process was lengthy and complex, suiting the gravity of the crime, with the added advantage of elevating the event to a major public spectacle. Giving allowance for tokens of individual creative talent on the part of the executioner, the procedure was this:

1. The traitor was 'drawn' to the gallows from his place of incarceration. At first this was achieved with great economy of effort by simply tying the prisoner to the tail of a horse and dragging him along the ground; and with the optional aggravation of having sharp stones scattered along the route, this proved a great favourite with the crowds that customarily lined the route. However, the method proved less satisfactory when, in the majority of cases, the leading actor in this spectacle was dead long before the more imaginative scenes could be played out. Thus developed drawing on an ox-hide, and later a hurdle which in its turn was replaced by a sledge.

2. The prisoner was hanged by the neck from a gallows and cut down while still alive. This was not difficult, as even a 'standard' hanging was little better than slow strangulation at the end of a rope, frequently allowing the felon to linger for hours on the edge of death.

3. The 'privy members', or 'private parts', were cut off, and the bowels hacked out and 'thrown into the fire before your eyes'.

4. The head was severed from the body by the executioner who was expected to hold it aloft, addressing the crowd with such words as 'Behold the head of a traitor'.

5. What remained of the corpse was butchered into four quarters and customarily displayed above the city gates or, in the case of London, London Bridge.

In his *History of the Life of Thomas Ellwood written by his own hand*, Ellwood, a Quaker imprisoned in Newgate at the beginning of Charles II's reign, described the barbaric preparation of the relics for display:

When we came first into Newgate, there lay the quartered bodies of three men who had been executed some days before for a real or pretended plot; and the reason why their quarters lay so long there was, the relations were all that while petitioning to have leave to bury them, which at length, with much ado, was obtained for the quarters but not for the heads, which were ordered to be set up in some part of the City. I saw the heads when they were brought up to be boiled. The hangman fetched them in a dirty dust basket, out of some by-place, and setting them down among the felons, he and they made sport with them. They took them by the hair, flouting, jeering and laughing at them, and then giving them some ill names, boxed them on the ears and cheeks. Which done, the hangman put them into his kettle, and parboiled them with bay-salt and cumin seeds that keep them from putrefaction, and this to keep off the fowls from seizing on them. The whole sight (as well as that of the bloody quarters first, and this of the heads afterwards) was both frightful and loathsome, and begat an abhorrence in my nature.

It remained only to find a rational justification for this singularly distasteful practice, a job enthusiastically espoused by the celebrated lawyer and politician, Sir Edward Coke (1552–1634). Coke was a veteran of a number of more or less contentious parliamentary and legal debates, and his early championship of the royal prerogative ensured his involvement in the prosecution of Essex, Raleigh, and Guy Fawkes and his fellow Gunpowder Plotters, themselves perhaps the most famous traitors to suffer hanging, drawing and quartering. Sir Edward's approval of the punishment relied heavily upon biblical support:

The conclusion shall be from the admirable clemency and moderation of the king, in that howsoever these traitors have exceeded all others their predecessors in mischief, and so '*Crescente malitia, cres-*

cere dobuit et paena'; yet neither will the king exceed the usual punishment of law, nor invent any new torture or torment for them; but is graciously pleased to afford them as well an ordinary course of trial, as an ordinary punishment, much inferior to their offence. And surely worthy of observation is the punishment by law provided and appointed for High-Treason, which we call *crimen laesae majestatis*. For first after a traitor that had his just trial and is convicted and attained, he shall have his judgement to be drawn to the place of execution from his prison as not being worthy any more to tread upon the face of the earth whereof he was made: also for that he hath been retrograde to nature, therefore is he drawn backward at a horse tail. And whereas God hath made the head of man the highest and most supreme part, as being his chief grace and ornament, '*Pronaque cum spectent animalia caetera terram os homini sublime dedite*', he must be drawn with his head declining downward, and lying so near the ground as may be, being thought unfit to take the benefit of the common air. For which cause also he shall be strangled, being hanged up by the neck between heaven and earth, as deemed unworthy of both, or either; as likewise, that the eyes of men may behold, and their hearts condemn him. Then he is to be cut down alive, and to have his privy parts cut off and burnt before his face as being unworthily begotten, and unfit to leave any generation after him. His bowels and inlay'd parts taken out and burnt, who inwardly had conceived and harboured in his heart such horrible treason.

After, to have his head cut off, which had imagined the mischief. And lastly his body to be quartered, and the quarters set up in some high and eminent place, to the view and detestation of men, and to become a prey for the fowls of the air. And this is a reward due to traitors whose hearts be hardened.

Of course treason, like all 'political' crimes, is in the eye of he who feels wronged. Sir William Wallace, for example, may well have got up the nose of his Majesty King Edward I, but to the nationalists of his native Scotland, Wallace was the great patriot – a man for whom a charge of treason was meaningless as he viewed England as a foreign country anyway. Nevertheless, William Wallace was hanged, drawn and quartered at Smithfield in 1305, his head being the first to adorn old London Bridge, and his quarters distributed for display in Newcastle, Berwick, Perth and Stirling.

Drowning

Aside from accidents resulting from over-zealousness at the **ducking stool** or in **swimming** witches, punishment or execution by drowning was not widespread in Europe apart from in Germany.

During the German Middle Ages, execution by drowning was for the most part inflicted on women for infanticide, and on both genders for high treason. The usual method was to bind the prisoner's wrists and ankles and throw him or her into the river from a bridge. If the water was too shallow, the unfortunate victim was simply prodded under by means of long poles. When no suitable river or pond could be located, a large wooden barrel could serve the purpose, the felon being tied into a sack and pitched head first into the tub and held there.

Drunkard's Barrel
(see **Mantles**)

Ducking Stool

The ducking stool method of punishing women is funny enough. They fasten an armchair to the end of two strong beams twelve or fifteen feet long and parallel to each other. The chair hangs on a sort of axle on which it plays freely, so as always to remain in the horizontal position. The scold being well fastened in her chair, the beams are then placed as near in the centre as possible across a post on the waterside and, being lifted up behind the chair, of course, drops into the cold water. The ducking is repeated according to the degree of shrewishness possessed by the offender, and generally has the effect of cooling her immoderate heat – at least for a time.

(*Travels in England*, Messori, 1700)

In England the ducking stool has a history stretching back at least as far as the Norman conquest, when it was brought across the channel from mainland Europe and later joined the **pillory** and the **stocks** as a responsibility of the Courts Leet. There are even mentions of the use of a *fossa*, or ducking pond, following the Roman invasion.

From most early reports it seems that in Britain the punishment of ducking has always been reserved for scolds and female brawlers. The apparatus enjoyed great popular favour, and few villages were not equipped with facilities for ducking its shrews when the need arose. Indeed, many of the machines have survived to this day in local museums.

The Coventry stool was given official status in the leet book of 1597: 'Whereas there are divers and sundrie disordered persons within this citie that be scolds, brawlers and disquieters of their neighbours, to the great offence of Almighty God and the breach of Her Majestie's peace; for the reformation of such abuses it is ordered and enacted at this leet that if any disordered and disquiet persons of this citie do from henceforth scold or brawle

with their neighbours or others, upon complaint to the alderman or the mayor they shall be committed to the stoole lately appointed for the punishment of such offenders, and thereupon be punished for their deserts, except they do presently paye eleven shillings and eleven pence for their redemption from that punishment to the use of the poore of this citie.'

There is a note of such a sentence being passed in the Wakefield Sessions book for 1671: 'Forasmuch as Jane, the wife of William Farrett of Selby, shoemaker, stands indicted at this sessions for a common scold, to the great annoyance of her neighbours and a breach of His Majesty's peace. It is therefore ordered that the said Jane Farrett for the said offence be openly ducked and ducked three times over the head and ears by the constables of Selby aforesaid, for which this shall be their warrant.'

In his *Beverley Street Names*, J. R. Witty passes on this cautionary verse:

There stands, my friend, in yonder pool,
An engine called the ducking-stool.
By legal power handed down,

The joy and terror of the town.
If jarring females kindle strife,
Give language foul, or not be wife,
If noisy dames should once begin
Too drive the house with horrid din –
'Away,' you cry, 'You'll grace the stool,
We'll teach you how your tongue to rule!'

There were wide variations in the design of ducking stools, which sometimes consisted simply of a chair attached to a rope and pulley lowered from a fixed beam at the edge of the pond; others worked on a pivot or 'see-saw' mechanism. There are records enough of fatalities resulting from ducking – either directly by drowning or subsequently through pneumonia or exposure. In 1731 the mayor of Nottingham ordered to the stool a woman who was ducked so long and so violently by the mob that she died; this dreadful incident resulted in the prosecution of the mayor and the destruction of the ducking stool.

The prison reformer John Howard (*State of the Prisons in England and Wales*, 1777–80) described a ducking stool still in use for a novel purpose at the Liverpool Bridewell: 'In it all the female vagrants (not males) at their entrance were placed, with a flannel shift on, and underwent a thorough ducking, three times repeated – a use of the bath which I dare say legislators never thought of when, in their recent Act, they ordered baths with a view to cleanliness and preserving the health of the prisoners, not for the exercise of a wanton and dangerous kind of severity.'

The ducking stool remained in use, as much as a popular entertainment as a punishment, up to the beginning of the nineteenth century. Although it is clearly impossible to trace the last instance of ducking, records survive of its use in Plymouth in 1808, and at Leominster in 1809. In the latter case a woman named Jenny Pipes was paraded around town seated on the chair before being ducked from Thenwater Bridge.

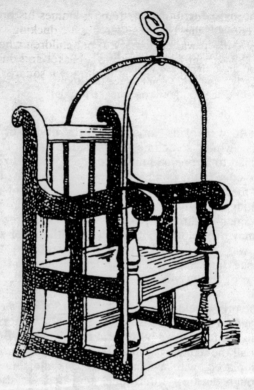

Ipswich ducking stool

Baker's Baptism

Ducking stools were in regular use throughout Germany in the sixteenth century for the punishment of bakers who sold underweight bread – hence the description 'Baker's Baptism'. Often very elaborate ducking cages were constructed and at the Crime Museum in Rothenburg there stands a magnificent structure with see-saw pivots and counterbalances. For each 16.66 grammes his bread was underweight the baker suffered one ducking. Also at Rothenburg it was customary to put children who unlawfully shook fruit from trees into a basket and duck them several times in the fountain in the town square.

Plymouth ducking stool

EF

Electric Chair

A growing dissatisfaction with the still somewhat crude and uncertain method of **hanging** in the United States led, in 1885, to New York Governor David B. Hill establishing a legislative committee to examine other possibilities (abolition not being among them). Under the chairmanship of Elbridge T. Gerry, a noted campaigner against cruelty to children, the 'Death Commission' is said to have examined no fewer than forty methods of execution, settling in the end for the four considered the most humane – the **garotte**, which was subsequently considered too unreliable; the **guillotine**, abandoned because shedding so much blood 'does not accord with the temperament of the American people'; **lethal injection**; and death by electricity.

There was no shortage of strong opinions on the delicate subject of killing criminals, and in the end the application of electricity won most votes among the legal and medical experts canvassed. In a paper published in 1888, Dr J. Mount Bleyer, a New York physician, wrote:

> Last April [1887], in the Legislature of Pennsylvania, a bill was introduced providing that the penalty for the crime of murder in the first degree should be death by electricity.
>
> This method of taking human life certainly possesses all the requisites of a fitting mode of capital execution. It is decorous, involving no brutal or barbarous intervention of the executioner; it is humane, involving no prolonged agony for the condemned. The duration of an electric spark amounts to only an extremely small fraction of a second of time – about one five-hundredth part. The nervous system

requires no appreciable length of time to act or react. A puncture made with a pin on the arm is not *instantly* noted by the brain, or felt, as we say; a man may lose a finger or a hand by the action of a rapidly revolving circular saw, and feel no pain at the instant. In death by the electric current life is undoubtedly extinct before the afferent nerves can carry to the brain intelligence of the stroke that has fallen. It follows that death by such means – death by electricity – must be absolutely painless.

The mode of execution would be about as follows:

Electric wires connecting with the main wires which supply light through the city's streets might be laid to the place assigned for executions, being so concealed and guarded as to be inaccessible to the condemned criminal or his friends, and otherwise protected against accident. At the assigned place a small wooden house, like a sentry box or a watchman's hut should be erected. Spring locks, which close around both limbs, neck and arms, should be so attached to this hut that it will take but a few seconds to enclose the criminal in order that the body will not fall to the ground after death. A metallic plate connecting with one of the wires and serving as an electrode is placed evenly with the floor of the hut; on this plate the criminal is to stand. A second electrode is introduced through the roof of the hut, and its end descends just so far within the hut as just to touch the top of the head when the criminal is introduced into the box. His feet should be bare, and his hair cropped short. When the time for the execution has come, the electrodes are to be tested to determine whether the current flows in sufficient force, and the whole apparatus is in proper working order. If so, the sheriff, or his deputy, or other representative of the law, touches a push-button, thus closing the circuit. The electric current passes through the body of the criminal, and even before the bystanders have consciousness of the act of pressing the button all is over.

Post-mortem examinations show the blood coagulated throughout its vessels. Experiments made by me upon the lower animals prove that after death by electricity decomposition proceeds with extreme rapidity. Perhaps this circumstance is to be regarded as an incidental advantage of this mode of execution: it would tend to abridge, if not to abolish, the customary 'wake' over the criminal's carcass.

This plan was tried on a large dog. The animal never made a perceptible movement or uttered a sound. Rabbits were experimented upon in the same manner. In every instance death was instantaneous and presumably painless.

In the event this proved to be an utterly naive scenario, and the 'absolutely painless' 500th of a second electric shock woefully inadequate – as the first execution of a human being two years later was to emphasise.

The following account of the execution of murderer William Kemmler was written by Dr Carlos MacDonald, head of the Auburn Asylum for Insane Criminals, and one of the medical witnesses of Kemmler's death:

THE FIRST EXECUTION BY MEANS OF ELECTRICITY

The execution of William Kemmler, alias John Hart, at Auburn Prison, New York, on August 6, 1890, marked the first case in the world's history of the infliction of the death penalty by electricity. The execution was under the immediate direction and control of the prison warden [C. F. Durston], and took place in a room set apart for the purpose, in the basement of the prison's administrative building, to which the electric current was conducted by means of an ordinary electric-light wire.

The apparatus consisted of a stationary engine, an alternating-current dynamo and exciter, a

THE INFLICTION OF THE

DEATH PENALTY BY MEANS OF ELECTRICITY

BEING A REPORT OF SEVEN CASES

*With Remarks on the Methods of Application and the
Gross and Microscopical Effects of Electrical Currents of Lethal Energy
on the Human Subject*

BY

CARLOS F. MacDONALD. M. D.

PRESIDENT OF THE NEW YORK STATE COMMISSION IN LUNACY ;
PROFESSOR OF MENTAL DISEASES IN THE BELLEVUE HOSPITAL MEDICAL COLLEGE;
LECTURER ON INSANITY IN THE ALBANY MEDICAL COLLEGE

*REPRINTED FROM
THE NEW YORK MEDICAL JOURNAL
FOR MAY 7 AND 14, 1892*

NEW YORK
D. APPLETON AND COMPANY
1892

Cardew volt meter with extra resistance coil, cali-
brated for a range of from 30 to 2000 volts, an
ammeter for alternating currents from 0.10 to 3
amperes, a Wheatstone bridge, rheostat, bell signals, and necessary switches; a 'death chair' with
adjustable head-rest, binding tapes, and two
adjustable electrodes. The chair, a square-framed
heavy oaken one with a high, slightly sloping back
and broad arms, was fastened to the floor, the feet
of the chair being properly insulated.

Attached to the back of the chair, above the head-
rest, was a sliding arrangement shaped like a figure
four (4), the base or horizontal arm of which projected forward, and from which was suspended the
head electrode, so as to rest on the vertex, or top
of the head, against which it was firmly held by
means of a spiral spring. The spinal, or body electrode was attached to the lower part of the back of
the chair and projected forward horizontally on a
level with the hollow of the sacrum. The electrodes
each consisted of a bell-shaped rubber cup about
four inches in diameter, the part corresponding to
the handle of the bell being of wood, through the
long axis of which the wire passed into the bell,
terminating in a metallic disc about three inches in
diameter, and faced with a layer of sponge. The
lower electrode was also provided with a sliding
arrangement and spiral spring to hold it in place,
while a broad strap fastened to the back of the chair
and passed round the lower part of the prisoner's
abdomen rendered the contact secure. The head was
firmly secured by means of conjoined broad leather
bands, which encircled the forehead and chin, concealing the eyes and upper portion of the face, and
were fastened at the back of the almost perpendicular head-rest, while the chest, arms and legs were
secured by broad straps attached to corresponding
portions of the chair. The wire attached to the head
electrode descended from the ceiling, and that of

the lower one passed along the floor to the chair, being protected by a strip of wood.

The dynamo and engine were located in one of the prison [work] shops several hundred feet distant from the execution room; the voltmeter, ammeter, switchboard, etc., were located in a room adjoining the execution room, which contained the death chair, electrodes and connecting wires. Communication between the meter room and dynamo room was by means of electric signals.

Of the twenty-five official witnesses present, fourteen were physicians. Before Kemmler was brought into the room the warden asked the physicians how long the contact should be maintained. Dr MacDonald suggested twenty seconds but subsequently assented to ten seconds.

The preliminary arrangements having been completed, Kemmler was brought into the execution room by the warden and introduced to the witnesses who were seated in a semi-circle facing the death chair. On entering the room the prisoner appeared strikingly calm and collected. In fact, his manner and appearance indicated a state of subdued elation, as if gratified at being the central figure of the occasion, his somewhat limited intellect evidently rendering him unable to fully appreciate the gravity of his situation. He was given a chair near the death chair and, on being seated, in response to the warden's introduction, said: 'Well, I wish every one good luck in this world, and I think I am going to a good place, and the papers has been saying a lot of stuff about me that wasn't true. That's all I have to say.'

At the warden's bidding he then arose, removed his coat, and without the least display of emotion or nervousness, took his seat in the execution chair, calmly submitting to the adjustment of the electrodes and binding straps, himself aiding the proceedings by suggestions and fixing his body and limbs in the proper position. Observing the nervousness of the prison officers who were adjusting the straps he admonished them not to hurry, and to 'be sure that everything is all right'.

He pressed his bared back firmly against the spinal electrode and requested that the head electrode be pressed down more firmly on the top of his head, from which the hair had been imperfectly clipped before he entered the room, remarking at the same time that he desired to perform his part to the best of his ability. The preparations terminated with a final moistening of the electrodes, the whole occupying at most between three and four minutes. Everything being seemingly ready, the warden signalled to his assistants in charge of the switches in the adjoining room to turn the lever which closed the circuit and instantly sent the deadly current through the prisoner's body. The instant the contact was made the body was thrown into a state of extreme rigidity, every fibre of the entire muscular system being apparently in a marked condition of tonic spasm. Synchronously with the onset of rigidity, body sensation, motion and consciousness were apparently absolutely suspended, and remained so while electrical contact was maintained. At the end of seventeen seconds Kemmler was pronounced dead, none of the witnesses dissenting, and the warden signalled to have the contact broken, which was immediately done.

For obvious reasons, the only means of determining the question of death while the body was in circuit was by ocular demonstration; so that it can not be positively asserted that the heart's action entirely ceased with the onset of unconsciousness, though most of the medical witnesses present thought that it did.

When the electrical contact was broken the condition of rigidity noted above was instantly succeeded by one of complete muscular relaxation. At the same time superficial discolorations resembling commencing capillary post-mortem changes were observed on the exposed portions of the face. The body remained limp and motionless for approximately half a minute, when there occurred a series of slight spasmodic movements of the chest, accompanied by the expulsion of a small amount of mucus from the mouth. There were no evidences of a return to consciousness or of sensory function; but in view of the possibility that life was not wholly extinct, beyond resuscitation, and in order to take no risk of such a contingency, the current was ordered to be reapplied, which was done within about two minutes from the time the first contact was broken. The sudden muscular rigidity noted on the first closure of the circuit was again observed and continued until the contact was again broken, when the opposite state of complete muscular relaxation re-occurred. The second closure of the circuit was inadvertently maintained for about seventy seconds, when a small volume of vapour, and subsequently of smoke, was seen to issue from the point of application of the spinal electrode, due, as was subsequently found, to scorching of the edge of the sponge with which the electrode was faced, and from which the moisture had been evaporated by prolonged electrical contact. The odour of burning sponge was faintly perceptible in the room.

There was also some dessication of the already dead body, immediately underneath the electrodes, especially under the lower one. A careful examination of the body was now made in which the medical witnesses participated to a greater or less extent. The radial pulse and heart's action had ceased, the pupils were dilated and the corneas were depressed and flaccid on pressure. In other words, William Kemmler was dead, and the intent and purpose of the law to effect sudden and painless death in the execution of criminals had been successfully carried out.

In the excitement and confusion of the moment, occasioned by the belief on the part of some that death was not complete, the second application of the current in Kemmler's case was maintained too long – nearly a minute and a half. If there was a spark of unconscious vitality remaining in the prisoner's body after the first contact was broken, it was absolutely extinguished the instant the second and last contact was made. That the man was dead, however, comparatively long before the burning of the sponge and desiccation of the tissue occurred, there is no reason to doubt.

Despite this complacent conclusion it was an execution which had clearly been bungled, for though Dr MacDonald seemed to have no problem accepting the inevitability of prisoners reviving after the initial charge, or with smoke and 'vapour' rising from the charring flesh, other witnesses were less sanguine. The *New York Times* on the following day reported one expert declaring that 'the execution was an awful botch, Kemmler was literally roasted to death'; and New York's deputy coroner gave his opinion that 'It was fearful. No humane man could witness it without the keenest agony.'

Nevertheless electrocution was there to stay for many decades, and despite the fact that there are still appalling incidents in the death chamber many states continue to use the electric chair as their means of effecting judicial execution. As recently as May 1990, Jesse Joseph Tafero was also 'literally roasted to death'. Convicted of shooting a highway patrolman in 1976, Tafero was finally strapped into 'Old Sparky' at Florida's Starke Prison on 4 May 1990. It is customary to require only one surge of electricity to immobilise and kill the condemned man, but in Tafero's case the technicians needed to switch the current on and off three times during the course of four minutes. Each time it was turned on flames shot from the helmet on Tafero's head and black smoke poured from beneath the mask covering his face. Only after the third attempt did the prisoner stop breathing and moving his head. A Press Association reporter said: 'This is the first time I have seen sparks and flames coming from the head.' The Governor of Starke launched an immediate inquiry, the result of which was a period of tests carried out on the machine by the Florida Prisons Administration, who finally attributed its temperamental nature to the use of artificial instead of natural sponges to cushion the electrodes to the prisoner's head. At any rate, less than three months after the Tafero fiasco, on 27 June 1990, Anthony Bertolotti was executed in the same chair without undue incident. However, there is some sign that botched electrocutions such as that at Starke have begun to persuade even the most devoted retentionists that some change is needed. This has shown itself in the gradual replacement of death with gas and electricity by death through **lethal injection**.

Execution Broadsheets

Of all the ballads and broadsheets published during the eighteenth and nineteenth centuries the most popular by far were the 'Murder' sheets. One good killing could spawn a whole series of sheets, starting with the discovery of the corpse, passing through the investigation, apprehension, trial, death-cell lament and finally execution of the culprit.

Execution sheets generally follow a similar format and contain a combination of the following elements:

The Trial Described briefly, particularly if a separate sheet has not already covered it.

The Sentence

Prisoner's confession A great deal of importance was attached to extracting a confession from the condemned man, as this had the composite value of proving God's intervention in the affairs of man, the vindication of the sentence and, in days more orthodoxly religious than our

The Life, Trial, Execution, Lamentation, and Letter written by the unfortunate man

James Ward,

Aged 25, who was hung in front of the Gaol,

For the Wilful Murder he committed on the body of his Wife, near Edminton.

TRIAL.

At an early hour on the morning of the trial, the court was crowded to excess, the Judge taking his seat at nine o'clock. The Prisoner, on being placed at the bar, pleaded 'Not Guilty' in a firm tone of voice. The trial lasted many hours, when, having been found 'GUILTY,' the learned Judge addressed the prisoner as follows:—

"Prisoner, you have been found guilty of a most cold-blooded murder, a more deliberate murder I never heard of. You and your wife had been to a neighbouring town, and were returning home, when you did it. She was found in a ditch, and I hold out the slightest hope of mercy towards you in this case." During this address the whole court was melted into tears. His Lordship then put on the black cap and passed the sentence as usual, holding out no hope of mercy to the prisoner.

Letter written after his Condemnation.

Dear Sister,   Condemned Cell.

When you receive this you will see that I am condemned to die; my Father and Mother are coming to take their last farewell, and I should very much liked to have seen you, but knowing that you are on the eve of bringing into the world another to your family, I beg that you will refrain from coming; if that you do serious may be the consequences, therefore, dear Sister, do not attempt to come. I hope that no one will upbraid you for what I have done; so may God bless you and yours; farewell! dear sister for ever.

J. WARDE

EXECUTION.

The Execution of the above prisoner took place early this morning at eight o'clock, the people flocking to the scene at an early hour. As the period of the wretched man's departure drew near, the chaplain became anxious to obtain from him a confession of the justice of the sentence. He acknowledged the justice of his sentence, and said he was not fit to live, and that he was afraid to die, but he prayed to the Lord for forgiveness, and hoped through the merits of his Saviour that his prayer would be heard. Having received the sacrament, the executioner was not long in performing his office. The solemn procession moved towards the place of execution, the chaplain repeating the confession words, "In the midst of life we are in death." Upon ascending the platform he appeared to tremble very much. The cap being drawn over his eyes and the signal given, the wretched man was launched into eternity. He died almost without a struggle. After the body had hanged the usual time it was cut down and buried according to the sentence, in the gaol,

LAMENTATION.

Come all you feeling hearted christians, wherever you may be,
Attention give to these few lines, and listen unto me;
Its of this cruel murder, to you I will unfold,
The bare recital of the same will make your blood run cold.

Confined within a lonely cell, with sorrow I am opprest,
The very thoughts of what I've done deprives me of rest;
Within this dark and gloomy cell in the county Gaol I lie,
For murder of my dear wife I am condemned to die.

For four long years I'd married been, I always lov'd her well,
Till at length I was overlooked, oh shame for me to tell;
By Satan sure I was beguiled, he led me quite astray,
Unto another I gave way on that sad unlucky day.

I well deserve my wretched fate, no one can pity me,
To think that I in cold blood could take the life away;
I took a stake out of the hedge and hit on the head,
My cruel blows I did repeat until she were dead.

I dragged the body from the stile to a ditch running by,
I quite forgot there's One above with an all-seeing eve,
Who always brings such deeds to light, as you so plainly see,
I questioned was about it and took immediately.

The body's found, the inquest held, to prison I was sent,
With shame I do confess my sin, with grief I do repent;
And when my trial did come on, I was condemned to die,
An awful death in public scorn, upon the gallows high.

While in my lonely cell I lie, the time draws on apace,
The dreadful deeds that I have done appear before my face;
While lying on my dreadful couch those horrid visions rise,
The ghastly form of my dear wife appears before my eyes.

Oh may my end a warning be now unto all mankind,
And think of my unhappy fate and bear me in your mind;
Whether you are rich or poor, your wives and children love,
So God will fill your fleeting days with blessings from above.

Roeliff, Printer, Old Gravel Lane, London.

own, the hope of salvation in the afterlife for the criminal. Where no confession was forthcoming from the condemned it was considered quite acceptable for the printer to write one for him.

Copy of Verses (sometimes called a 'Lamentation') The verses were an essential part of the execution sheet, being a summary, in verse, of the life, crimes and apologia of the criminal – almost always written in the first person, though never by the prisoner. Said one hack, 'I gets a shilling a copy for the verses written by the wretched culprit the night previous to his execution.' It seems that the price was a standard one – 'no more nor a bob for nothing' – which reflects in the quality of the verse, which is for the most part unimaginative in the extreme. Little attention was paid to the facts of the case under treatment, and scant respect paid to any poetic convention. Sometimes special broadsheets were issued consisting solely of the copy of verses or lamentation, with perhaps a standard woodcut to illustrate them; on the whole these were somewhat better compositions and written to be set to a currently popular tune.

Dying Speech However illogical a sequence of events that allowed a copy of a dying speech to be on sale beneath the gallows many hours before the condemned man stood upon it, it made no difference to the popularity of this traditional section of the 'gallows sheet'.

Execution Another purely fictitious piece of prose hastily prepared to be in time for the first sales on the day of execution. Clearly, as it was written without the benefit of witnessing the event, accuracy was a matter of the purest chance. Indeed, there are execution broadsheets claiming the 'launching into eternity' of prisoners who are known to have been given last-minute reprieves.

Execution Diary

AD 35	Saint Stephen becomes the first, or 'proto', martyr after suffering **stoning to death** by the Jews for bearing witness that Christ was the Messiah.
1076	Waltheof, Earl of Northumberland, is the first person in England to be executed by the axe.

1241   William Marise, a pirate, is the first to be hung drawn and quartered in England.

1305   The head of Scottish patriot William Wallace is the first to adorn the ramparts of London Bridge.

1307   1 April: Raphael Holinshed records the execution by an early **guillotine** of Murcod Ballagh, near Merton, Ireland.

1312–77   Introduction of the so-called **Halifax Gibbet**, a form of mechanical decapitator.

1406   The punishment of **pressing** (or peine forte et dure) is adopted in England.

1447   The **rack** is first introduced from Europe into the Tower of London by John Holland, Duke of Exeter, the Tower Constable.

1486   Introduction of the 'Mannaia', a form of guillotine, to Italy.

1531   **Boiling to death** enters the English statute by order of Henry VIII as a punishment for the crime of poisoning. Abolished under Edward VI in 1547.

1580   James Douglas, Fourth Earl of Morton, Regent of Scotland is executed on the Scottish '**Maiden**', a mechanical guillotine designed by the Regent himself and based on the Halifax Gibbet.

1644   Only recorded instance of an execution by **beheading** in the United States, at Massachusetts.

1648   Abolition of **burning alive** as a punishment for heresy in England (in fact the last actual such execution was of Edward Wightman in 1612).

1649   Most famous beheading to be carried out on a 'murderer and traitor' in England takes place – that of King Charles I.

1659   27 October: Quaker missionary Mary Dyer becomes the first woman sentenced to hang in the New World; the execution is carried out before a large crowd on Boston Common.

1686	Alice Molland is the last person to be hanged as a witch in England (in Scotland the last witch burning is thought to have been as late as 1722).
1747	9 April: Simon Fraser, eleventh Baron Lovat, is the last person publicly beheaded in Britain; Lord Lovat had been condemned for his part in the Jacobite rebellion of 1745.
1752	An Act of this year allows the bodies of executed murderers to be sent for dissection to Surgeons' Hall, conveniently situated close to the Old Bailey. Skeletons of notorious criminals (like that of **Mrs Brownrigg**) were publicly displayed.
1757	Robert Francois Daumiens is executed in Paris by being torn in quarters by horses. Daumiens had been convicted of the unsuccessful regicide of Louis XV.
1760	Laurence Shirley, Earl Ferrers, is the first to be hanged using 'the new drop', a far cry from the later more efficient 'long drop', but the first advance in the craft of the hangman.
1772	**Pressing** (peine forte et dure) abolished in England.
1783	7 November: John Austin, a thief, is the last person to be hanged on the notorious gallows at Tyburn.
—	9 December: first batch of prisoners is publicly hanged at the new gallows erected outside Newgate Gaol.
1786	Last public burning of a felon (in this case a woman) at Newgate; she had been hanged previously until dead.
1803	After execution by hanging for murder, George Foster is delivered to a Professor Aldini who tries unsuccessfully to revive him by 'Galvanism'.
1809	Possible last use of **ducking stool** in England, at Leominster. Jenny Piper is paraded through

town before being ducked off Thenwater Bridge.

1813 **Garotte** introduced in Spain to replace hanging as the official means of judicial execution.

1814 Beheading abolished as a means of capital punishment in Britain.

1818 The first **treadmill**, designed by Sir William Cubitt, is built at Brixton Prison.

1827 Abolition in England of **benefit of clergy** (last recorded use in 1855, in Carolina, USA).

1829 31 December Thomas Maynard is executed at the Old Bailey, the last in England to die for forgery.

1832 Capital punishment abolished in Britain for cattle, horse and sheep stealing.

1833 Capital punishment for housebreaking abolished in Britain.

1834 James Cook, a bookbinder of Leicester, is executed for the murder of a Mr Paas, and becomes the last man in England to suffer **hanging in chains** after death.

1835 Abolition of capital punishment in Britain for sacrilege; also for Post Office workers stealing mail.

1836 Capital punishment abolished in Britain for coining and forgery.

1837 Capital punishment abolished for burglary and stealing from dwelling houses in Britain.

1856 **Scold's bridle** reported to be still in use at Bolton-le-Moore, Lancashire.

1860 13 July: Private John Dalliger the last to suffer **hanging from the yardarm**, off China.

1861 27 August: Martin Doyle becomes the last person in England to be executed for attempted murder.

1862 26 December: America's largest mass execution – 38 Sioux Indians are hanged at Mankato, Minnesota.

1866   Last public execution in Scotland, of Joe Bell, by hanging, at Perth.

1868   2 April: last public execution of a woman in England – Frances Kidder at Maidstone.

—   29 May: Michael Barrett, the Fenian who caused the Clerkenwell explosion, becomes the last person in England to be publicly hanged.

—   29 May: Capital Punishment Within Prisons Bill receives Royal Assent.

—   13 August: at Maidstone, Thomas Wells is the first person to be executed behind prison walls, for the murder of a railway stationmaster at Dover.

1873   **Hara-kiri** officially abolished in Japan.

1899   20 March: first woman to be executed by electricity, Martha Garretson Place, dies in the **electric chair** at Sing Sing.

1908   Children's Act abolishes the death penalty for persons under the age of sixteen years (later eighteen).

1922   Passing of the Infanticide Act, reducing the penalty for women who kill their children within a certain period after birth to one for manslaughter instead of murder.

1924   8 February: lethal gas used for the first time as a means of execution when Gee Jon, convicted of murder is put into the gas chamber in Nevada.

1936   Last public execution (a hanging) in the United States, at Owensboro, Kentucky.

1939   17 June: last public execution in France, of Eugen Weidmann on the guillotine at Versailles.

1941   Juanita Spinelli becomes the first woman to be executed in the gas chamber (she is also the first woman to be executed in California).

1955   13 July: for the shooting of her lover, David Blakely, Ruth Ellis becomes the last woman to be hanged in Britain.

1964   13 August: last two executions in Britain – Peter Anthony Allen at Walton Prison, Liverpool, and Gwynne Owen Evans at Manchester's Strangeways Prison.

1965   9 November: Murder (Abolition of Capital Punishment) Act is passed by Parliament, suspending the death penalty for a trial period of five years.

1969   16 December: Parliament reaffirms its commitment to abolition.

1982   7 December: first execution by **lethal injection** of Charlie Brookes at Huntsville, Texas.

1984   2 November: 52-year-old Velma Barfield is the first woman executed by lethal injection, at Central Prison, Raleigh, North Carolina.

Execution Dock

An appropriately watery end was reserved for English pirates and other criminous seamen at Execution Dock. Sited on the bank of the River Thames at East Wapping, 'opposite Blackwall', it was the tradition to hang pirates from chains to drown there (though they were sometimes extended the 'mercy' of being hanged on a gallows first). John Stow, the historian, records in his *Survey of London* (1598–1603) that it was 'The usual place for hanging of pirates and sea-rovers, at the low-water mark, and there to remain till three tides had overflowed them'. The practice had been carried out since the reign of Henry VI, when there is a record of two bargemen being convicted of the 'murder of three Flemings and a child in a Flemish vessel' and were 'hanged till the water had washed them by ebbying and flowyd, so the water bett upon them'.

An Elizabethan tragi-comedy, *Fortune by Land and Sea* by Heywood and Rowley, has one scene set at Execution Dock, where Purser and Clinton, two pirates, are to be hung in chains; they lament:

But now our sun is setting; night comes on;
The watery widerness o'er which we reigned
Proves in our ruins peaceful. Merchants trade,
Fearless abroad as in the river's mouth,
And free as in a harbour. Then, fair Thames,
Queen of fresh water, famous through the world,
And not the least through us, whose double tides
Must overflow our bodies; and, being dead,
May thy clear waves our scandals wash away,
But keep our valours living.

As late as 1844, Charles Knight wrote in his *London*: 'There are some now alive who yet remember the bodies of the pirates opposite Blackwell wavering in the wind – a gibbet's tassel.'

Execution Dock's most famous son was the notorious Scottish privateer Captain William Kidd. In 1696 a consortium of London merchants equipped Kidd with a 30-gun ship for the purpose of eliminating pirates ranging the Indian Ocean, but within two years there were rumours that Kidd had himself turned pirate, and he was arrested on landing at Boston harbour. Although he was tried in London, convicted and hanged, most of the exploits associated with Captain Kidd are purely legendary; indeed, it is even possible that he was, as he claimed, innocent. The *Newgate Calendar* records that 'He suffered with one of his companions (Darby Mullins) at Execution Dock on the 23rd day of May, 1701. After Kidd had been tied up to the gallows the rope broke and he fell to the ground; but was immediately tied up again.'

Eye-cups

For this dreadful contribution, said to have originated in Iran when that country was called Persia, I am indebted to an anonymous reporter in *Famous Crimes Past and Present*:

They have, too, an ingenious and fiendishly cruel eye-torture in that country. A leather strap contains two cups which, when the contrivance is fastened to the head, just fit on the eyes. The cup is so made that the bottom rim presses the eyelids open in a rather painful manner, but that is the least severe part of the torture. The cup is made to hold corrosive acids, and these, fed from a holder, leak into the eyes through ingeniously contrived channels in the bottom of the cup. The culprit's eyes are thus slowly eaten away, and if the torture is continued for any length of time, the unfortunate wretch dies in dreadful agony.

Flagellation

The use of the whip, in all its variations, has been so widespread throughout time and geographical location that the punishment of flagellation has become a study in its own right.* It is impossible, of course – even within centuries – to determine when one man first flogged another; what we can be sure of is that, according to reports from around the world, they are still doing it. What follows, then, is less a historical narrative than a miscellany of facts, features and anecdote.

*Such a work is the excellent *History of Corporal Punishment*, by George Ryley Scott.

Whipping Among the Romans
The Romans made considerable use of flagellation as a
punishment for slaves and soldiers, but rarely for free
men. The culture recognised several basic instruments for
the infliction of punishment, their use being dictated by
the seriousness of the offence. A simple, flat strap called
a *ferula* was used to impart minor punishments; there
followed three variations on the 'cat' (see below) – the
scutia was a whip fashioned from twisted thongs of parch-
ment, the *plumbatae* had many thongs, each tipped with
lead or bronze balls, and the *flagellum*, with three ferocious 'tails' of ox leather. The Romans also used rods
to effect flagellation, and this method invariably preceded
execution by **beheading**.

The Cat
Although its ancestry clearly lies in the Roman *scutia* and
plumbatae, the cat is a quintessentially British flogging
instrument with particular military and nautical connections; it was frequently used in the British navy of Nelson's
day, when a cruel captain could order as many as 500
lashes. Commonly called the 'cat-o'-nine-tails', there were
nine separate thongs, or 'tails', of leather or whipcord,
knotted in three places along their two-foot length. The
effect of the strokes was twofold – the tail itself would
cut through a prisoner's skin, while the knots would eat
out small pieces of flesh. The following description of
a flogging at sea (albeit aboard a Transport) uses the
'boatswain's cat', and derives from *Experiences of Flagellation*, an anonymous ('Compiled by an Amateur Flagel-
lant'), privately printed volume dated 1885:

Amongst the recruits assigned to his command on

his passage outwards was an unfortunate man named Green, who had formerly kept a hatter's shop in Catherine Street, Strand, and who, under a conviction for some crime was sentenced to transportation for fourteen years. His wife, an amiable but heartbroken woman, was permitted to accompany him on the voyage, and shortly after the vessel sailed from the Downs symptoms of mutiny were discovered amongst the convicts; several had sawed off their irons, and Green was charged not with any act of mutiny, but with furnishing the convicts with money to procure implements to take off their irons. The unfortunate man stated in his vindication that he had only lent some of the wretches a few shillings to take some sheets and other necessaries out of pawn. But this defence would not do. He was brought to the gangway by order of the Governor, without drum-head, or any other court-martial, and flogged with a boatswain's cat until his bones were denuded of flesh. Still the unhappy man never uttered a groan. The Governor, who superintended the punishment, swore he would cure the rascal's stubbornness and make him cry out, or whip his guts out. The surgeon remonstrated on the danger of the man's death, but in vain. Ensign Wall, the Governor's brother, a humane young man, on his knees entreated that the flogging should cease; but also in vain; and his importunity only served to provoke a threat of putting himself in arrest. He then entreated the unfortunate Green to cry out and save himself. But he said it was too late now, as he felt himself dying, and unable to cry out, and that he had not avoided it through stubbornness but concealed his pangs lest his wretched wife, who was down below and knew nothing of his situation, should hear his cries and die with anguish. The flogging was continued until the convulsions of his bowels appeared through his lacerated loins, when he fainted under the lash, and was consigned to the surgeon.

That this kind of severe punishment was often fatal is no
surprise, and such was the widespread abuse of power by
captains of His Majesty's navy that several serious mutin-
ies took place during the late eighteenth century. In the
spring of 1797, British sailors at anchor in Spithead had
risen against their ill-use and appalling conditions, and on
17 May the Admiralty had been forced to implement a
package of concessions which included the dismissal of
officers accused of unnecessary brutality. Between 30 May
and 13 June a further serious mutiny broke out among
the ships resting at the Nore. The self-styled 'Floating
Republic' led by 'President' Richard Parker was this time
crushed mercilessly. Parker himself was hanged from the
yardarm of the *Sandwich* as an example, and 29 fellow
conspirators were also executed; nine others were flogged,
and 29 imprisoned. Conditions failed to improve for
almost another century, and it was not until 1881 that the
cat was finally abolished by the British services.

Unsurprisingly, the cat also featured heavily in the punishment routine of most British prisons, and judges would
sentence offenders to imprisonment plus an additional
punishment of flogging – often stipulating the number
of lashes. Although whipping was abolished as a court
sentence in 1948, the use of the cat-o'-nine-tails to impose
prison discipline and punish adult transgressors was available to governors into the 1960s. Prisoners received their
punishment spread-eagled to a specially designed frame
(see *Whipping Beds* below); one concession to humani-
tarianism was that wide leather belts were used to protect
the kidneys and neck from damage.

It remains to add that flagellation, and the use of the
cat in particular to punish slaves, was extensive throughout the British Colonies, and nowhere more brutally than
in the West Indies. In Barbados, for example, flogging
was never removed from the statute book – the last criminal sentenced to the cat being a teenage rapist in 1969.
However, according to a report sent by Garry Steckles
from Bridgetown to the *Sunday Times* in March 1991,
Barbados has revived the use of the cat-o'-nine-tails in a

Whipping in the press yard at Newgate

desperate attempt to halt the rise in drug trafficking. Steckles concluded: 'The problem facing the local judiciary, apart from the protests of church leaders and others who regard the punishment as inhumane, is finding a suitable whip. The only cat-o'-nine-tails on the island is a treasured museum exhibit that may fall apart if cracked enthusiastically after decades of idleness. Edgar Hendy, superintendent of prisons, will extend his search to Britain while convicts await their fate.'

Knout

According to Scott, 'In no country in the world is whipping so widely practiced, so savagely and so vindictively inflicted, as in the Russia of the Tsars.' The special instrument of flagellation uniquely favoured by the Russians was the fearful knout: 'it was a wooden-handled whip usually consisting of several thongs of raw hide twisted together and terminating in a single strand projecting some eighteen inches farther than the body of the knout. In some cases wire was plaited with the hide, in others rings or hooks were attached to the ends of the thongs; in other instances, the barbaric sadism of the individual wielding the whip caused him to harden the raw hide by dipping it in water or other liquid and allowing it to freeze.'

The use of the knout was prescribed for a wide range of crimes, and in the time of Peter the Great the maximum sentence was 101 lashes. It was applied without favour both to men and to women, and even the aristocracy was not exempt. Being discovered involved in a treason plot, a Madame Lapuchin, attached to the court of Elizabeth, was publicly stripped to the waist and savagely whipped with the knout before having her tongue cut out and being sent into Siberian exile. It is even fabled that Peter the Great knouted his own son to death.

However, there is one apparently authentic description of the knouting of a man and a woman relayed in the *Anecdotes* of Reuben and Sholto Percy (1820–23). The eye-witness was none other than the great philanthropist and prison reformer John Howard:

> When the philanthropic Howard was in Petersburg, he saw two criminals, a man and a woman, suffer the punishment of the *knout*. They were conducted from prison by about fifteen hussars and ten soldiers. Whey they had arrived at the place of punishment, the hussars formed themselves into a ring round the whipping post; the drum beat a minute or two, and then some prayers were repeated, the populace taking off their hats. The woman was first taken, and after being roughly stripped to the waist, her hands and feet were bound with cords to a post made for the purpose. A servant attended the executioner and both were stout men. The servant first marked his ground, and struck the woman five times on the back; every stroke seemed to penetrate deep into her flesh; but his master thinking him too gentle, pushed him aside, took his place, and gave all the remaining strokes himself, which were evidently more severe. The woman received twenty-five blows, and the man sixty. 'I,' continues Mr Howard, 'pressed through the hussars, and counted the number as they were chalked on a board for the purpose. Both of the criminals seemed just alive, especially the man, who had yet strength enough remaining to receive a present with some signs of gratitude. I saw the woman in a very weak condition some days after, but could not find the man any more.'

The use of the knout was abolished in 1845.

Jamaican Cart Whip
Used extensively for the punishment of slaves, this comprised a two-foot handle to which was attached a leash four or five yards long, tapering from two and a half inches where it joined the handle to the thickness of a

cord at its tip. So savagely were slaves treated that a member of the Jamaica Assembly claimed: 'The cart-whip is a cruel, debasing instrument of torture, a horrible, detestable instrument when used for the punishment of slaves. I claim that thirty-nine lashes with this can be made more grievous than five hundred lashes with the cat.' Indeed, so powerful were the representations made that in 1826 the Assembly made it an offence punishable by a £10 fine for any slave-driver to administer more than ten lashes at a time; and for any slave-owner to administer more than 39 lashes for a single offence.

Jamaican cart whip

Bullet Whip
Made from a string of bullets (ball shot) covered with leather and attached to a leather strap:

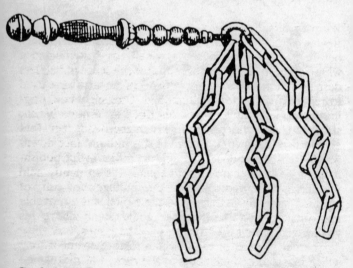

Chain Whip

To a very strong wooden handle are attached a number of lengths of chain with flat, sharp-edged links. It was said that wielded by a strong arm this fearsome weapon could flay a man's back with a few strokes.

Gaoler's Whip

Intended to be used as a weapon of self-defence by the men set to guard the inmates of Britain's roughest gaols, in the hands of a brutal warder this whip could inflict terrible gratuitous punishment. In form it resembles the medieval 'mace and chain', and consists of a wooden

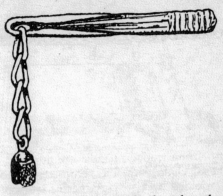

handle to which is attached a single short length of chain with a weight at its end.

Whipping Beds

It was always necessary to somehow secure a prisoner before flogging commenced – usually by fastening to a whipping post. However, to reinforce the sense of helpless despair and terror, a number of special devices were used to render a victim totally immobile. One such 'bed' originated in Germany and was described as 'a large bench, strongly made, with straps to fasten the head, legs, feet and arms of the victim. Bound in this fashion, face downwards, the executioner was able to inflict awful punishment upon his unhappy captive who was so tightly held that it was quite impossible even to indulge the luxury of writhing in agony. Attached to the bench was a movable platform, so that the whipper could stand above his victims and put all his strength into the lashes.'

Another product of the German torture chamber, one which incorporated elements of the **rack**, was nicknamed 'Schlimme Liesel', or 'Fearful Eliza': 'At the foot of the device there are strong iron rings into which the man's feet were placed. His hands were then fastened to a triangular piece of wood which was raised by pulleys until he was stretched beyond endurance. The flagellation would thus be more horribly effective.'

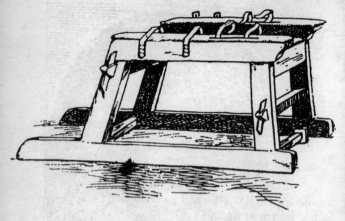

Whipping bed

Until comparatively recently, corporal punishment was an everyday feature of prison and Borstal life in Britain. Whipping – usually with the cat for adults, the birch for young offenders – was carried out at a whipping frame. Pettifer, in his *Punishments of Former Times*, illustrates the frame used at Wandsworth Prison, London.

Whipping at the Cart's Tail

With the dissolution of the monasteries during the reign of Henry VIII, there arose a considerable problem with the number of displaced vagrants wandering the country, and in 1530 the Statute of Labourers allowed for whipping them. In the same year a Whipping Act was also directed at vagrants, and stipulated that they should be stripped naked, tied to the end of a cart and flogged through the town 'till the body shall be bloody by reason of such whipping'. The Act was later amended, and to avoid causing offence to public decency, the victim was to be naked only from the waist up. At the same time most towns and villages had responded to encouragement to set up a permanent whipping post so that they might be prepared for any visitation of vagabonds.

TITUS OATES. D.D.

Whipping at the cart's tail was expanded to be used as a punishment for a variety of offences outside vagrancy, and the length of the route to be taken by the cart, and hence the number of lashes to be administered related directly to the seriousness of the offence.

One of the most notorious cases of whipping at the cart's tail was the punishment inflicted by Judge **Jeffreys** on Titus Oates in 1658.

The rascally Oates, a British cleric who had already spent some years as a spy infiltrating Jesuit colleges abroad, approached adherents of the Protestant cause

Oates Whipt from Algate to Tyburn.

with a list of fanciful allegations – the '43 Articles' – which claimed a conspiracy by Papists to assassinate the king and overthrow the Protestant religion in favour of Charles's Roman Catholic brother James, Duke of York: the so-called 'Popish Plot'. Between 1678–80 many quite innocent Catholics were executed as a result of Oates's false testimony. Finally he was carried before 'Bloody' Jeffreys,

who imposed one of the most savage sentences of the day
– even judged by Jeffreys's own harsh standards. Titus
Oates was condemned to the pillory, whipping at the
cart's tail and imprisonment. The following description of
the ordeal was given by Thomas Macaulay in his *History
of England*:

> On the day on which Oates was pilloried in Palace-
> yard he was mercilessly pelted and ran some risk of
> being pulled to pieces. But in the City his partisans
> mustered in great force, raised a riot and upset the
> pillory. They were, however, unable to rescue their
> favourite. On the following morning he was brought
> forth to undergo his first flogging. At an early hour
> an innumerable multitude filled all the streets from
> Aldgate to the Old Bailey. The hangman laid on the
> lash with such unusual severity as showed that he
> had received special instructions. The blood ran
> down in rivulets. For a time the criminal showed a
> strange constancy: but at last his stubborn fortitude
> gave way. His bellowings were frightful to hear. He
> swooned several times, but the scourge continued
> to descend. When he was unbound it seemed that
> he had borne as much as a human frame can bear
> without dissolution. James was entreated to remit
> his second flogging. His answer was short and clear:
> 'He shall go through with it, if he has breath in his
> body.' An attempt was made to obtain the Queen's
> intercession; but she indignantly refused to say a
> word in favour of a wretch. After an interval of
> forty-eight hours, Oates was again brought out of
> his dungeon. He was unable to stand, and it was
> necessary to drag him to Tyburn on a sledge. He
> seemed quite insensible; and the Tories reported
> that he had stupefied himself with strong drink. A
> person who counted the stripes on the second day
> said that there were 1,700.

Finger Pillory
(see **Pillory**)

The torture of flaying alive

Flaying

As far back as the second century before Christ, stripping the skin from the bodies of his prisoners was a firm favourite with Asdrubal, founder of the Phoenecian city of Carthage. Flaying was also one of the 'slow deaths' so beloved of the Chinese, and closely associated with **death by the thousand cuts**. The Turks flayed criminals convicted of serious crimes such as piracy, and though it was by no means common, there are a number of instances of flaying in Europe. George Ryley Scott quotes two notable examples; one was the execution of the Count de Rouci's Chamberlain in 1366, and the other of Paolo Garnier of Roras, who was first castrated and then stripped of his entire skin while still alive.

The followers of Pierre Waldo – the 'Poor Men of Lyons', or Waldenses – were a band of wandering preachers whose rejection of the sacramental claims of the orthodox priesthood earned them centuries of intermittent persecution by a succession of Popes. During a particularly virulent period in the middle of the seventeenth century two brothers, Jacopo and David Perrin, were partially flayed, 'having the skin stripped off their arms and legs in long slices, till the flesh was quite bare'. I have been unable to trace any reliable reference to flaying alive in Britain.

Footscrew
(see **Thumbscrew**)

Frying

An early form of torture – usually resulting in death – which differed very little from **boiling to death**, except that a shallow pan was used to contain oil or pitch and the victim was fried alive rather than boiled. The use of the **gridiron** completed the 'culinary' tortures.

G

Galvanism

At 8.03 a.m. on 18 January 1803, George Foster was hanged at Newgate for the murder of his wife and child by drowning them in the Paddington Canal.

After it had been cut down from the gallows, Foster's corpse was conveyed to the house of Professor Aldini, where it was subjected to the galvanic process – a 'science' discovered by the professor's uncle, Luigi Galvani, an Italian who had observed that the dismembered legs of frogs appeared to return to life when touched with pairs of different metals.

> On the first application of the process to the face, the jaws of the deceased criminal began to quiver, and the adjoining muscles were horribly contorted, and one eye was actually opened. In the subsequent part of the process the right hand was raised and clenched and the legs and thighs set in motion. Mr Pass, beadle of the Surgeons' Company, who was an observer, was so alarmed that he died of fright soon after his return home. Other bystanders thought the wretched felon was on the eve of being restored to life; this, however, was impossible, as several of his friends who were beneath the scaffold, had violently pulled his legs in order to put a more speedy termination to his sufferings.
>
> (*The Newgate Calendar*)

In fact, Galvani's assumption that it was an inherent 'animal electricity' that had re-animated the frogs' legs was incorrect; the stimulus simply arose from current electricity unwittingly generated by the rudimentary battery cell acting on the nerves and muscles.

Gaol Fever

This malignant distemper was fatal and frequent in old Newgate and other county jails in different parts of England.

The Assize held at Oxford in the year 1577, called the Black Assize, was a dreadful instance of the deadly effects of the gaol fever. The judges, jury – in fact everyone in court except the prisoners – were killed by a foul air, which at first was thought to have arisen out of the bowels of the earth; but that great philosopher, Lord Bacon, proved it to have come from the prisoners taken out of a noisome jail and brought into court to take their trials; and they alone, inhaling the foul air, were not injured by it. Three hundred, more or less, succumbed. Others attributed the cause of this sudden mortality at Oxford to witchcraft, the people in those times being very superstitious. In Webster's *Display of Witchcraft*, we find the following account of the Black Assizes:

The 4th and 5th days of July were holden the assizes at Oxford, where was arraigned the condemned, one Rowland Jenkes, for his seditious tongue, at which time there arose such a damp, that almost all were smothered. Very few escaped that were not taken at that instant. The jurors died presently – shortly after died Sir Robert Bell, Lord Chief Baron, Sir Robert De Olie, Sir William Babington, and other Gentlemen. There died at Oxford 300 persons, and sickened there, but died in other places, 200 and odd, from the 6th of July to the 12th of August, after which day died not one of that sickness, for one of them infected not another, nor any one woman or child died thereof . . . Just at the conjuncture of time when Jenkes was condemned, there being none before, and so it could not be a prison infection; for that would have manifested itself by smell or operating sooner. But to take away all scruple, and to assign the true cause, it was thus: it fortuned that a manuscript fell into my hands, collected by an ancient gentleman of York, who was a great observer and gatherer of strange things and facts, who lived about the time of this accident happening at Oxford, wherein it is related thus: 'That Rowland Jenkes, being imprisoned for treasonable words, spoken against the Queen [Elizabeth I], and being a popish recusant, had, notwithstanding, during the time of his restraint, liberty to walk some time abroad with a keeper; and that one day he came to an apothecary, and showed him a receipt [i.e. recipe] which he desired him to make up; but the apothecary, upon view of it, told him that it was a strong and dangerous receipt, and required some time to prepare it; but also asked him to what use he would apply it. He answered, to kill the rats, that, since his imprisonment, spoiled his books. So being satisfied, he promised to make it ready. After a certain time he cometh to know if it were ready; but the apothecary said the ingredients were so hard to procure that he had not done it, and so gave him the receipt again, of which he had taken a copy, which mine author had there precisely written down, but did seem so horribly poisonous, that I cut it forth, lest it fall into the hands of wicked persons. But after, it seems, he had it prepared, and, against the day of his trial, had made a wick of it (for so is the word, that is, so fitted, that like a candle it might be fired) which, as soon as ever he was condemned, he lighted, having provided himself a tinder-box, and steel to strike fire. And whosoever should know the ingredients of that wick, or candle, and the manner of the composition, will easily be persuaded of the virulency and venomous effect of it.'

In the year 1730, the Lord Chief Baron Pengelly, with several of his officers and servants, died at Blandford, on the Western Circuit of the Lent Assizes, from the infected stench brought with the prisoners from Ilchester Jail to

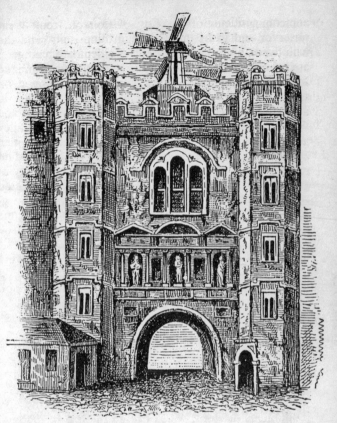

*A view of old Newgate, showing the windmill installed as part
of George Dance's improvements, with a view to higher levels
of sanitation. In fact, several of the workmen engaged in
connecting up the ventilation shaft died of the fever*

their trials at Taunton, where the infection later spread
and carried off some 100 persons.

In 1754 and 1755, this distemper prevailed in Newgate
to a degree which took a toll of more than one-fifth of
the prisoners.

Sir Stephen Theodore Jansen, one of the most philanthropic magistrates of the City of London, took great interest on behalf of the regulation of prisons, and the amelioration of the miseries of the unfortunate prisoners. When Chamberlain of London, in the year 1767, he published a pamphlet, addressed to the Lord Mayor, on the cause of gaol fevers. He was Sheriff of London in 1750, when the putrid fever, the consequence of filth and foul air, made such dreadful havoc in the Old Bailey Sessions. Sir Theodore strongly recommended a plan similar to that of York Castle, which, he said, covered no less than two acres and a rood of ground, with plenty of water and other conveniences. He warmly remonstrated against the spot then proposed for the rebuilding of Newgate. He said it did not occupy more than three-quarters of an acre, and that the number of convicts in that prison was more than treble that at York Castle.

In the year 1772 the assizes for the Summer Circuit were adjourned for Hampshire from 17 July to 2 September, on account of an infectious distemper in Winchester Gaol. One who wrote on the subject under the signature of 'A Philanthropist', declared:

> The public may be rather concerned than surprised at the deplorable consequences of gaol distempers, and at the fatal instances of their contagion. Several judges, sheriffs, magistrates, juries, and whole courts of judicature, have been infected by those contagious diseases, which caused the loss of many valuable lives, particularly at the Old Bailey, and formerly at the assizes at Oxford, all owing to the horrid neglect of gaolers, and even of the sheriffs and magistrates, whose office it is to compel gaolers, to the most rigorous repeated orders and attention to their duty, without the least indulgence or remission; as the gaolers are (some excepted) frequently low bred, mercenary and oppressive, barbarous fellows, who think of nothing but enriching themselves by the most cruel extortion; and who have less regard for the life of a poor prisoner than

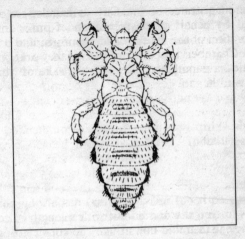

Pediculus humanis, *the typhus-carrying body louse*

for the life of a brute. The felons of this kingdom lie worse than dogs or swine, and are kept much more uncleanly than those animals are in kennels and sties, according to all accounts from clergymen, who are obliged to go to the gaols. From them I have been assured that the stench and nastiness are so nauseous, that the very atmosphere is pestiferous, and that no persons enter therein, without the risque of their health or lives, which prevents even many clergymen and physicians from going there, and assisting their sick and dying fellow-creatures; so that they live and die like brutes, even worse than many beasts, to the disgrace of human nature. Every person endowed with the least principle of real humanity, and of true policy, must be affected with such barbarities, neglects, uncleanliness and dangers. A contagion of that kind may spread over a whole country and kingdom; the greatest precaution ought therefore to be taken in time. The gaolers ought to be forced to have all the rooms sprinkled and fumigated with vinegar every day: for some hundred prisoners, particularly criminals, are early killed by a sort of pestilence and vermin among them, occasioned by filth and nastiness, and a corrupted air. All hospitals, prisons, and workhouses, should have bathing places, for the sake of cleanliness and health.

Gaoler's Whip
(see **Flagellation**)

Garotte

Strangling (other than by **hanging**) has a long pedigree, and was historically carried out with a length of cord or, as in ancient China, a bowstring. The convicted prisoner would be tied to a post and the cord wound once around his neck and pulled tight by the executioner.

In Spain and Spanish América a mechanised form of strangling – the garotte – was introduced by the grace of Ferdinand II during his reign (1808 and 1814–33) as an alternative to the crude method of hanging then current. At its simplest the garotte consists of a post with two holes bored in it; a cord is passed through one hole, round the front of the prisoner's neck and out the other. The two ends could be pulled tightly, or a noose tied which could be tightened by inserting a stick or bar and twisting. Later the instrument was refined and a special chair provided in which the seated prisoner was tied to the arms and legs. A metal collar, which at first fits loosely round the victim's neck, can be tightened from behind by means of a hand-operated lever. In his *Gatherings From Spain* (1847) Richard Ford describes the execution of a robber named José de Roxas by this means:

He was clad in a coarse yellow baize gown, the colour of which denotes the crime of murder, and is associated always with Judas Iscariot in Spanish paintings. He walked slowly on his last journey, half supported by those around him, and stopping often, ostensibly to kiss the crucifix held before him by a friar, but rather to prolong existence – even for a brief moment. When he arrived reluctantly at the scaffold, he knelt down on the steps, the threshold of death, and the reverend attendants covered him over with their blue robes; his dying confession was listened to unseen. Then he mounted the platform attended by a single friar . . .

Meanwhile the executioner, a young man dressed in black, was busied with the preparations for death. The fatal instrument is simple: the culprit is placed on a rough seat. His back leans against a strong upright post, to which an iron collar is attached, enclosing his neck, and so contrived as to be drawn home to the post by turning a powerful screw. So tightly did the executioner bind the prisoner's legs that they swelled up and became black – a precaution not unwise, as his own father had been killed in the act of executing a struggling criminal. The priest who attended was a bloated, corpulent man, more occupied with shading his own face from the sun than in his ghostly office. The robber sat with a writhing look of agony, grinding his clenched teeth. When all was ready, the executioner took the lever of the screw in both hands, gathered himself up for a strong muscular effort, and at the moment of a prearranged signal drew the iron collar tight, while an attendant threw a black handkerchief over the face. A convulsive pressure of the hands and a heaving of the chest were the only visible signs of the passing of the robber's spirit. After a pause of a few moments the executioner peeped cautiously under the handkerchief, and after giving another turn to the screw, lifted it off, folded it up, carefully put it into his pocket, and then proceeded to light a cigar . . .

The face of the dead man was slightly convulsed, the mouth open, the eye-balls turned into their sock-

ets from the wrench. A black bier, with two lanterns
fixed on staves, and a crucifix was now set down
beside the scaffold – also a small table and a dish
into which the mob threw alms to be paid to the
priests who sang Mass for his soul . . .

The body remained on the scaffold till the afternoon; then it was thrown in the scavenger's cart and
led by the *pregonero* (the common crier) beyond the
jurisdiction of the city to a square platform called
La Mesa del Rey (the king's table) where the bodies
of the executed are quartered and cut up – 'a pretty
dish to set before the king'. Here the carcass was

hacked and hewed into pieces by the bungling executioner and his attendants, with that inimitable defiance of anatomy for which they and Spanish surgeons are equally renowned.

The quite extraordinary device illustrated, called a 'garotting chair' is described and illustrated by the English hangman **James Berry** in his autobiography *My Experiences as an Executioner*: it has an iron spike attached to the inside of the collar, and when the lever is pulled and the collar tightened the spike enters between two vertebrae and severs the spinal cord. In fact later modifications in the form of a double collar did ensure a comparatively swift death.

Gas Chamber

Like the **electric chair** and **lethal injection**, gassing as a means of judicial execution is a phenomenon confined to the United States.

The gas chamber is a small, airtight room with an observation window, a chair with straps attached to it, and a container of acid beneath it. The prisoner is strapped into the chair and at the appointed moment a remote-control mechanism drops sodium cyanide (NaCN) pellets into the acid-filled bucket below the chair, causing the release of the deadly gas hydrogen cyanide (HCN).

To suffer an *almost* instantaneous, *almost* painless death, the victim must inhale the fatal gas deeply as soon as it is released into the chamber. If the instinctive reaction of self-preservation forces the prisoner to hold his breath, or take only a timid sniff, he will suffer a slow and painful end with dizziness, headache, nausea, vomiting and difficult breathing, until unconsciousness leads to final oblivion. A doctor is able to monitor extinction of life via earphones attached to a stethoscope strapped to the prisoner's chest.

Nevada, 1924

The first state to introduce lethal gas was Nevada. Up to 1921 condemned prisoners had been offered a choice between the rope and the firing squad, which were generally held to be, respectively, unreliable and messy. While other states were turning increasingly to the electric chair, Dr Allen McLean Hamilton, a Nevada toxicologist, was busy promoting an entirely new method of execution – gas. As far as the state legislators could see, it was set to put them in the forefront of the nationwide search for a quick, painless judicial death. In 1921 lethal gas became the official means of execution in the state of Nevada. On 27 August of the same year a crime was committed which would, three years later, provide the gas chamber with its very first human victim.

The shooting was as cold-blooded as they come; indeed it was a ruthless execution, carried out as part of a long-standing feud between two rival Chinese 'tong' gangs. The victim was elderly Tom Quong Kee, his killer was Gee Jon, an assassin sent by the California Hop Sing tong.

On 7 February 1924, the day before Gee Jon's execution, the gassing apparatus was tested on two cats which had been sealed in the airtight gas chamber. Outside was a tank containing hydrocyanic acid which was forced into the death chamber via a hand-pump and hosepipe, entering as a gaseous spray. The cats obligingly dropped dead within seconds. On the following morning it was Gee Jon who occupied the single chair in the bare cubicle, strapped to it hand and foot. As there was then no accurate way of determining from the outside whether a prisoner was dead or not, gas was pumped in for around six minutes, and after some initial struggling, Gee Jon had slumped, apparently unconscious. To make sure, his body was left in the cubicle for thirty minutes while a fan extracted the gas. When he was removed from the chair Gee Jon was quite dead. It was a first for Nevada, and by 1960 another ten states had installed gas chambers.

Cell 2455, Death Row
The Gas Chamber's most colourful and best known victim was Caryl Chessman, for eleven years an inmate on San Quentin's Death Row, awaiting execution on a charge of sexual assault which he vigorously denied. It was in 1948 – a year after Chessman's release from imprisonment on theft convictions – that he was accused of being responsible for a series of robberies and sexual assaults. After unsuccessfully conducting his own defence, Caryl Chessman was sentenced to death and spent more than a decade fighting execution and writing best-selling autobiographical books to fund his legal battles (*Cell 2455, Death Row* was also made into a successful movie).

Chessman's death was as ironic as his fight against it was heroic. At 10.03 on the morning of 2 May 1960 the cyanide pellets finally dropped into the acid under the chair in which he was strapped; at *exactly* the same time Judge Goodman ordered a stay of execution. The prison authorities claimed that by the time they received the telephone message it was too late to save Chessman's life; others have violently disagreed. One thing is certain: it would have solved one mystery – Caryl Chessman would have been able to tell the world what it was really like to be judicially gassed, if it really was as he had described it in his book *Death By Ordeal*:

You inhale the deadly fumes. You become giddy. You strain against the straps as the blackness closes in. You exhale, inhale again. Your head aches. There's a pain in your chest. But the ache, the pain is nothing. You're hardly aware of it. You're slipping into unconsciousness. You're dying. Your head jerks back. Only for an awful instant do you float free. The veil is drawn swiftly. Consciousness is forever gone . . .

Gladiators
(see **Roman Circus**)

Gridiron

Saint Laurence roasted on the gridiron

Often featured in the martyrdoms – both real and fictional – of the early Christians, there is no evidence that the gridiron survived on any consistent scale into later centuries, or was widespread in Europe. The most commonly depicted form is a simple metal frame, about six feet by two and a half, raised off the ground on legs to enable a fire to be lit beneath it.

Roasting Alive
Other forms of torture related to the gridiron ranged from the simple – suspending a victim over a fire – to the more exotic, such as that described by Fox in his *Book of Martyrs* as the slow roasting of a Christian on a spit, accompanied by 'pouring vinegar and salt' on his genitals.

An early martyr roasted alive on the spit

Guillotine

Origins

It has long been a common misconception that the guillotine was a purely Gallic contraption devised for the purposes of the French Revolution. In reality, similar machines had been in use for some five hundred or more years before Dr Joseph-Ignace Guillotin refined the design for his *machine à decoller* which he obligingly presented to the National Assembly in Paris in 1792.

Whether it is the Irish or the English who can lay claim to the doubtful title of grandfather of the guillotine is disputed still, though each has its supporters. Of course, it is possible that the decapitating instrument (as a simple means of mechanising the work of the headsman) had its origins earlier than either the Irish or the English versions – though many of these early claims remain unverified. The following is a brief chronology:

1266 Naples, Italy Decapitation of Conrad of Swabia. (Unverified)

1300 Zittau, Germany Five unnamed men executed by means of a beheading machine. (Unverified)

1307 April 1st, near Merton, Ireland In his *Chronicles of England*, Raphael Holinshed recounts the execution of Murcod Ballagh. The text is illustrated by a woodcut depicting an unmistakable guillotine.

Reign of Edward III (1312–77), Halifax, England Introduction of the **Halifax Gibbet**.

1486 onwards, Italy The *mannaia*, or 'headsman's axe', in frequent use. Described in 1730 by Père Jean-Baptiste Labat:

A framework four to five feet in height measuring about fifteen inches across between the inner surfaces. It is composed of two uprights measuring about three inches square and with grooves in them. The two uprights are joined to each other by three cross-pieces fixed with tenons and mortices, one at each end and another fifteen inches above the one closing the bottom of the frame. It is on this last cross-piece that the victim places his head. Above this cross-piece is the movable cross-piece which slides in the grooves of the uprights. The lower part is furnished with a large sharp blade nine or ten inches long and six inches across. The upper part carries a weight of sixty to eighty pounds. This murderous cross-piece is raised to within an inch or two of the upper cross-piece, to which it is attached by a thin cord; when the captain of the guard signs to the executioner, he simply cuts this thin cord and the blade, falling directly on the victim's neck, cuts it cleanly.

1581, Scotland The execution of the Regent Morton on the machine called the **Maiden**.

Guillotin's Guillotine
The one thing that is certain, then, is that Dr Guillotin did not *invent* the device which to this day bears his name. So what part did the good doctor play in this scheme of things?

In 1788 Dr Joseph-Ignace Guillotin was the Professor of Anatomy and Physiology at the Paris Faculty of Medicine, and entertaining ideas of entering politics. The following year found him taking great personal interest in a debate on the Penal Code which had opened in the Assembly on 9 October. Guillotin submitted a proposition to the debate which consisted of six articles, including his soon-to-be-famous recommendation that all criminals sentenced to death in France should be executed by means of *mechanical* decapitation. Although Dr Guillotin was cheered from the floor of the Assembly, discussion of his proposal was adjourned. On 1 December, 1789, he was obliged to remind the learned politicians by once again presenting his 'six articles':

1. Crimes of the same kind shall be punished in the same manner regardless of the rank or social class of the convicted person.
2. Where the law calls for the death penalty to be imposed, the means of execution shall be the same for all capital crimes; that is, decapitation by means of a simple mechanism.
3. As crimes are committed by individuals, no punishment of a guilty person shall involve discredit to his family – they shall be no less acceptable for employment in the professions, general trade or public office.
4. A citizen shall not be reproached for a crime committed by another member of his family. Those who do so reproach shall have sentence passed upon them and a notice of that sentence be written up on their door.
5. A condemned person's property shall not be confiscated.
6. The mortal remains of an executed offender shall be handed over to his family for normal burial. No reference shall be made in the register of deaths to the nature of his passing.

This time round Guillotin emphasised the efficacy of his proposed 'mechanism of decapitation' compared with the awful tortures inflicted past and present, and both press and public applauded these new 'humane' proposals. The Assembly was less enthusiastic, and adopted only the first of Guillotin's six articles. They were then conveniently forgotten until 21 January 1790, when the cause was taken up by the Abbé Papin. This time, after a lengthy debate, a further three of the six articles were adopted – they did not include Article 2. It was not until June 1791 that the debate on capital punishment was reopened; on the 3rd of the month the Assembly approved universal decapitation, but did not mention a machine, and on 25 September decapitation was written into the French Penal Code. After much agitating – in which Dr Guillotin himself had long since lost interest – it was decreed on 20 March 1792 that decapitation should be carried out by means of a machine.

The first *official* victim of the guillotine was a man named Nicolas-Jacques Pelletier, who had been convicted of a violent robbery in December 1791. After much persuasion, the Minister for Justice sanctioned the use of the guillotine, and in April 1792, Pelletier publicly lost his head.

The machine which came into official use throughout France was based on a design drawn up by Dr Antoine Louis, the septuagenarian secretary of the Academie Chirurgical. The instrument was made by the state carpenter and scaffold specialist, Monsieur Guidon. According to Louis's specifications the machine consisted of* two parallel oak uprights, ten feet high, joined at the top by a cross-bar and held firm at the bottom by a solid base with supporting braces at the front, back and sides. The uprights were set one foot apart on the inside, with square grooves running from top to bottom, one inch deep, to take the blade (or *couperet*). The top of the blade was drilled with holes so that a heavy weight could be strapped on to give greater impetus. This blade is fitted into a blade holder, which itself fits into, and slides up and down between, the longitudinal grooves. To the blade holder a strong rope is attached, through a pulley, by which means it is raised to the top of the cross-beam, and held there by the rope being fastened to the foot of the upright. At the lower end and between the uprights the wooden block is set on which the victim's neck is laid; the top of the block is carved out in a concave so that the neck fits

* Details derived in part from Alister Kershaw's exhaustive study, *A History of the Guillotine*.

'comfortably'. To hold the neck firmly in place an iron crescent encircles the back of the neck and is held in place by bolts. The victim is strapped to a tilting table which slides forward positioning his neck on the block (or *lunette*) beneath the blade. When all is prepared the executioner need only slacken the rope for the weighted blade to fall . . . The victim, claimed Dr Louis, felt no more than 'a slight chill on the neck'.

Within a year of claiming its first victim, the guillotine had decapitated Louis XVI, King of France, and become the bloody symbol of the French Revolution's Reign of Terror; in fact so many aristocrats and perceived 'enemies of the Revolution' lost their lives on the machine that it took on the nickname 'The People's Avenger'. When order was subsequently restored to France following the fall of Robespierre and the end of the Terror, the guillotine remained, as Dr Guillotin had advised, the official means of effecting the death penalty throughout the country.

Executions were held in public until as late as 1939, when the serial killer Eugen Weidmann was decapitated at Versailles. It is recorded that when Weidmann's body was slid beneath the blade, the executioner misjudged the distance and failed to get the correct position in the *lunette*; his assistants were obliged to pull on Weidmann's ears and hair in order to align his neck with the knife. The use of the guillotine declined sharply during the 1960s and 70s, but it was not until pressed by the European Parliament in 1980 to align itself with the rest of Europe that France effectively abolished the death penalty. According to a report in the English *Independent* newspaper on 13 June 1989, an oak guillotine, fourteen feet high, came under the hammer at the Paris auction house of Drouot for 270,000 francs (£25,000); it was bought by a German collector.

Talking Heads
On 25 June 1905, at Orléans, what began as the routine execution of a bandit turned into one of the most extraordinary episodes in the colourful history of France's guillotine. The following account of Henry Languille's death has been derived from contemporary newspaper reports:

> The day breaks with that pale light that makes figures look like ghosts. Now and again agitated shouts resound from behind the barriers to the left and the right of the Rue de Bel-Air; barriers which have several times almost been broken down despite the three ranks of soldiers holding back the crowd and the knots of gendarmes. Suddenly a movement is seen in the Rue Verte; it is the enclosed wagon, escorted by a detachment of gendarmes, which transports Languille from prison. It is half-past three.
>
> The melancholy procession arrives at the end of Rue Verte and emerges on the Place, the wagon being reined in beside the guillotine. The prison chaplain, the Abbé Marcais, himself as pale as the prisoner, steps from the wagon first. Behind him comes Languille, his arms tied behind him, supported by the executioner's assistants.
>
> The killer of Nibelle is white as a shroud, his half-bare shoulders shivering with the morning chill. Nevertheless he seems resolved, and to the end maintains his previous courage. Despite his apprehension Languille hurls an insult into the expectant crowd: 'Muck-heap of peasants!'
>
> The assistant executioners now take hold of their prisoner and push him on to the *bascule*. It seems almost as if the condemned man's muscles conspire to throw him backwards, but he is swiftly laid on the plank. His neck is encircled with the *lunette*. A few seconds pass, then the young Deibler – quicker and more off-hand than his illustrious father, who

was always hesitant – steps up to the machine. 'Monsieur de Paris' puts the spring in motion, the glittering knife falls with a dry sound; a thin stream of blood spurts up into the air, and the head falls into the tray. The decapitated corpse is rolled to the right into the coffin-shaped basket of sawdust.

The Head of Languille

As soon as Languille's head drops into the tray, a Dr Beaurieux, with the permission of the Public Prosecutor, lifts it out in order to conduct a most bizarre experiment. The doctor holds the severed head between his hands, and looking into the apparently dead face of the bandit, calls 'Languille! Languille!' Slowly, but deliberately, the eyelids open, revealing eyes still sparkling with life; they stare into the eyes of Beaurieux for a long moment, and then the lids fall again. 'Languille,' the doctor calls for a second time. And again the eyelids are raised; again the eyes stare out from the disembodied head, before closing for the last time. When his name is called for the third time, Languille's eyes remained for ever more shut tight. Although the experiment lasted some thirty seconds according to the newspaper, other medical experts at the foot of the guillotine are said to have insisted that the spark of life lasted no longer than ten seconds after the execution. This may be purely academic, because since that June day in 1905 so much scorn has been poured on the remarkable occurrence at Orléans that many are inclined to view the original newspaper report a hoax!

H

Halifax Gibbet

The gibbet is supposed to have been introduced into Halifax during the reign of Edward III (1312–77)*; later, according to the parish register, the machine was used to despatch 49 offenders between March 1541 and April 1650. Of several reliable descriptions, the most graphic derive from Pennant and Holinshed respectively:

> The Maiden [as it was sometimes called] seems to have been confined to the limits of the forest of Hardwicke, or the eighteen towns and hamlets within its precincts. The time when this custom took place is unknown; whether Earl Warren, lord of this forest, might have established it among the sanguinary laws then in use against the invaders of the hunting rights, or whether it might not take place after the woollen manufactures at Halifax began to gain strength, is uncertain. The last is very probable, for the wild country around the town was inhabited by a lawless set, whose depredations on the cloth-tenters might soon stifle the efforts of infant industry. For the protection of trade and for the greater terror of offenders by speedy execution this custom seems to have been established, so as at last to receive the force of the law, which was that 'If a felon be taken within the liberty of the forest of Hardwicke, with goods stolen out or within the said precincts, either hand-habend, back-berend or confessioned, to the value of thirteenpence-halfpenny, he shall, after three market-days, within the town

*There are even those who claim that the Halifax machine was introduced into England by the Normans.

of Halifax, next after such his apprehension, and being condemned, be taken to the gibbet, and there have his head cut from his body'. The offender had always a fair trial, for as soon as he was taken he was brought to the lord's Bailiff at Halifax; he was then exposed on the three markets, which were held thrice in a week, placed in the stocks with the goods stolen on his back, or if the theft was of the cattle kind they were placed by him; and this was done both to strike terror into others and produce new informations against him. The bailiff then summoned four freeholders of each town within the forest to form a jury. The felon and prosecutors were brought face to face, and the goods, the cow or the horse, or whatsoever was stolen, produced. If he was found guilty he was remanded to prison, had a week's time allowed for preparation, and then was conveyed to the spot where his head was struck off by this machine. I should have promised that if the criminal, either after apprehension, or on the way to execution, could escape out of the limits of the forest (part being close to the town), the bailiff had no further power over him; but if he should be caught within the precincts at any time after, he was immediately executed on his former sentence. This privilege [the gibbet] was very freely used during the reign of Elizabeth; the records before that time were lost. Twenty-five suffered in her reign and at least twelve from 1623 to 1650; after which, I believe, the privilege was no more exerted. This machine of death is now destroyed, but I saw one of the same kind in a room under the Parliament House in Edinburgh [see **Maiden**].

(Pennant)

There is, and has been, of ancient time, a law or rather custom, at Halifax, that whosoever doth commit any felony, and is taken with the same, or confesses the fact upon examination, it be valued by

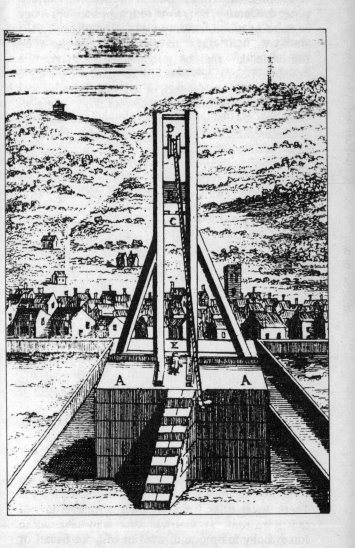

The Halifax gibbet

four constables to amount to the sum of thirteen pence-halfpenny, he is forthwith beheaded upon one of the next market days (which fall usually upon the Tuesdays, Thursdays, and Saturdays), or else upon the same day that he is convicted, if market be holden. The engine wherewith the execution is done is a square block of wood, of the length of four feet and a half, which doth ride up and down in a slot, rabet, or regall, between two pieces of timber that are framed and set upright, of five yards in height. In the nether end of a sliding block is an axe, keyed or fastened with an iron into the wood, which, being drawn to the top of the frame, is there fastened by a wooden pin (with a notch made in the same, after the manner of a Samson's post), unto the midst of which pin is a long rope fastened, that cometh down among the people; so that when the offender hath made his confession, and hath laid his neck over the nethermost block, every man there present doth either take hold of the rope, or putteth forth his arm so near to the same as he can get, in token that he is willing to see justice executed, and pulling out the pin in this manner, the head-block wherein the axe is fastened both fall down with such violence, that if the neck of the transgressor were so big as that of a bull, it should be cut in sunder at a stroke.

(*Chronicles of England*, Raphael Holinshed)

William Camden (1722) adds the following detail in his *Britannia*:

If it was a horse, an ox, or any other creature, that was stol'n, it was brought along with him to the place of execution, and fasten'd to the cord by a pin that stay'd the block. So that when the time of execution came (which was known by one of the Jurors holding up one of their hands) the Bailiff or his Servant, whipping the beast, the pin was pluck'd

out and execution done. But if it was not done by
a beast, then the Bailiff or his Servant cut the rope.

Halters

Used as 'shame' punishments, the wearing of various ridiculous or derisory objects and notices around the neck
has been known world-wide; however, most records survive from Europe and China. There is an obvious relationship between these halters and **shame masks**, and between
these and the **stocks** and the **pillory**.

Cangue

A form of neck pillory used for the punishment of a wide
variety of minor crimes in China; also called the *tcha*, the
kea, and *kian hao*.

It is a great thick board, four or five palms square,
with a hole cut in the middle of it about the bigness
of a man's neck. This they fasten about their necks,
and to it are hung two scrolls of paper wherein are
written his crime, and the cause of his punishment;
they also serve to show that the board has not been
opened. And so with these great boards about their
necks, these poor wretches are brought out every
day and exposed to shame in the public streets,
for fifteen, twenty or thirty days, according to their
sentence, whose greatest rigour is that during all
that time these boards are not taken off their necks
neither night nor day.
(*History of China*, F. Alvarez Semedo, London,
1655)

It is obvious (from the illustration) that by far the greatest
hazard resulted from the size of the board preventing the
prisoner feeding himself or taking drink; a man or woman
without friends or family to feed them could simply perish
before their release was due.

The cangue

Shame Boards
The European equivalent of the cangue, shame boards bore an inscription detailing the name, address and offence committed by the prisoner, who was frequently put in the **pillory** at the same time. Laziness carried the additional humiliation of wearing a fool's cap, and wooden shame boards in the shape of a neck-ruff were reserved for women who failed to observe modesty in their dress.

Neck Violins

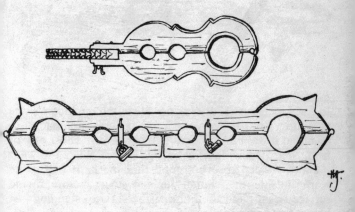

A restraint used mainly on women during the Middle Ages and having many variations of design, though most actually looked like a violin (sometimes with additional carving or paintwork to emphasise the effect). The shaped board had holes cut out for the neck and the hands, and a hinge and padlock so that it might be locked in place. Double violins were also available to accommodate two women who had been convicted of quarrelling or brawling in public. The wearing of violins, or 'fiddle-yokes' was frequently an additional punishment for women sentenced to the pillory.

Shame Flute
A heavy metal representation of a wind instrument attached to a lockable collar was ordered to be worn in public by musicians accused of being incompetent tune-smiths.

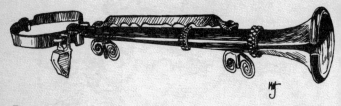

Rosary

In former centuries, attendance at church on Sundays was obligatory, and as everyone in the congregation had their own seat it was easy to identify malingerers. Those absent from their pew without good cause were obliged to wear a giant wooden rosary around their neck. It had to be worn outside the church for the hours before divine service began, and then during the service, standing just below the pulpit in view of the whole congregation. This punishment was also inflicted on those caught snoozing during the sermon.

Cheater's Chain

Similar to the **rosary**, the cheater's chain had suspended from it oversized, heavy wooden representations of playing cards and dice – and was worn as a mark of shame by anybody caught cheating at those games.

Slander Stone

These originated in an early form of ecclesiastical penance and necessitated an offender wearing a heavy stone around his neck in public. In Germany it was developed as a punishment for a range of different offences including slander, adultery, false pretences, blasphemy, swearing and theft. Regional variations in the name for the stone emphasise the slander aspect – *bagstein* ('bicker-stone'), *lasterstein* ('slander-stone'), *kakstein* ('pillory-stone'), *schandstein* ('shame-stone'), etcetera. The stone was hung round the offender's neck by the town bailiff, and he was ordered to walk a certain distance with this burden. If he

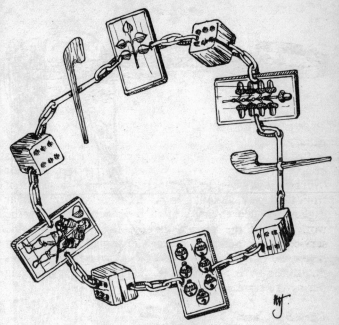

Cheater's chain

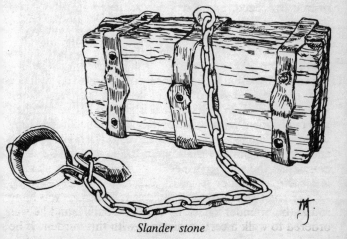

Slander stone

Neck-weight for thieves

or she set the stone down to rest, a further punishment
was incurred.

Hanging

Hanging as an instrument of judicial execution entered
England by way of the Anglo-Saxons, who had inherited
the method from their German ancestors. It became the
established punishment for a great many crimes when
Henry II organised trial by jury and the assize courts in
the twelfth century. By the Middle Ages, the power to
try, sentence and hang felons was vested in every town,
abbey, and manorial lord.

Until the present century executions were extremely
crude affairs – carried out publicly and often preceded
and succeeded by additional barbaric torture. Elabor-
ations such as **drawing and quartering** became popular
spectator events.

But even at best, a simple hanging was little better than
slow strangulation – sometimes lingering on for hours;
indeed, it was considered a great act of kindness on the
part of the executioner to allow some relative or well-
wisher to pull on the victim's legs, and so hasten death.

Public executions took place, of course, all over Britain,
but the most notorious were those carried out at the
'triple tree' erected at Tyburn specifically for the purpose.
Condemned prisoners would be conveyed through
London from the prison at Newgate, to their death at
Tyburn (near modern-day Marble Arch).

Early Spectacles

The actual ceremony was to the last degree cold-blooded
and wanting in all the solemn attributes befitting the awful
scene. The doomed was carried in an open cart to Tyburn
or other appointed place; the halter already encircled his
neck, his coffin was at his feet, by his side the chaplain
or some devoted amateur philanthropist and preacher
striving earnestly to improve the occasion. For the mob
it was a high day and holiday; they lined the route taken

by the ghastly procession, encouraging or flouting the
convict according as he happened to be a popular hero
or unknown to criminal fame. In the first case they
cheered him to the echo, offered him bouquets of flowers,
or pressed him to drink deep from St Giles's Bowl*; in
the latter they pelted him with filth and overwhelmed him
with abuse. The most scandalous scenes occurred on the
gallows. The hangman often quarrelled with his victim
over the garments, which the former looked upon as a
lawful perquisite, and which the latter was disposed to
distribute among his friends; now and again the rope
broke, or the drop was insufficient, and Jack Ketch had to
add his weight to the hanging body to assist strangulation.
Occasionally there was a personal conflict, and the hangman was obliged to do his office by sheer force. The
convicts were permitted to make dying speeches, and
these orations were elaborated and discussed in Newgate
weeks before the great day; while down in the yelling
crowd beneath the gallows spurious versions were hawked
about and rapidly sold. It was a distinct gain to the decency and good order of the metropolis when Tyburn and
other distant points ceased to be the places of execution,
and hangings were exclusively carried out in front of
Newgate, just over the debtors' door. But some of the
worst features of the old system survived. There was still
the melodramatic sermon, the chapel hung with black,
before a large congregation collected simply to stare at
the convicts squeezed into one pew, who in their turn
stared with mixed feelings at the coffin on the table before
their eyes. There was still the same tumultuous gathering
to view the last act in the tragedy, the same bloodthirsty
mob swaying to and fro before the gates, the same blue-
blooded spectators, George Selwyn or my Lord Tom
Noddy, who breakfasted in state with the gaoler, and so
got a box seat or rented a window opposite at an exhorbit-

*At the church of St Giles it was customary for the procession
to stop so that the condemned man might be refreshed by
drinking a jug of ale.

Early Christians wrapped in animal skins and
thrown to the dogs

Above: St Catherine of Alexandria

Left: Austrian folk carving of St Vitus boiling to death

Right: Judge
George Jeffreys

Below: Block
and axe used to
execute Lord
Lovat and now
in the Tower of
London

Pressing to death

Prison ship at Woolwich, south London, 1828

Mr Baron Martin puts on the Black Cap to sentence Franz Muller, the first man convicted of murder on an English train

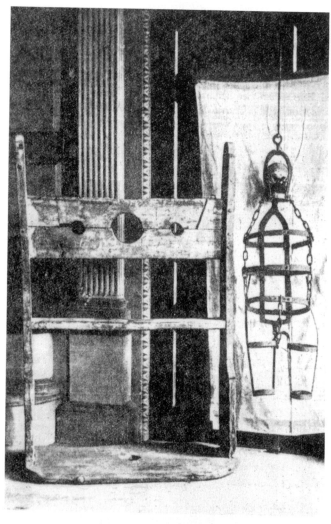

Breeds' gibbet, now in Rye Town Hall;
beside it is the town pillory

Executioner James Berry

A rare photograph of executioner Calcraft

The electric chair

ant rate. The population were like degenerate Romans in the amphitheatre waiting for the butchery to begin. They fought and struggled desperately for front places: people fell and were trampled to death, hoarse roars came from the thousands of brazen throats, which swelled into a terrible chorus as the black figures of the performers on the gallows stood out against the sky. 'Hats off!' 'Down in front!' these cries echoed and re-echoed in increasing volume, and all at once came abruptly to an end – the bolt had been drawn, the drop had fallen, and the miserable wretch had gone to his long home.

(*Chronicles of Newgate*, Arthur Griffiths, 1883, pp. 7–8)

Fatal Accident at Newgate!

On 6 November 1802 Mr John Cole Steele, who owned a lavender-water warehouse in Catherine Street, Strand, journeyed to Bedfont where he kept a lavender plantation. When he did not return on the same or the following day, friends began to worry over Steele's safety.

The corpse of John Steele was found in a ditch beneath some bushes on Hounslow Heath. The terrible wounds to his head left no doubt as to the cause of his death.

It was just short of four years after John Steele's untimely death that a man named Benjamin Hanfield was convicted at the Old Bailey of grand larceny and, in accordance with custom, Hanfield was taken on board one of the prison hulks at Portsmouth. Here he contracted a severe illness, and in delirium he raved constantly about some murder and demanded to see a magistrate. Accordingly an officer was dispatched from Bow Street and Hanfield related the circumstances to him, implicating John Holloway and Owen Haggerty in the awful crime.

On Monday 9 February 1807 Holloway and Haggerty stood before Joseph Moser Esq., sitting magistrate at the police court in Worship Street, charged with the murder of John Cole Steele on Hounslow Heath. Hanfield, an accomplice by his own admission, turned King's evidence under the promise of a pardon. John Holloway and Owen Haggerty were convicted and ordered for execution on the following Monday morning, and it is estimated that a crowd upwards of forty thousand crammed into the area around Newgate to witness the event.

However a situation was developing among the spectators that was to leave 36 dead and countless injured, as panic spread through the crushed throng desperately trying to escape from suffocation. A contemporary account of this horrific scene is given in the *Newgate Calendar*:

The crowd which assembled to witness this execution was unparalleled, being, according to the best calculation, nearly forty thousand; and the fatal catastrophe which happened in consequence will for long cause the day to be remembered. By eight o'clock not an inch of ground was unoccupied in view of the platform. The pressure of the crowd was such that, before the malefactors appeared, numbers of persons were crying out in vain to escape from it; the attempt only tended to increase the confusion. Several females of low stature who had been so imprudent as to venture among the mob were in a dismal situation; their cries were dreadful. Some who could be no longer supported by the men were suffered to fall, and were trampled to death. This also was the case with several men and boys. In all parts there were continued cries of 'Murder! Murder!' – particularly from the females and children among the spectators, some of whom were seen expiring without the possibility of obtaining the least assistance, everyone being employed in endeavours to preserve his own life.

Those who once fell were never more suffered to rise, such was the violence of the mob. At this fatal place a man of the name of Herrington was thrown down, who had by the hand his youngest son, a fine boy about twelve years of age. The youth was soon trampled to death; the father recovered, though much bruised, and was among the wounded in St Bartholomew's Hospital. A woman who was so imprudent as to bring with her a child at the breast was one of the number killed. Whilst in the act of falling she forced the child into the arms of the man nearest to her, requesting him, for God's sake, to save its life. The man, finding it required all his exertion to preserve himself, threw the infant from him, but it was fortunately caught at a distance by another man, who, finding it difficult to ensure its safety or his own, got rid of it in a similar way. The child was again caught by a man, who contrived to struggle with it to a cart, under which he deposited

it until the danger was over, and the mob had dispersed.

In other parts the pressure was so great that a
horrible scene of confusion ensued, and seven persons lost their life by suffocation alone. It was shocking to behold a large body of the crowd, as one
convulsive struggle for life, fight with the most
savage fury with each other; the consequence was
that the weakest, particularly the women, fell a sacrifice. A cart which was overloaded with spectators
broke down and some of the persons who fell from
the vehicle were trampled underfoot, and never
recovered. During the hour that the malefactors
hung, little assistance could be afforded to the
unhappy sufferers; but after the bodies were cut
down, and the gallows removed to the Old Bailey
Yard, the marshals and constables cleared the street
where the catastrophe occurred, and, shocking to
relate, there lay nearly one hundred persons dead,
or in a state of insensibility, strewed round the
street! Twenty-seven dead bodies were taken to St
Bartholomew's Hospital, four to St Sepulchre's
Church, one to *The Swan* on Snow Hill, one to a
public-house opposite St Andrew's Church, Holborn; one, an apprentice, to his master's; Mr Broad-
wood, pianoforte maker, to Golden Square. A
mother was seen carrying away the body of her dead
boy; Mr Harrison, a respectable gentleman, was
taken to his house at Holloway.

There was a sailor-boy killed opposite Newgate,
by suffocation; he carried a small bag, in which he
had some bread and cheese, and was supposed to
have come some distance to behold the execution.
After the dead, dying and wounded were carried
away, there was a cartload of shoes, hats, petticoats
and other articles of wearing apparel picked up.
Until four o'clock in the afternoon most of the surrounding houses had some person in a wounded
state; they were afterwards taken away by their

friends on shutters, or in hackney-coaches. The
doors of St Bartholomew's Hospital were closed
against the populace. After the bodies of the dead
were stripped and washed they were ranged around
a ward on the first floor, on the women's side; they
were placed on the floor with sheets over them, and
their clothes put as pillows under their heads; their
faces were uncovered. There was a rail along the
centre of the room: the persons who were admitted
to see the shocking spectacle went up on one side
of the rail, and returned on the other. Until two
o'clock the entrances to the hospital were beset with
mothers weeping for their sons, wives for their husbands and sisters for their brothers, and various
individuals for their relatives and friends.

The next day (Tuesday) a coroner's inquest sat in
St Bartholomew's Hospital, and other places where
the bodies were, on the remains of the sufferers.
Several witnesses were examined with respect to the
circumstances of the accident, which examination
continued till Friday, when the verdict was, 'That
the several persons came by their death from compression and suffocation'.

The Appliance of Science

With the last public hanging in 1868, and the confinement
of such practices to the execution shed of prisons, a more
enlightened and humane procedure was developed to dispatch the prisoner with the greatest speed and least pain.
The act of hanging became a science based on the accurate
relationship of weight to distance, and the hangman
became its craftsman. Of this new breed of executioner,
men who thought long and hard about the practice and
consequences of their craft, the first was William Marwood, official hangman between 1874 and 1883. It was
Marwood who developed what became known as the 'long
drop', scientifically calculated according to the weight and
build of the prisoner. Marwood sought to break the spine
at the neck, thus causing instant death rather than slow

strangulation. Sadly, William Marwood left no convenient autobiography or memoirs, and so these early experiments with 'humane' hanging reach us through his successor, **James Berry**.

James Berry's Method of Execution
Calculation and Apparatus

My method of execution is the outcome of the experience of my predecessors and myself, aided by suggestions from the doctors, and it is rather the result of gradual growth than the invention of any one man.

The Drop

The matter which requires the greatest attention in connection with an execution is the allowance of a suitable drop for each person executed, and the adjustment of this matter is not nearly so simple as an outsider would imagine.

It is, of course, necessary that the drop should be of sufficient length to cause instantaneous death, that is to say to cause death by dislocation rather than by strangulation; on the other hand the drop must not be so great as to outwardly mutilate the victim. If all murderers that have to be hanged were of precisely the same weight and build it would be very easy to find out the most suitable length of drop and always give the same, but as a matter of fact they vary enormously. In the earliest days of hanging it was the practice of the executioner to place his noose round the victim's neck, and then to haul upon the other end of the rope, which was passed through a ring on the scaffold pole, until the culprit was strangled, without any drop at all. After a while the drop system was introduced, but the length of drop given was never more than three feet, so that death was usually caused by strangulation and not by dislocation, as it is at present. One after another, all our English executioners followed the same plan without thought of change or improvement until Mr Marwood took the appointment. He, as a humane man, carefully considered the subject, and came to the conclusion that the then existing method, though certain, was not so rapid or painless as it ought to be. In consequence he introduced his long-drop system with a fall of from seven to ten feet, which caused instantaneous death by severance of the spinal cord. I was slightly acquainted with Mr Marwood before his death, and I had gained some particulars of his method from conversation with him; so that when I undertook my first execution, at Edinburgh, I naturally worked upon his lines. This first commission was to execute Robert Vickers and William Innes, two miners who were condemned to death for the murder of two game-keepers. The respective weights were 10 stone 4 lbs. and 9 stone 6 lbs., and I gave them drops of 8 ft. 6 in. and 10 ft. respectively. In both cases death was instantaneous, and the prison surgeon gave me a testimonial to the effect that the execution was satisfactory in every respect. Upon this experience I based a table of weights and drops. Taking a man of 14 stones as a basis, and giving him a drop of 8 ft., which is what I thought necessary, I calculated that every half-stone lighter weight would require a two inches longer drop, and the full table, as I entered it in my books at the time, stood as follows:

14 stones	8 ft.	0 in.
13½ "	8 "	2 "
13 "	8 "	4 "
12½ "	8 "	6 "
12 "	8 "	8 "
11½ "	8 "	10 "
11 "	9 "	0 "
10½ "	9 "	2 "
10 "	9 "	4 "
9½ "	9 "	6 "
9 "	9 "	8 "
8½ "	9 "	10 "
8 "	10 "	0 "

This table I calculated for persons of what I might call 'average' build, but it could not by any means be rigidly adhered to with safety. For instance, I have more than once had to execute persons who had attempted suicide by cutting their throats, or who had been otherwise wounded about the neck, and to prevent reopening the wounds I have reduced the drop by nearly half. Again in the case of persons of very fleshy build, who often have weak bones and muscles around the neck, I have reduced the drop by a quarter or half the distance indicated in the table. If I had not done so, no doubt two or three of those whom I have executed would have had their heads jerked entirely off – which did occur in one case to which I shall again refer. In the case of persons with scrofulous tendencies it is especially necessary that the fall should be unusually short, and in these cases I have at times received useful hints from the gaol doctors.

Until November 30th, 1885, I worked to the scale already given, but on that date I had the awful experience above referred to [the execution of Robert Goodale at Norwich Castle, when the prisoner's head *was* 'jerked entirely off'] which caused me to reconsider the whole subject and to construct a general table on what I believe to be a truly scientific basis.

The Rope

The apparatus for carrying out the extreme penalty of the law is very simple. The most important item is the rope, which must necessarily possess certain properties if the death of the condemned person is to be instantaneous and painless.

For successful working the rope must, of course, be strong, and it must also be pliable in order to tighten freely. It should be as thin as possible, consistent with strength, in order that the noose may be free running, but of course it must not be so thick as to be liable outwardly to rupture the blood vessels of the neck.

Before undertaking my first execution I gave careful consideration to the question of the most suitable class of rope, and after trying and examining many varieties, I decided upon one which I still use. It is made of the finest Italian hemp, three quarters of an inch in thickness. Before using a rope for an execution, I thoroughly test it with bags of cement of about the weight of the condemned person, and this preliminary testing stretches the cord and at the same time reduces its diameter to five-eighths of an inch. The rope consists of five strands, each of which has a breaking strain of one ton dead weight, so that it would seem unnecessary to test it from any fear of its proving too weak, but the stretching and hardening which it undergoes in the testing makes it far more 'fit' and satisfactory for its work than a new, unused rope would be.

It has been said that I use a rope with a wire strand down the centre, but the notion is so ridiculous that I should not refer to it if it were not that many people seem to believe it, and that more than once it has been stated in the newspapers. A rope with a wire strand would possess no possible advantage that I can see, and it would have so many practical disadvantages that I do not think anyone who has studied the matter would dream of using such a thing. At any rate, I have not done so, and I know that neither Mr Binns nor Mr Marwood ever did. Mr Marwood used ropes of about the same quality and thickness as my own, while Mr Binns used a much thicker rope (about one and a quarter inch diameter after use), of a rougher and less pliable class of hemp.

Until the commencement of 1890 I supplied my own ropes, some of which, however, were made to order of the Government, and I was able to use the same rope again and again. One I used for no less than sixteen executions, and five others I have used for twelve executions each. These are now in the possession of Madame Tussaud. At the beginning of 1890 a new rule was made under which a new rope is ordered to be supplied and used for most of the executions in England, and to be burned, together with the clothes of the person executed (which were formerly the perquisite of the executioner) by the prison officials immediately after the execution. In Scotland and Ireland I still supply my own ropes.

The rope I use is thirteen feet long and has a one-inch brass ring worked into one end, through which the other end of the rope is passed to form the noose. A leather washer which fits the rope pretty tightly is used to slip up behind the brass ring, in order to prevent the noose slipping or slackening after it has been adjusted.

In using the rope I always adjust it with the ring just behind the left ear. This position I never alter, though of course if there were any special reason for doing so, for instance if the convict had attempted suicide and were wounded on the side of the throat, death could be caused by placing the ring under the chin or even behind the head. The position behind the ear, however, has distinct advantages and is the best calculated to cause instantaneous and painless death because it acts in three different ways towards the same end. In the first place it will cause death by strangulation, which was really the only cause of death in the old method of hanging, before the long-drop was introduced. Secondly it dislocates the vertebra, which is now the actual cause of death. And thirdly, if a third factor were necessary, it has a tendency to internally rupture the jugular vein, which in itself is sufficient to cause practically instantaneous death.

Pinioning Straps, etc.

The pinioning arrangement, like the rest of the arrangements for an execution, is very simple. A broad leathern body-belt is clasped round the convict's waist, and to this the two arm straps are fastened. Two straps, an inch and a half wide, with strong steel buckles, clasp the elbows and fasten them to the body-belt, while another strap of the same strength goes round the wrists, and is fastened into the body belt in front. The legs are pinioned by means of a single two-inch strap below the knees. The rest of the apparatus consists of a white cap, shaped somewhat like a bag, which pulls down over the eyes of the criminal to prevent his seeing the final preparations.

The Scaffold

Until recently, the scaffolds in use in the various gaols differed very much in the details of their construction, as there was no official model, but in each case the local authorities followed their own idea. In 1885, however, a design was drawn, in the Surveyors' Department of the Home Office, by Lieut.-Col. Alton Beamish, R.E. Before being finally adopted, the design was submitted to me; and it seemed a thoroughly good one, as, indeed, it has since proved to be in actual practice. The design is supplied to the authorities of any gaol where a scaffold is to be erected, from the Engineers' Department at the Home Office; and, with a slight alteration, has been the pattern in general use to the present day. The alteration of which I speak is a little one suggested by myself, and consists of the substitution of a slope, or a level gangway, in place of the steps. I had found in some cases, where the criminals were nervous or prostrated, that the steps formed a practical difficulty. The slope, or gangway, was approved by the Home Office, and was first introduced on April 15th, 1890, at Kirkdale Gaol, for the execution of William Chadwick. It was a simple improvement, but it turned out to be a very useful one.

At most of the gaols in the country the scaffold is taken to pieces and laid away immediately after use, but in Newgate, Wandsworth, Liverpool, and Strangeways (Manchester), it is kept standing permanently.

The essential parts of the scaffold are few. There is a heavy cross-beam, into which bolts terminating in hooks are usually fastened. In some cases this cross-beam stands on two upright posts, but usually its ends are let into the walls of the scaffold house. Of course the hooks fastened to it are intended to hold the rope.

The scaffold proper, or trap, or drop, as it is variously called, is the portion of the structure to which most importance is attached, and of which the Government

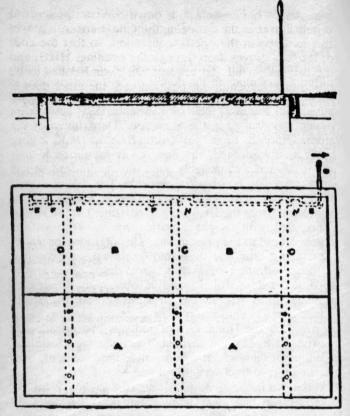

Plan and elevation of the drop

furnishes a plan. It consists of two massive oaken doors,
fixed in an oak frame-work on a level with the floor, and
over a deep bricked pit. The plan and section will explain
the arrangement. The two doors are marked AA and BB
on the plan. The door AA is hung on three strong hinges,
marked CCC, which are continued under the door BB.
When the trap is set the ends of these long hinges rest on
a draw-bar EE, as shown in the plan. The draw-bar is of
iron, one and one quarter inches square, sliding in strong

iron staples FFF, which fit it exactly. When the lever D is pulled over in the direction of the little arrow, it moves the draw-bar in the opposite direction, so that the ends of the long hinges drop through the openings HHH, and the two doors fall. To set the trap door BB has to be raised to a perpendicular position until the other door is raised and its hinges placed on the draw-bar. The arrangement is a very good one; as both doors must necessarily fall at exactly the same moment. Their great weight – for they are of three-inch oak – causes them to drop very suddenly, even without the weight of the criminal, and they are caught by spring catches to prevent any possibility of rebound.

(My Experiences as an Executioner)

Modern Times

James Berry went on to describe his procedure for actually carrying out the execution which, along with the apparatus used, changed very little between then and 1964, when the last two people were executed in Britain. The following is an extract from the Home Office memorandum presented to the Royal Commission set up in 1949 to consider limiting capital punishment or modifying the condemned prisoner's routine in the days before execution:

Immediately a prisoner sentenced to death returns from court, he is placed in a cell for condemned prisoners and is watched night and day by two officers. Amenities such as cards, chess, dominoes, etc. are provided in the cell and the officers are encouraged to – and invariably do – join the prisoner in these games. Newspapers and books are also provided. Food is supplied from the main prison kitchen, the prisoner being placed on a hospital diet, with such additions as the medical officer considers advisable. A pint of beer or stout is supplied daily on request and ten cigarettes or half an ounce of pipe tobacco are allowed unless there are medical

reasons to the contrary. The prisoner may smoke in
his cell as well as exercise.

It is the practice for the Governor, medical officer,
and chief officer to visit a prisoner under sentence
of death twice daily, and the chaplain or minister of
any other denomination has free access to him. He
may be visited by such of his relations, friends and
legal advisers as he desires to see and as are authorised to visit him by the Visiting Committee and the
commissioners, and he is given special facilities to
write and receive letters.

The executioner and his assistant arrive at the
prison by 4 p.m. on the day preceding the execution,
and are not permitted to leave the prison until the
execution has been carried out. They see the prisoner at exercise and test the execution apparatus
with a bag of sand approximately of his weight. The
bag is left hanging overnight to stretch the rope.

On the morning of the execution it is usual for
the chaplain to spend the last hour with the prisoner
and remain with him until the execution is over.
Some twenty minutes before the time is fixed for
execution the High Sheriff – or more usually the
Under Sheriff – arrives at the prison, and a few
minutes before it is due, proceeds with the Governor
and medical officer to the place of execution. The
executioner and his assistant wait outside the condemned cell with the chief officer and the officer
detailed to conduct the prisoner to the execution
chamber. On a signal given by the Sheriff they enter
the cell and the executioner pinions the prisoner's
arms behind his back. He is escorted to the drop
with one officer on either side. The Sheriff, the
Governor and the medical officer enter the
execution chamber directly by another door. The
prisoner is placed on the drop on a marked spot so
that his feet are directly across the division of the
trap doors. The executioner places the white cap
over the prisoner's head and places the noose round

his neck, while the assistant pinions his legs. When the executioner sees that all is ready he pulls the lever.

The medical officer at once proceeds to the pit and examines the prisoner to see that life is extinct. The shed is then locked and the body hangs for one hour. The inquest is held the same morning. Burial of the body takes place in the prison graveyard during the dinner hour; the chaplain reads the burial service. Burial within the prison precincts, where suitable space is strictly limited, gives rise to increasing difficulties. In some prisons bodies are already buried three deep.

The duty thrown on prison staff and others concerned is a distasteful one, not only in carrying out the execution itself, but in the long-drawn preliminary stages. Indeed the actual execution may come as a relief from the mounting tension of the previous days. Anything tending to increase this atmosphere of tension in the prison generally has been, as far as possible, eliminated. The hoisting of a [black] flag and the tolling of a bell were discontinued many years ago, and today the prisoners are no longer locked in the cells during an execution. The time fixed is after the normal routine of the prison is under way, and all prisoners are out at work or about their normal business.

Hanging from the Yardarm

An entirely nautical punishment which differed from ordinary hanging only in that it took place aboard ship and the 'gallows' was a horizontal beam across the mast which supported a sail. The following case study is taken from an edition of the *Newgate Calendar* published in 1926; the execution took place in November, 1812:

The Execution of Lieutenant Gamage aboard the Griffon

This unfortunate young officer fell a victim to ungovernable passion. He had ordered a sergeant of marines upon some duty which the sergeant, conceiving it incompatible with his rank, refused to carry out. He was, withal, insolent in his replies. The Lieutenant burst into a violent passion, ran to his cabin, seized his dirk, returned and stabbed the sergeant in the heart. For this crime he was tried by a court martial and sentenced to death.

The execution took place aboard the sloop-of-war *Griffon*. Gamage bore his fate with manly fortitude. About eight o'clock he was attended by the clergyman who remained with him till about half-past nine, when the procession began from his cabin to the platform from whence he was to be launched into eternity. The clergyman walked first, then Lieutenant Gamage attended on each side by two officer friends, several officers followed behind; everyone present was deeply affected at the unfortunate fate of this young gentleman, the ship's company particularly. Boats from the different ships attended, as usual, round the execution, and the same sympathy and pity was observable in each. 'God receive his soul!' frequently burst forth from different seamen. He bowed and thanked them three times, and seemed deeply affected by the sympathy he aroused. He spoke briefly to his own crew, warning them to beware of giving way to sudden passion. As soon as he reached the platform he prayed again with the clergyman, and at precisely ten o'clock, the signal gun being fired, he was run up to the yardarm, amidst the repeated exclamations from the seamen of 'God bless and receive him!' He appeared to suffer little.

The body was brought on shore for interment at two o'clock, and was received at landing by Perrer Downer, Esq., Governor of the Naval Hospital who, with a number of naval and military officers, attended this unfortunate young gentleman's remains to the burial ground of the Naval Hospital, where they were deposited. General Trollope and the officers of the *Griffon*, with several of the crew, were present and bore ample testimony, by their appearance, to the regret they felt at his untimely fate.

Hanging in Chains

> . . . . but they kill'd him, they
> Kill'd him for robbing the mail,
> They hanged him in chains for a show.
>
> (Alfred, Lord Tennyson, 'Rizpah')

There gradually arose, side by side with the capital punishment of hanging on the gallows – which may be said to be as old as the world itself – the custom of publicly exposing human bodies upon gibbets as warnings to others.

In England, we gather from the Vocabulary of Archbishop Alfric of the tenth century, and from early illuminated manuscripts, that the gallows ('galga') was the usual mode of capital punishment with the Anglo-Saxons. It can hardly be doubted that in certain cases, as with the Romans, the body of the 'fordemned' remained *in terrorem* upon the gibbet. As Robert of Gloucester states in 1280, 'In gibet hil were an honge.'

In the numerous enactments concerning the administration of the criminal law, from the Statute of Westminster the First in 1277, to the Act of George II in 1752, no recognition is given to the hanging of bodies of criminals in chains. Such treatment was rather devised by the state than by the law. However, in Chauncy's History of Hertfordshire, it is stated:

Soon after the King came to Easthampstead to

recreate himself with hunting, where he heard that the bodies which were hanged here were taken down from the gallowes, and removed a very great way from the same; this so incensed the King [Richard II] that he sent a writ, tested the 3rd of August, Anno 1381, to the bailiffs of this borough, commanding them on sight thereof, to cause chains to be made, and to hang the bodies in them upon the same gallowes, there to remain as long as one piece might stick to another, according to the judgement; but the townsmen, not daring to disobey the King's command, hanged the dead bodies of their neighbours again, to their great shame and reproach, when they could not get any other for any wages to come near the stinking carcasses, but they themselves were compelled to do so vile an office.

Again, during the Second Northern Rising in 1536, the Duke of Norfolk hung and quartered (as the usual punishment for high treason) 74 men at Carlisle, but the bodies of Sir Robert Constable and Ashe, as special cases, were hung in chains at Hull and York respectively.

The numerous allusions to gibbets by Shakespeare show how common they were in his day.

In Scotland, Lord Dreghorn, writing in 1774, says, 'The first instance of hanging in chains is in March 1637, in the case of Macgregor, for theft, robbery, and slaughter; he was sentenced to be hanged in chenzie on the gallowlea till his corpse rot.' Thus hanging in chains formed part of the sentence in Scotland which it never did in England for any crime, if we except the solitary instance at Easthampstead in 1381.

It will be convenient to give a variety of examples further illustrating the subject:

We learn from the parish registers of Bourne, in Cambridgeshire, that Richard Foster, his wife, and his child, were buried on Shrove Wednesday 1671. All three were murdered the preceding Sunday by a miscreant named George Atkins. He evaded the law for seven years, but

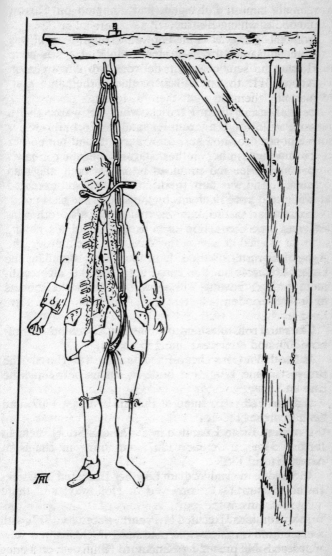

A pirate hanging in chains

was finally captured, hanged, and gibbeted on Caxton
Common, adjoining Bourne.

In 1674 Thomas Jackson, a notorious highwayman, was
executed for the murder of Henry Miller. He was hung
in chains on a gibbet set up between two elm trees on
Hampstead Heath, one of which retained the name 'Gallows Tree'.

In 1690 one William Barwick, while out walking with
his wife at Cawood, a few miles south of York, threw her
into a pond, drowned her, drew her out, and buried her
there and then, in her clothes. Barwick's brother-in-law's
suspicions arose, and enquiries were set about; the man
confessed, and was duly tried, condemned and executed
at York, and hung in chains by the side of the fatal pond.
A curious part of this case was that Barwick's brother-in-
law was urged to action in consequence of his having
seen, or fancied he saw, a few days after the murder, the
ghost of his sister by the side of the water, at midday.

For examples in the early years of the eighteenth
century the following will show how thick the gibbets
were near London:

Edward Tooll Executed on Finchley Common, February 1700, and afterwards hung in chains.

Michael Von Burghem Executed at the Hartshorne
Brewery, June 1700, and hung in chains between Mile
End and Bow.

William Felby Executed at Fulham, August 1707, and
hung in chains there.

Hermann Brian Executed in St James's Street, near St
James's House, October 1707, and hung in chains at
Acton Gravel Pits.

Richard Keele and William Lowther Executed on Clerkenwell Green, 1713, conveyed to Holloway, and there
hung in chains.

John Tomkins Executed at Tyburn, February 1717, with
fourteen other malefactors, and hung in chains.

Joseph Still Executed on Stamford Hill Road, and hung
in chains in the Kingsland Road.

John Price Executed in Bunhill Fields, and hung in chains near Holloway, 1717.

In 1742 John Breeds, a butcher of Rye, conceived a violent animosity against Mr Thomas Lamb of the same place, and as the old Statute of High Treason would put it, 'compassed and imagined' his death. He was tried and found guilty, and condemned to death and to be hung in chains. For this purpose a gibbet was set up in a marsh at the west end of town, later called Gibbet Marsh. The carcass of Breeds swung for many years on the morass, and when all but the upper part of the skull had dropped away the chains and frame were rescued by the Corporation of Rye.

In 1747 Christopher Holliday was beaten to death with his own staff by one Adam Graham, on Beck Moor, near Balenbush, on the English side of the Border. Graham was executed at Carlisle, and his body hung in chains upon a gibbet twelve yards high on Kingsmoor, with twelve thousand nails driven into it to prevent it being 'swarmed', or cut down, and the body carried off.

By this time it became usual for the court, in atrocious cases, to direct that the murderer's body should be hung upon a gibbet in chains, near the place where the fatal act was committed; but this was no part of the legal judgement. By an Act of 25 George II (1752), gibbeting in chains was first legally recognised. By this statute it was enacted that the body should, after sentence delivered and execution done, be given to the surgeons to be dissected and anatomised, and that the judge might direct the body afterwards to be hung in chains, but in no wise to be buried without dissection. This Act seems to have cleared the way considerably, and from this date gibbeting rapidly increased. It may here be recalled that the idea of being gibbeted was ever a very terrifying one to the sufferer, and many a strong man who had stood fearless under the dread sentence broke down when he was measured for his irons.

At Newgate, as at other gaols, it was the custom after

execution to convey the body into a place grimly called 'The Kitchen'. Here stood a cauldron of boiling pitch, and into this the carcass was thrown. Shortly after it was withdrawn, packed in chains, and these cold-riveted – truly 'fast bound in misery and iron'. We can picture the brutal work, with, no doubt, the coarse jesting when the malefactor was finally riveted up in what was called 'his last suit'.

A notorious highwayman, John Whitfield, was executed and gibbeted on Barrock, near Wetheral, Cumberland, about the year 1777. It is said he was gibbeted alive, and that the guard of a passing mail-coach put him out of his misery by shooting him. Later a sergeant was reduced to the ranks for shooting at the dead body in chains of Jerry Abershaw, a notorious brigand, on Wimbledon Common. Towards the year 1808, a man named Thomas Otter, alias 'Tom Temporal', was hanged at Lincoln for the murder of a woman with whom he cohabited. It appears that she had followed him when he returned to Nottinghamshire where his wife lived. At the junction of the two counties he turned on her like a wild beast, and slew her, and flung her body into a drain dividing the two counties. He was executed and hung in chains on the fatal spot. Subsequently, some inquiring tomtits made their nest and hatched seven young ones in the upper part of the iron frame where the head was fixed, and a local poet produced the following riddle:

10 tongues in one head
9 living and one dead
1 flew forth to fetch some bread,
To feed the living in the dead.
(Answer: The tomtit that built a nest in Tommy Otter's head)

The last example of hanging in chains is that of a man named Cook, a bookbinder, who murdered Mr Paas with the iron handle of his press at Leicester in 1834. He was sentenced to death and the body ordered to be gibbeted. This was done in Saffron Lane, outside the town, and the

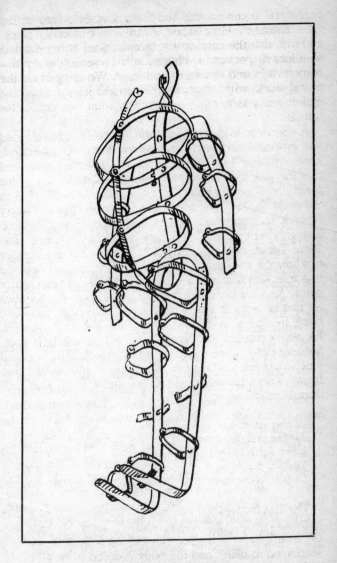

Miles's irons, 1791

disgraceful scene around the gibbet, as described by an eye-witness, was like a fair. A Dissenter mounted upon a barrel and preached to the people, who only ridiculed him, and the general rioting soon led to an order for the removal of the body. In the same year hanging in chains was abolished by Statute (4 William IV).

The Life
and Unparalleled
Voyages and Adventures
of
Ambrose Gwinett

Written by Himself*

I was born of reputable parents in the city of Canterbury, where my father dealt in slops [sailors' clothing and bedding]. He had but two children, a daughter and myself; and having given me a good school education, at the age of sixteen he bound me apprentice to Mr George Roberts, an attorney of the same town, with whom I staid four years and three quarters, to his great content, and my own satisfaction.

My sister being come to woman's estate, had now been married something more than a twelvemonth to one Sawyer, a seafaring man, who having got considerable prizes (my father also gave him £200 with my sister) quitted his profession, and set up a public house within three miles of the place of his nativity, which was Deal, in the county of Kent.

I had frequent invitations to pass a short time with them; and in the Autumn of the year 1709, having obtained my master's consent for the purpose, I left the city of Canterbury on foot on a Wednesday morning, being the 17th day of September; but through some unavoidable delays on the road, the evening was considerably advanced before I had reached Deal; and so tired was I, being unused to that way of travelling, that, had

*In fact, it was written by Isaac Bickerstaffe.

my life depended on it, I could not have got as far as my sister's that night. At this time there were many of her Majesty Queen Ann's ships lying in the harbour, the English being then at war with the French and Spaniards; besides which, I found this was the day for holding the yearly fair; so that the town was filled to that degree that a bed was not to be gotten for love or money. I went seeking a lodging from house to house to no purpose, till, being quite spent, I returned to the public house where I had first made inquiry, desiring leave to sit by their kitchen fire to rest myself till morning.

The publican and his wife where I put up happened, unfortunately for me, to be acquainted with my brother [-in-law] and sister, and finding by the discourse that I was a relation of theirs, and going to visit them, the landlady presently said she would endeavour to get me a bed, and going out of the kitchen, she quickly after called me into a parlour that led from it. Here I saw sitting by the fire side a middle-aged man in a night gown and cap, who was reckoning money at a table. 'Uncle,' said the woman as soon as I had entered, 'this is a brother of our friend Mrs Sawyer: he cannot get a bed anywhere, and is tired after his journey. You are the only one that lies in this house alone, will you give him part of yours?' To this the man answered that she knew he had been out of order, that he was blooded [bled] that day, and consequently a bedfellow could not be very agreeable. 'However,' said he, 'rather than the young man shall sit up, he is welcome to sleep with me.' After this we sat a while together, when, having put his money in a canvas bag into the pocket of his night gown, he took the candle, and I followed him up to bed.

How long I slept I cannot exactly determine, but I conjectured it was about three o'clock in the morning when I awakened with a cholic, attended with the most violent gripes; I attributed this to some cabbage and bacon I had eaten that day for dinner, after which I drank a large draught of milk. I found my chum awake as well as myself. He asked me what was the matter. I informed

him, and at the same time begged him direct me to the
necessary. He told me, when I was downstairs, I must
turn on my right hand, and go straight into the garden,
at the end of which it was, just over the sea. 'But (adds
he) you may find some difficulty opening the door, the
string being broken which pulls up the latch. I will give
you a pen knife, which you may open it with through a
chink in the boards.' So saying, he put his hand into his
waistcoat pocket, which lay over him on the bed, and
gave me a middle-sized pen knife.

I hurried on a few of my clothes and went downstairs;
but I must observe that in unclasping the pen knife to
open the door of the necessary, according to his directions, a piece of money which was stuck between the blade
and the groove in the handle, fell into my hand. I did not
examine what it was, nor indeed could I well see, there
being then but a very faint moonlight; so I put them
together carelessly into my pocket.

I apprehended I staid in the garden pretty near half an
hour, for I was extremely ill, and, by over-heating myself
with walking the preceding day, had brought on the piles;
a disorder I was subject to since my youth. These seem
trifling circumstances, but afterwards turned out of infinite
consequence to me. When I returned to the chamber, I
was surprised to find my bedfellow gone; I called several
times, but receiving no answer, took it for granted he
had withdrawn into some adjoining closet for his private
occasions. I therefore went to bed and again fell to sleep.

About six o'clock I arose, nobody yet being up in the
house. The gentleman was not yet returned to bed, or if
he was, had again left it. I dressed myself with what
haste I could, being impatient to see my sister; and the
reckoning being paid over-night, I let myself out at the
street door.

I will not trouble you with a relation of the kindness
with which my sister and her husband received me. We
breakfasted together, and I believe it might have been
about eleven o'clock in the fore-noon when standing at
the door, my brother-in-law by my side, we saw three

horsemen galloping towards us. As soon as they came up they stopt, and one of them lighting suddenly seized me by the collar, crying, 'You are the Queen's prisoner.' I desired to know my crime. He said I should know that as soon as we came back to Deal, where I must immediately go with them. One of them told my brother that the night before I had committed murder and robbery.

Resistance would have proved as vain as my tears and protestations of my innocence. In a word a warrant was produced, and I was carried back to Deal attended by the three men; my brother and another friend accompanying us, who knew not what to say, or how to comfort me.

Being arrived in town, I was immediately hurried to the house where I had slept the previous night, the master of which was one of the three men that came to apprehend me, though in my first hurry I did not recollect him. We were met at the door by a crowd of people, every one crying 'Which is he? which is he?' As soon as I entered, I was accosted by the publican's wife, in tears. 'Oh! Cursed wretch, what hast thou done? Thou hast murdered and robbed my poor dear uncle, and all through me, who put thee to lie with him! But where has thou hid his money? And what hast thou done with his body? Thou shalt be hanged upon a gallows as high as the May pole.' My brother begged her to be pacified, and I was taken into a private room. They began to question me as the woman had done, about where I had put the money, and how I had disposed of the body. I asked them what money, and whose body they meant? They then said I had killed the person I had lain with the preceding night for the sake of a large sum I had seen him with. I fell down upon my knees, calling God to witness I knew nothing of what they accused me. Then somebody cried out, 'Carry him up the stairs;' and I was brought to the chamber where I had slept. Here the man of the house went to the bed, and turned down the sheets, pillows and bolster dyed with blood. He asked me did I know anything of that? I declared to God that I did not. Says a person who was in that room, 'Young man, something very odd must have passed here last night, for lying in the next chamber I heard groanings, and going up and down stairs more than once or twice.' I told them the circumstance of my illness and that I had been up and down myself, with all that passed between my bedfellow and me. Somebody proposed to search me; several began to turn my pockets inside out, and from my waistcoat tumbled the pen knife and the piece of money I have already mentioned. Upon seeing these, the woman immediately screamed out, 'O God! There is my uncle's pen knife!' Then taking up the money and calling the people about her, 'here is what puts the villain's guilt beyond a doubt; I can swear to this William and Mary Guinea; my uncle has long had it by way of a pocket-piece and engraved the first letters of his name upon it.' She began to cry again, while I could do nothing but continue to call Heaven to witness that I was as innocent as the child unborn.

After this they carried me down to the necessary, and here fresh proofs appeared against me. The constable, who had never left me, perceived blood on the edges of the seat, (which might have been the haemorrhage the night before). 'Here,' said he, 'after having cut the throat, he let the body down into the sea.' This every body immediately assented to. 'Then,' said the master of the house, 'it is vain to look for the body any further, for there was a spring tide last night, which has carried it off.'

The consequence of these proceedings was an immediate examination before the justice of the peace; after which I suffered long and rigorous imprisonment in the county town of Maidstone. For some time my father, my master, and my relations were inclined to think me innocent; and in compliance with my earnest request, an advertisement was published in the *London Gazette*, representing my deplorable circumstances and offering a reward to any person who could give tidings of Mr Richard Collins (the name of the man I was supposed to have murdered), either alive or dead. No information, however, of any kind came to hand. At the Assizes therefore, I was brought to trial; and circumstances appearing strong against me, I received sentence to be carried in a cart the Wednesday fortnight, to the town of Deal, and there to be hanged before the inn-keeper's door where I had committed the supposed murder; after which I was to be hung in chains within a little way of my brother's house. Nothing could have supported me under this dreadful condemnation, but a consciousness of my not being guilty of the crime for which I was to suffer. My friends now began to consider my declarations of innocence as persisting in falsehood to the perdition of my soul; many of them discontinued their inquiries after me, and those few who still came to visit me, only came to urge me to confession. But I was resolved I would never die with a lie like that in my mouth.

The Monday was now arrived before the fatal day, when an end was to be put to my miseries. I was called down into the court of the prison; but I own I was not a little shocked when I found it was to be taken measure for the irons in which I was to be hung after execution. A fellow prisoner appeared before me in the same woeful plight (he had robbed the mail) and the smith was measuring him when I came down; while the gaoler, with as much calmness as if he had been ordering a pair of stays for his daughter, was giving directions in what manner the irons should be made so as to support the man, who was remarkably heavy and corpulent.

Between this and the day of my execution, I spent my time alone in prayer and meditation. At length Wednesday morning came, and about six o'clock I was put into the cart; but sure such a day of wind, rain, and thunder, never blew out of the Heavens. It pursued us all the way; and when we arrived at Deal, it became so violent that the sheriff and his officers, who had not a dry thread upon them, could scarce sit their horses. For my own part, my mind (God help me) was with long agitation become so unfeeling, that I was in a manner insensible to every object about me; I therefore heard the sheriff whisper to the executioner to make what despatch he could without the least emotion, and suffered him to tuck me up like a log of wood, unconscious of what he was doing.

I can give no account of what I felt while I was hanging, only that I remember, after being turned off, something for a little appeared about me like a blaze of fire; nor do I know for how long I hung, no doubt the violence of the weather favoured me greatly in that circumstance. What I am now going to tell you I learned from my brother, which was that after having hung about half an hour, the sheriff's officers went off and I was cut down by the executioner; but when he came to put the irons upon me, it was found a mistake had been made, and that the iron of the other man had been sent instead of mine. This they remedied as well as they could, by stuffing rags between my body and the hoops that surrounded it. After a while I was taken according to my sentence, to the place appointed, and hung upon a gibbet which was ready prepared.

The cloth over my face being but lightly tied, and suffering no pressure from the iron, which stood a great way from it, was, I suppose, soon detached by the wind, which was still rather violent, and probably its blowing on my face expedited my recovery; certain it is, that in this tremendous situation I came to myself.

It was, no doubt, a very great blessing that I did not immediately return so perfectly to my senses as to have a feeling of things about me; yet I had a sort of recollection of what had happened, and in some measure was sensible where I was.

The gibbet was placed in one corner of a small common-field, where my sister's cows usually ran, and it pleased God that about that time a lad who took care of them came to drive them for evening milking. The creatures which were feeding almost under me, brought him near the gibbet; when, stopping to look at the melancholy spectacle, he perceived that the cloth was from off my face and, in the very moment he looked up, saw me opening my eyes and moving my under jaw. He immediately ran home to inform the people at his master's. At first they made some difficulty to believe his story; at length, however, my brother came out, and by the time he got to the field I was so much alive that my groans were very audible.

It was now dusk. The first thing they ran for was a ladder. One of my brother's men mounted, and, putting his hand on my stomach, felt my heart beating very strongly. But it was found impossible to detach me from the gibbet without cutting it down. A saw, therefore, was got for that purpose and, without giving you a detail of trifling circumstances, in less than half an hour, having freed me from my irons, they got me blooded, and put me into a warm bed in my brother's house.

It is an amazing thing, that, though upwards of eight persons were entrusted with this transaction, and I remained three days in the place after it happened, not a creature betrayed the secret. Early next morning it was known that the gibbet was cut down, and immediately it occurred to every body that it was done by my relations in order to put a slight veil over their own shame by burying the body; but when my brother was summoned to the mayor's house in order to be questioned, and he denied knowing anything of the matter, little more stir was made about it; partly because he was so greatly respected by all the neighbouring gentlemen, and in some measure, perhaps, because it was known that I continued to persist strongly in my being innocent of the fact for which I suffered.

Thus, then, was I most miraculously delivered from an ignominious death, if I may call my coming to life a delivery after all I had endured. But how was I to dispose of my life now I had regained it? To stay in England was impossible without exposing myself again to the terrors of the law. In this dilemma a fortunate circumstance occurred. There had lain for some time at my brother's house, one or two of the principal officers of a privateer that was preparing for a cruise, just then ready to sail. The captain kindly offered to take me aboard with him. You may guess little difficulty was made on our side to accept of such a proposal; and proper necessaries being quickly provided for me, my sister recommended me to the protection of God and the worthy commander, who most humanely received me as a sort of under-assistant to his steward . . .

[*There follows an account of the 'Voyages and Adventures . . . to the West Indies, and being taken by the Spaniards, amongst whom he met with the supposed Murdered Mr Collins, and proposed to return to England together. The Accident that threw Ambrose into the hands of Pirates; his Extraordinary adventures with them; and being again taken by the Spaniards, and there condemn'd to the Galleys. His being taken by the Algerines, and carried into Slavery, and, after many Hardships, returned to England'.*]

Hangmen of England

> Ye hangmen of Old England,
> How sturdily you stood,
> A-smoking pipes by Tyburn Tree,
> A-swigging pots in the Old Bailee,
> And strung up all you could.
>
> (from an old ballad)

Many discrepancies are encountered in attempting the task of listing Ye Hangmen of Old England, but the following represents an attempt to make sense out of the available records*. Some exist merely as disembodied names – like Bull, known to be active in 1593 (in the reign of Elizabeth I), though nothing more is recorded of him. Some became household names – like Jack Ketch, himself no better than the villains who swung from his rope; a man despised even beyond the despised rank of hangman. Some, like **William Calcraft** attracted legends so extravagant that even his flamboyant character could

*Based on Horace Bleackley, *Hangmen of England*, 1929

not live up to them; it is said of him that in his professional capacity he favoured the short drop, so that he could leap on to the back of the still-conscious victim and thus strangle him. Some, like **James Berry** and Albert Pierrepoint, changed their views so sharply that conscience hastened their retirement – Berry's in 1892 and Pierrepoint's in 1964. Both subsequently spoke strongly in favour of abolition; Berry claiming that 'My experiences have convinced me we shall never be a civilised nation while executions are carried out in prison.'

The Hangmen

Bull	1593
Derrick	1601
(Assistant: G. Brandon)	
Gregory Brandon	1616 (active)-c. 1640
Richard Brandon	c. 1640–49
Lowen	1649
Edward Dun	164(9)–63
Jack Ketch	1663–86
(In 1686 Ketch was replaced for a short period by Pasha Rose)	
John Price	1714–15
William Marvell	1715–17
Banks	1717–28
Richard Arnet	
John Hooper	1728–35
John Thrift	1735–52
Thomas Turlis	1752–71
Edward Dennis	1771–86
William Brunskill	1786–1814
John Langley	1814–17
James Botting	1817–20
James Foxen	1820–29
William Calcraft	1829–74
William Marwood	1874–83
Bartholomew Binns	1883–84
James Berry	1884–92

James Billington	1894–1902
William Billington	1902–05
Henry Pierrepoint	1905–11
Thomas Pierrepoint	1903–48
James Ellis	
Albert Pierrepoint	1940–64

The hangman Edward Dennis – called the 'Yeoman of the Halter' – served during the 1770s and was active in

the Gordon Riots (see illustration facing, thought to be a likeness of Dennis). The riots were initially inspired by anti-Catholic sentiments, but quickly turned by the mob into a debauch of drunkenness, pillage and destruction, including the burning of the infamous Newgate prison by a rabble led by James Jackson. The gaol was razed to the ground and those prisoners who were not consumed in the blaze or crushed under falling masonry were released. Also destroyed were the Fleet prison, New Gaol in Southwark, the King's Bench prison, and the Surrey House of Correction.

When the rising had been quelled and most of the 2,000 escaped prisoners restored to makeshift prisons, more than sixty were sentenced to death for their part in the riot. Ironically, one of their number was Edward Dennis. After the City Alderman had rejected Dennis's plea that his son take over his duties (presumably on the grounds that the boy would have to hang his own father), the 'Yeoman' was reprieved in order to dispatch 25 of his fellow-rioters.

The Hangman Hanged

In the year 1718, while George I ruled Great Britain and Ireland, John Price, ex-sailor and confirmed villain, reigned as Common Hangman. His occupancy of this throne was a short one, culminating in his ignominious death at the end of his successor's rope – hanged for the murder of a woman whose audacious crime was to resist Price's attempt to assault her. It is recorded of John Price that he 'first drew his breath in the fog-end of the suburbs of London, and, like Mercury, became a thief as soon as ever he peeped out of the shell. So prone was he to vice, that as soon as he could speak he would curse and swear with as great a passion and vileness as is frequently heard round any gaming table. Moreover, to this unprofitable talent of profaneness he added that of lying.'

Sentenced to death the first time by the Chelmsford magistrate, he was reprieved on the recommendation of his former master, whose position of High Sheriff of the

County of Essex, entitled him to such gratuitous – and in this case undeserved – kindness.

On his way once more to London, Price was next apprehended as a pickpocket, and cast into the Bristol Newgate and flogged. He fared little better at sea, discovering that life on board a man o' war, far from leading him out of temptation, encouraged him to pilfer from his fellow-seamen, a habit which even such characteristically nautical punishments as whipping at a gun, pickling with brine, and keel-hauling failed to break by the time the ship re-entered Portsmouth harbour two years later.

Price's career in crime was marginally more successful on dry land – at least in so far as he tended to get caught less often, though the good times finally came to an end and, chastened by a spell in Newgate and another flogging at the cart's tail, Price endeavoured to change his fortune by marriage.

His wife, Betty, was employed at Newgate Gaol – where probably they met – in the capacity of a run-around; that is, she ran errands for such of the prisoners as had money to pay for the service. It was through his wife's contacts that John raised himself to the position of hangman for the county of Middlesex.

Nevertheless the new hangman, shiftless by nature, could not long stay out of trouble, and despite a salary approaching £40 per year, and the customary perquisite of the condemned man's clothing to sell, John Price soon found himself in the Marshalsea Prison, and out of a job as executioner.

When we next encounter the fortunes of John Price, he has been released from the Marshalsea, and is about to slip into even deeper trouble.

What brought him to this end was his going one night over Bunhill Fields in his drunken airs, when he met an old woman, named Elizabeth White, a watchman's wife, who sold pastry-ware about the streets. He violently assaulted her in a barbarous manner, almost knocking one of her eyes out of her head, giving her several bruises about her body, breaking one of her legs, and wounding her in the belly. Whilst he was acting this inhumanity two men came along at the same time, and hearing dreadful groans supposed somebody was in distress, and having the courage to pursue the sound as well as they could, at last came up to the distressed woman, which made Price damn them for their impudence. However, they secured him, and brought him to the watch-house in Old Street, from whence a couple of watchmen were sent to fetch the old woman out of Bunhill Fields, who within a day or two died, under the surgeon's hands.

Newgate. Enter Price yet again.

At length the fatal day came wherein he was to bid adieu to the world, which was on a Saturday, the 31st of May, 1718. As he was riding in the cart he several times pulled a bottle of Geneva out of his pocket to drink before he came to the place of execution, which was in Bunhill Fields, where he committed the murder. Having arrived at the fatal tree, he was, upon Mr Ordinary's examination, found so ignorant on the ground of religion that he troubled himself not much about it; but valuing himself upon his former profession of being hangman, styled himself finisher of the law, and so was turned off the gibbet, aged upwards of forty years.

(The Annals of Newgate)

Hara-Kiri

By the Japanese code, death was preferable to dishonour, and suicide preferable to death at the hands of the executioner. Strictly speaking, execution by suicide – Hara-kiri, or 'happy dispatch' – was reserved for members of the Japanese aristocracy and senior government and military officers, who required permission from the Mikado to take their own lives. The ceremony was carried out at a specified time and a specified place and the subject, dressed in the white robe reserved for such use, would give a final address to assembled friends and official observers. He then knelt on the floor, and with a short, razor-sharp knife made first a horizontal cut across his abdomen followed by another, vertical cut, making a cross penetrating to the bowel. Immediately the official called the *kaishaku* lifted up his sword and struck off the dying man's head.

Although it was the privilege of class, many common criminals also took the option of suicide in the hope of avoiding disgrace for their family, and of gaining some public redemption for their courage. Practised from medieval times, hara-kiri ceased to be obligatory in 1868, and was officially abolished in 1873.

IJK

Impaling Alive

Impaling alive was once popular with the Romans, and among certain eastern nations. The Assyrians impaled their prisoners of war, and the practice was still being used by the Turks as a means of execution during the Bulgarian atrocities of 1876. There is a record of the death by impaling of the Turk Solyman Illeppy, convicted of the assassination of General Jean Baptiste Kleber in June 1800; it is said he remained alive on his stake for almost two hours without once crying out.

Impaling was an uncommon punishment in western Europe, though by no means unknown among the Teutonic peoples, among whom it was a punishment for various sexual offences such as adultery. In one variation, depicted in all its graphic horror in the Statute Book of the City of Zwickau (1348), two adulterers are shown tied one upon the other while two fiendish-looking executioners hammer a single long stake through both bodies.

Impalement was frequently the accompaniment to **burial alive**, in which a stake would be driven into the soil filling the pit and through the victim – it was thought that this would effectively prevent the evil spirit of the malefactor returning (this, of course, was also the reason for driving stakes through the hearts of witches, vampires and suicides). Sometimes a pile of bramble twigs were also heaped on the pit to further inhibit a return from the grave. Impalement was calculated to be a symbolically appropriate punishment for rapists, and in some areas it was customary for the rape victim to wield the mallet for the first three blows. There is a naive painting dated 1574, from Freiburg, Switzerland, in which a woman is shown buried alive and impaled with a stake through her heart, though neither of these punishments, together or separately, survived long into the 'modern' period.

Inevitably, isolated acts of barbaric cruelty are recorded, particularly in time of war, and from his remarkable document on the iniquities of the Napoleonic invasion of Spain in 1808, Francisco de Goya in the suite of etchings *The Disasters of War* offers a suitably awful example of the impalement of a captured prisoner.

Vlad the Impaler

One of the most celebrated torturers of all time – and a man whose name is familiar to anybody with a taste for the Gothic – was Vlad the Impaler, ruler of fifteenth-century Wallachia and also known as Vlad Dracula. The Impaler's life was chronicled many times since his assassination and references exist in such early European languages as Byzantine, Hungarian, Turkish, Genoese and French; in addition there is a large volume of regional folklore.

Even by the bellicose standards of the time and area, Vlad left no doubt that he was a torturer's torturer, and happily embraced blinding, dismemberment, burning and boiling alive. Nor was he particularly fussy which of his neighbours he tortured and killed – Hungarians, Bulgarians, Romanians, Turks – and representatives of most religions suffered his persecutions.

As for Vlad's favourite pastime, one authority on his life, Radu Florescu, comments: 'Dracula's sadistic pleasure was enhanced by watching his victims suffer a slow torture rather than immediate death. This is why he had the victims' stakes carefully rounded at the points so that entrails were not pierced with a fatal wound when the horses were put to the gallop with the victim's feet stretched apart.'

The fifteenth-century woodcut facing depicts Vlad dining *al fresco* surrounded by the impaled bodies of his victims. Unlike Bram Stoker's Dracula – to whom Vlad gave his name – the Impaler did not suck his victims' blood with fangs, but drank it from a cup.

Inquisition

Papal Inquisition
Following its own extensive suffering at the hands of the
pagan Romans, Christianity, when it became the official
Church of the Empire, itself turned persecutor. This was

for no reason of mere revenge, but the result of a single-minded policy of combined evangelism and self-preservation. It became essential, as the Roman Church spread, that the *status quo* of the ecclesiastical hierarchy be preserved and maintained. This it ensured, firstly by the acquisition of converts (even using coercion by fear), and secondly by the destruction of their perceived enemy, the 'heretics'. This destruction was, by AD 430, quite literal, with heresy liable under civil law to punishment of death.

The 1049 Church Council of Rheims recommended excommunication for heresy, and this was broadly ratified by the Toulouse Council of 1119 and the Lateran Council twenty years later. However, the Papal Inquisition proper was established in 1199 by a Papal Bull of Innocent III, which took the bishops' powers to investigate heresy back into the Vatican itself so that the Inquisition could be administered centrally. Five years later the first of the Roman Catholic purges began, with attacks on the sect known as the Albigenses, active in southern France and northern Italy. They were a type of Manichean, or followers of Mani, a Persian teacher of the third century who preached that the universe is under the control of two opposing forces – light and goodness (identified with God) and darkness and evil. It was one of Mani's beliefs that although Christ had been sent into the world to banish darkness and restore light, the Apostles had corrupted His doctrine; it was he, Mani, who had been sent to restore it. During the thirteenth century the Inquisition began its persecution of the Albigenses, and by the fourteenth they had been exterminated.

The first Holy Office of the Inquisition was set up at Toulouse in 1233, and another was established shortly afterwards at Aragon. Over the coming centuries the Inquisition would spread like wildfire throughout Europe and up into the Netherlands. The persecution would last for five centuries, with escalating corruption of both the Inquisitors and the principles of the Inquisition. It imposed a reign of terror under which even Catholics themselves were not safe from the excesses of the Inquisitors – men who had the power, for reasons entirely their own, or for no particular reason at all, to concoct charges in order to force victims into the torture chambers or, in the case of many women, into the Inquisitor's bed.

The discovery of heretics was to become a wider issue, and by 1320 sorcery and witchcraft had been added to heresy as proper subjects for investigation by the Inquisition. At the same time an entirely unwarranted 'witch mania' was *created* throughout Europe, and reached its peak with the Spanish Inquisition (see page 286). In 1484, Innocent VIII confirmed his earnest desire for the suppression of witchcraft in the influential Bull *Summis Desiderantes Affectibus* ('Desiring with the most profound anxiety') in which the Pope claims:

Recently it has come to our notice, much to our regret, that in some parts of Upper Germany, in the provinces, towns, territories, localities and sees of Mainz, Cologne, Treves, Salzburg and Bremen, a number of persons of both sexes, forgetful of their own salvation and contrary to their belief in the Catholic faith, have given themselves up to devils in the form of incubi and succubi. By their incantations, spells, crimes and infamous acts they destroy the fruit of the womb in women, in cattle and various other animals; they destroy crops, vines, orchards, meadows and pastures, wheat, corn and other plants and vegetables; they bring pain and affliction, great suffering and appalling disease (both external and internal) upon men, women and beasts, flocks and other animals; they prevent men from engendering and women from conceiving; they render both wives and husbands impotent; they sacrilegiously deny the faith they received in Holy Baptism; and they do not abstain from committing other fearful excesses and foul crimes, endangering their souls, mocking God and causing a serious scandal, at the instigation of the Enemy.

This must be seen as active support by Innocent VIII for his two Dominican Inquisitors, Jakob Sprenger and Heinrich Kramer, authors of the notorious 'guide to witch-hunting', the *Malleus Maleficarum*, which was being prepared that same year.

As early as 1252 the use of torture to extract infor-

Jews tortured as heretics by the Inquisition, 1475

Witches in the act of calling up a storm, from the De Lamiis,
1489

mation and confessions was sanctioned by a Bull of Innocent IV, and although it was officially only to be the
method of last resort, that was a rule that could conveniently be ignored. Having confessed during torture, a
prisoner was removed from the torture chamber in order

that he might repeat his confession 'freely and spontaneously' and without fear of further pain. He (or she, of course) was then obliged to provide the Inquisitor with the names of his accomplices in heresy – real or invented – thus ensuring a steady supply of victims through the Inquisition's courts. The confession had already put the prisoner's worldly possessions into the hands of the Church, and the wretched man was then sentenced, usually to death at the stake (see also **Burning Alive**). It must be emphasised that the Inquisition did not itself bear the distasteful responsibility for sentencing and execution – this was handed over to the secular authorities, who dared not flinch from their duty lest they themselves be accused of favouring heretics.

The Hammer of Witches

The *Malleus Maleficarum*, also called the *Hexenhammer* and *The Hammer of Witches*, was basically a manual for witch-hunters with chapters instructing potential inquisitors in the nature of witchcraft, the different types of *maleficia*, and the rules for trying, torturing and punishing suspected witches. The treatise was compiled by two Dominicans: Jakob Sprenger, the Dean of Cologne University, and Prior Heinrich Kramer. The arguments advanced in the book are highly illogical, but it nevertheless enjoyed huge circulation and was reprinted in dozens of editions between 1486 and 1669, in all the major European languages. *Malleus Maleficarum* became the indispensable companion of every judge, magistrate and priest during the fury of the Inquisition, being both a theological justification and practical handbook on each stage of the denunciation, trial and execution of 'witches'. However, its treatment of the subject of torture is uncharacteristically modest: '. . . and when the instruments of torture are prepared, the judge, both in person and through other good men, zealous in the faith, tries to persuade the prisoner to confess the truth freely; but if he will not confess, he bids the attendants prepare the prisoner for the stappado or some other torture. The attendants obey

MALLEVS
MALEFICARVM,
MALEFICAS ET EARVM
haeresim frameâ conterens,

EX VARIIS AVCTORIBVS COMPILATVS,
& in quatuor Tomos iustè distributus,

QVORVM DVO PRIORES VANAS DÆMONVM
versutias, præstigiosas eorum delusiones, superstitiosas Strigimagarum
cæremonias, horrendos etiam cum illis congressus; exactam denique
tam pestifera secta disquisitionem, & punitionem complectuntur.
Tertius praxim Exorcistarum ad Dæmonum, & Strigimagarum male-
ficia de Christi fidelibus pellenda; Quartus verò Artem Doctrinalem,
Benedictionalem, & Exorcismalem continent.

TOMVS PRIMVS.
Indices Auctorum, capitum, rerúmque non desunt.

Editio nouissima, infinitis penè mendis expurgata; cuique accessit Fuga
Dæmonum & Complementum artis exorcisticæ.

Vir siue mulier, in quibus Pythonicus, vel diuinationis fuerit spiritus, morte moriatur
Leuitici cap. 10.

LVGDVNI,
Sumptibus CLAVDII BOVRGEAT, sub signo Mercurij Galli.

M. DC. LXIX.
CVM PRIVILEGIO REGIS.

forthwith, yet with feigned agitation. Then, at the prayer
of some of those present, the prisoner is loosed again and
is taken aside once more and persuaded to confess, being
led to believe that he will in that case not be put to
death.'

Later demonologists added their own variations to the
Malleus Maleficarum. Nicholas Remy was born in 1530 in
the province of Lorraine, France; as a child he was present
at many of the early witch trials. Remy studied law at
Toulouse, and rose to the position of Attorney-General
of Lorraine. He was an enthusiastic witch-hunter, and his
classic work *Demonolatreiae* of 1595 became a close rival
of the *Malleus*. In it, Remy lays claim to having condemned to death no fewer than nine hundred witches in
the space of ten years. Remy's illustrious contemporary
was Jean Bodin – lawyer, philosopher and demonologist
– whose personal experiences as a witch-trial judge were
embodied in his *Demonomanie des Sorciers*, written with
the purpose of helping judges to counter witchcraft. Bodin
was himself an enthusiastic torturer and was known for
his particular cruelty to children and cripples. No suffering, he believed, was too great for witches, and he often
expressed regret that burning alive was too lenient a sentence as the torment rarely lasted longer than a half-hour.
Bodin went so far as to voice the opinion that a judge
who did not condemn a witch to the stake should himself
be put to death. Heinrich von Schultheis, a notorious
witch-hunter of the German Rhineland, was the author,
in 1634, of *Detailed Instructions how to Proceed in the
Inquisition against the Horrible Vice of Witchcraft*,
described as the most gruesome of all the most gruesome
literature of witch persecution.

By and large, England managed to escape the worst
excesses of witch mania, though there were those who
followed the trade of witch-hunter. Matthew Hopkins,
self-styled Witchfinder-General of England, was the best
known, and when not condemning innocent eccentrics to
the gallows found time to pen his own *Discovery of
Witches* (see also **Witch Trials**).

Illustration from Matthew Hopkins's Discovery of Witches

Chronology

Although the Spanish Inquisition is inextricably bound into the wider European Papal Inquisition, it is more convenient to treat it as a separate historical discussion. The following is a select chronology of the Papal Inquisition showing the key dates of events in Spain in square brackets.

1184 Pope Lucius III establishes an episcopal inquisition, giving powers to bishops to 'discover' deviations from official teachings and to hand over to the secular authorities for punishment those who were unable to establish their innocence. Officers entrusted with the administration of the civil law could be excommunicated for failing to do so.

1199 By a Papal Bull of 25 March, Innocent III takes power away from the bishops and administers the inquisitions from the Vatican, thus ensuring that the Church exercised its rightful claim on the confiscated propety of heretics.

1204 Inquisition institutes persecution of the Albigenses.

1215 The decree *Excommunicamus* ('Excommunication') confirms Innocent III's right to booty, and the obligation of the secular authorities to 'strive in faith' to exterminate heretics.

1233 Pope Gregory IX places responsibility for the Inquisition in the hands of the Dominicans (and sometimes Franciscans) under the direct control of the Pope but presiding from local monasteries, where the Inquisitions were frequently held. A Dominican named Alberic is recorded as operating in Lombardy under the title *Inquisitor haereticae pravitatis*.

1252 Papal Bull of Innocent IV, *Ad extirpanda*, sanctions the use of torture by the Inquisition.

1254 Pope Innocent IV grants witnesses appearing against an accused the right of anonymity.

1257 Pope Alexander IV asked to extend the Inquisition of heresy to include sorcery. Alexander consents only in so far as the sorcery was *also* heresy.

1320 Inquisition at Carcassonne authorised by Pope John XXII, to investigate allegations of witchcraft and sorcery. However, in 1333 the restriction that the charge must include heresy was reimposed.

1326 Major Inquisitorial witch hunts at Toulouse.

Protestants and Jews burned by the Inquisition for heresy and witchcraft, 1493

1330	Major Inquisitorial witch hunts at Narbonne.
1431	Pope Nicholas V authorises the Inquisition to flush out and eliminate sorcerers in the northern French district of Arras.
[1479	Spanish Inquisition established.]
1484	Papal Bull issued by Innocent VIII, *Summis Desiderantes Affectibus*, empowering the Inquisition to suppress witchcraft.
1486	First edition of Sprenger and Kramer's *Malleus Maleficarum*.
1501	Angelo of Verona given authority as Inquisitor General of all Lombardy by Pope Alexander VI.
1503	Pope Julius II issues a Bull to Giorgio de Casale, the Cremona Inquisitor, giving him special powers in Lombardy.
1523	On 20 July, Pope Adrian VI sends a Bull to the Inquisitor in Como, Modestus Vincentinus, reinforcing Julius II's order to exterminate the

heretics of Lombardy, and authorising Inquisitors to act without reference to the local bishops.

1529   Luxeuil witch trials.

1542   Congregation of the Inquisition established as a final court of appeal in heresy trials (see also 1908).

1585   Bull of Pope Sixtus V, *Coeli et terrae creator*, officially denounces all forms of sorcery – divination, astrology, incantation, summoning demons, etcetera.

[**1808**   Spanish Inquisition suspended.]

[**1814**   Spanish Inquisition reintroduced.]

1816   Authorisation of torture by Inquisition officially abolished by Pope Pius VII.

[**1834**   Spanish Inquisition finally terminated.]

1908   The Congregation of the Inquisition, established in 1542, is renamed Congregation of the Holy Office (see also 1965).

1965   The Congregation of the Holy Office established in 1908 is renamed the Sacred Congregation of the Doctrine of the Faith, and is to be solely concerned with the maintenance of ecclesiastical discipline.

Spanish Inquisition

Quite independent of the Papal, or Roman, Inquisition, the Spanish Inquisition was established under Ferdinand and Isabella in 1479 as an entirely nationalistic remedy for what was seen to be the uncontrollable spread of sorcery; some universities, for example, were running courses in astrology and necromancy. The Inquisition would survive until 1808, when Napoleon installed his brother Joseph Bonaparte, who suspended the terror, on the Spanish throne. After Bonaparte's abdication in 1813 the Inquisition was reinstated and not finally terminated for another twenty years, in 1834.

With Thomas de Torquemada as Grand Inquisitor, the initial programme of the Inquisition was the complete eradication, by any means, of heretical beliefs and practices – especially those of the Jews and the Moors. However, by the Bull of Pope Sixtus V, dated 1585, the Inquisition found its powers elastic enough to include – officially now – all forms of sorcery and divination, astrology and witchcraft. As an organised instrument of terror against dissenters, the Inquisition became unrivalled in the bloody violence of its torture chambers. Torture became inseparable from the process, and the most ingenious means of inflicting pain were developed – many of which are documented in separate entries throughout this book. It is impossible to measure the consequences of the Spanish Inquisition in terms of deaths, but one estimate suggests that in the year 1481, 3,000 'heretics' were burned in Andalucia alone, and a further 17,000 tortured.

The 'process' or method of inquisition followed an almost invariable pattern:

Evidence of heresy was gathered by the Holy Office of the Inquisition, either by voluntary confessions made in the hope of milder punishment, or by what was called the Edict of Faith, which made it the duty of all good Christians to testify against any person they knew or believed to hold heretical views – or face the painful consequence of excommunication or worse. If it seemed that there was *prima facie* evidence of a case against the accused, no matter how slim or unreliable the evidence might be, then he would be formally arrested – often at dead of night – and thrown into a 'secret' prison, a *carcelas secretas* run by the Inquisition. The accused's goods would be confiscated because, in the likely event of his being convicted, those goods would automatically become the property of the Church. The length of time that a prisoner might spend in these squalid, vermin-infested dungeons varied; it could be months before he even knew the nature of the charge against him, and then he would be pressed to make a full and voluntary confession of any sin that might be on his conscience. In order to detect frauds or recent hasty converts to Christianity, the accused would also be asked to recite the Lord's Prayer, the Ave Maria and the Pater

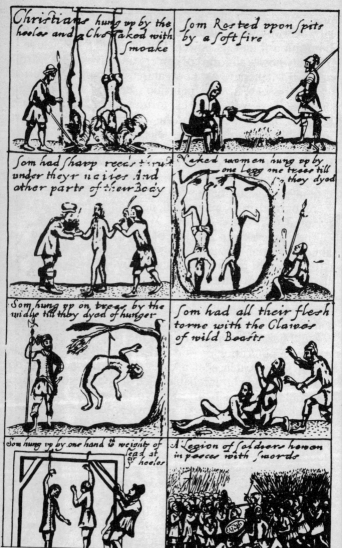

The many tortures of the Inquisition for heresy and witchcraft,
1493

Noster. There would follow a number of audiences with the Inquisitors over a period of months, sometimes years. It was only after these preliminary investigations that a trial at which evidence was presented was held. Some idea of the almost burlesque grandeur of these occasions is discernible in this description from Marchant: 'The hall is hung in black, without any windows, or light, but what comes in through the door. At the front there is an image of our Saviour on the cross, under a black velvet canopy, and six candlesticks with six thick yellow wax candles on the Altar's table: on one side there is a pulpit with another candle, where the secretary intones the crimes.'

The accused was allowed to make a defence, and was allowed a counsel – not of his own choosing, of course, but one nominated by the court; nor was it the counsel's duty to challenge evidence on behalf of his 'client'. It was the counsel's main preoccupation to persuade the prisoner that it would be better if he made a confession. He might also suggest that a suitable line of defence would be to name any particular enemies that the accused might believe would bring such infamous charges against him. If, by chance, the prisoner hit on the right name, then that person's evidence would be disallowed; but at best it was a hit-and-miss affair, as all witnesses remained anonymous and the accused was at no time told who had made allegations of heresy against him. An accused could also plead mitigation – that he was senile, too young to appreciate the seriousness of his actions, or drunk or insane; the problem with a plea of insanity was that the Inquisitor was likely to insist on it being tested under torture.

There followed a consultation, the *consulta da fé*, between the Inquisitor, the bishop and a couple of legal or theological experts, as to the verdict. Sometimes a verdict was reached immediately, and the prisoner sentenced. If there was any doubt as to the clarity of truth of the evidence, the court could, and frequently did, resort to torture.

This book is crammed with references to the

instruments of torture favoured by the agents of the Spanish Inquisition, but it should also be pointed out that the Holy Office employed secular executioners; consequently the torture methods initially used were also those available for use in the civil prisons. The most common forms of torture were suspension from the pulley (see **Squassation**) and water torture (see **Wooden Horse 1**); however, by the seventeenth century a range of more imaginative tortures had been added to the executioners' repertoire, and these continued to be refined throughout the duration of the Inquisition. Neither age nor gender was any safeguard against the horrors of the torture chamber, and ancient men were as enthusiastically put to the **rack** as young girls.

When a confession had been squeezed, often literally, out of a prisoner, it was essential that within 24 hours he should repeat these admissions in the presence of the Inquisitor and away from the intimidation of the torturer. The final stage of the proceedings was sentencing. If the offence was of a serious nature, then the convicted prisoner would not be advised of his punishment until the public *auto-da-fé*. For less serious offences he would be advised of his fate immediately, in the court. There was an escalating scale of possible punishments, to be imposed according to the seriousness of the heresy.

1. In the case of minor lapses of faith, to which the prisoner had freely confessed and repented, he was required publicly to face the cross and swear his allegiance to the Catholic faith and condemn heresy; he was also required openly to welcome any penance that he might be given. The prisoner may or may not have been given some light penance, but he would be forcefully warned against relapse – the penalty for which was certain death at the stake.

2. More serious lapses would attract a similar form of repentance, accompanied by more severe

penance, such as rigorous fasting and regular pilgrimages to the Holy Shrines.

3. The next level of punishment was exile – for periods of time ranging from a few months to a lifetime. The culprit might be banished from his town or village, from his district, or from the country. Time and distance would be determined by the gravity of the charges proved.

4. Flagellation was a frequent resort of the Inquisition; the penitent was stripped to the waist, seated on a donkey and, wearing a 'mitre' on his head describing the offence, was flogged through the open streets. According to one authority the average scourging consisted of 200 lashes, though this could be mitigated – for example, an 86-year-old man and a thirteen-year-old girl convicted in Valencia in 1607 were sentenced to only 100 stripes!

5. The most common punishment was imprisonment – from a few months to life, depending upon the seriousness of the heresy. In effect, lengthy sentences – those of more than five years – were impractical. Due to the heavy traffic of the courts and the reluctance of the Inquisition to invest in new prisons, there was always a severe shortage of space, resulting in periodic reviews when prisons were cleared in order to be filled anew.

6. The ultimate penalty for heresy was death; and the means of execution was the most terrible – burning alive at the stake. It must be remembered, however, that the Church *never* condemned prisoners to death – they were transferred to the jurisdiction of the secular authorities, and the heretic was executed by the state.

The great show-piece of the Inquisition was the *auto-da-fé* (Portuguese, 'act of faith'), a festival which attracted

Hanging of a woman accused by the Inquisition of being possesed by demons

crowds from miles around (not least because attendance was rewarded by a 40-day indulgence!). On the evening prior to the feast-day on which the *auto* was to take place, there would be a procession through the streets to the town square; here, an altar had already been installed on which was now placed a large green cross, eternal symbol of the Inquisition. A second cross was erected on the site where the executions were to take place.

On the early morning of the *auto-da-fé* all the prisoners were assembled at the Inquisition's special gaol and robed in their *sanbenitos*. This ritual dated back to the early years of the Inquisition, and in the time of Torquemada all the penitents' habits were black. More latterly, black was reserved for the worst category of prisoner – the relapsed heretic. On the front and back of these habits were painted the flames of Hell and the demons that dwelt in that place. Less obdurate heretics, according to the category of their offence, were dressed in yellow habits with either red or saffron St Andrew's crosses worked on to them, front and back. On their heads, mock mitres sat on which were written the details of their various heresies.

As the procession moved off from the prison they were led by a troop of halberdiers, behind whom the cross of the parish church was carried, shrouded in suitably solemn black. The penitents followed the cross, accompanied by more halberdiers. The less serious offenders led, with those destined for the stake at the rear. Effigies were swung aloft on poles, representing those heretics who had enjoyed the good fortune either to escape or to have died before the *auto*.

The penitents and effigies were followed by secular officials, and behind them the banner of the Inquisition was carried – a green cross on a black ground with an olive branch worked on to the left side to symbolise mercy, and a naked sword on the right, emblem of justice. Bringing up the rear of the procession were the Inquisitors themselves.

At the place of execution, the events began with a sermon, after which the long process of reading the prisoners' sentences started. As each penitent's name was called he advanced and stood before one of the two pulpits that had been erected either side of the altar, and listened to his fate. After sentence he fell to his knees to receive absolution and release from excommunication. Prisoners were then returned to prison to receive their punishment – incarceration, whipping, etc. There remained those under sentence of death, who were mounted astride donkeys and, accompanied by confessors, led to the place where they were to be burned.

The reason for burning being the prescribed method of execution was bound up in the Roman Catholic doctrine that *Ecclesia non novit sanquinem* ('The Church is untainted with blood'). The following is reputed to be an eye-witness account of an *auto-da-fé* that took place in Madrid in 1682. I have been unable to trace the original work of the Dr Geddes who has been credited with the account, but it accords with other reliable records of the Inquisition:

> The officers of the Inquisition, preceded by trumpets, kettle-drums and their banner, marched on the 30th of May, in cavalcade, to the palace of the great square, where they declared by proclamation that on the 30th of June the sentence of the prisoners would be put in execution. There had not been a spectacle of this kind at Madrid for several years before, for which reason it was expected by the inhabitants with as much impatience as a day of the greatest festivity and triumph. When the day appointed arrived, a prodigious number of people appeared, dressed as splendid as their respective circumstances could afford. In the great square was raised a high scaffold; and thither, from seven in the morning till the evening were brought criminals of both sexes; all the Inquisitions in the kingdom sending their prisoners to Madrid. Twenty men and women out of these prisoners, with one renegade Mahometan, were ordered to be burned; fifty Jews and Jewesses, having never before been imprisoned, and repenting of their crimes, were sentenced to a long confinement, and to wear a yellow cap; and ten others, indicted for bigamy, witchcraft and other crimes, were sentenced to be whipped and then sent to the galleys: these last wore large pasteboard caps, with inscriptions on them, having a halter about their necks, and torches in their hands. On this solemn occasion the whole court of Spain was present. The Grand Inquisitor's chair was placed in a sort of tribunal far above that of the king. The nobles here acted the part of the sheriff's officers in England, leading such criminals as were to be burned, and holding them when fast bound with thick cords; the rest of the criminals were conducted by the familiars of the Inquisition.

At the place of execution there are so many stakes

set as there are prisoners to be burned, a large quantity of dried furze being set about them. The stakes of the Protestants, or, as the inquisitors called them, the professed, are about four yards high, and have each a small board, whereon the prisoner is seated within half a yard of the top. The professed then go up a ladder betwixt two priests, who attend them the whole day of execution. When they come even with the aforementioned board, they turn about to the people, and the priests spend near a quarter of an hour in exhorting them to be reconciled to the see at Rome. On their refusing, the priests come down and the executioner ascending, turns the professed from off the ladder on to the seat, chains their bodies close to the stakes and leaves them. Then the priests go up a second time to renew their exhortations; and if they find them ineffectual, usually tell them at parting that they leave them to the devil, who is standing at their elbow ready to receive their souls, and carry them with him into the flames of hell-fire, as soon as they are out of their bodies. A general shout is then raised, and when the priests get off the ladder, the universal cry is: 'Let the dogs' beards be made!' (which implies, singe their beards). This is accordingly performed by means of flaming furzes thrust against their faces with long poles. This barbarity is repeated till their faces are burnt, and is accompanied with loud acclamations. Fire is then set to the furzes, and the criminals are consumed.

The intrepidity of the twenty-one men and women in suffering the horrid death was truly astonishing; some thrust their hands and feet into the flames with the most dauntless fortitude; and all of them yielded to their fate with such resolution that many of the amazed spectators lamented that such heroic souls had not been more enlightened. The near situation of the king to the criminals rendered their dying groans very audible to him; he could not, however, be absent from this dreadful scene, as it is esteemed a religious one, and his coronation oath obliges him to give a sanction by his presence to all acts of the tribunal.

Iron Collar
(see **Collars**)

Iron Maiden of Nuremberg

Probably the most notorious instrument of torture ever to have entered popular folklore is the Iron Maiden of Nuremberg. In its country of origin it is called the 'Eiserne Jungfrau', and this translates as 'iron virgin'. However, as the city of Toledo already boasts an **Iron Virgin**, the term 'maiden' is commonly substituted. The machine was widely used as a punishment for a variety of civil and ecclesiastical offences.

The person who has passed through the terrible ordeal of the Question Chamber, but has made no recantation, would be led along the tortuous passage by which we had come, and ushered into this vault, where the first object that would greet his eye, the pale light of a lamp falling on it, would be the Iron Virgin. He would be bidden to stand in front of the image. The spring would be touched by the executioner – the Virgin would fling open her arms and the wretched victim would straightway be forced within them. Another spring was then touched, and the Virgin closed upon her victim; a strong wooden beam, fastened at one end to the wall by a moveable joint, the other placed against the doors of the iron image, was worked with a screw and, as the beam was pushed out, the spikey arms of the Virgin slowly but irresistibly closed upon the man and did their work.

When the dreadful business was ended, it needed

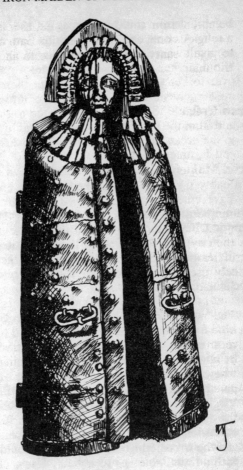

not that the executioner should put himself to the
trouble of making the Virgin unclasp the mangled
carcase of her victim; provision had been made for
a quick and secret disposal. At the touching of a
third spring, the floor of the image would slide aside,
and the body of the victim drop down the mouth of
a perpendicular shaft in the rock. Down this pit, at

a great depth, could be discerned the shimmer of water. A canal had been made to flow underneath the vault where stood the Iron Virgin, and when she had done her work upon those who were delivered over to her tender mercies, she let them fall, with quick descent and sudden plunge into the canal underneath, where they were floated to the Pegnitz, and from the Pegnitz to the Rhine, and by the Rhine to the ocean, there to sleep beside the dust of Huss* and Jerome . . .

(*The History of Protestantism*, Revd Dr Wylie)

Iron Virgin of Toledo

On the entry of the French into Toledo during the Peninsular War (1808–14), General Lasalle visited the palace of the Inquisition. The great number of the instruments of torture, especially the instruments to stretch the limbs, and the drop baths, which caused a lingering death, excited horror even in the minds of soldiers hardened in the field of battle. One of these instruments, singular in its kind for refined torture, and disgraceful to reason and religion in the choice of its object, deserved particular description. In a subterraneous vault, adjoining the secret audience chamber, stood in a recess in the wall a wooden statue made by the hands of monks, representing the Virgin Mary. A gilded glory beamed around her head, and she had a standard in her right hand. It immediately struck the spectator, notwithstanding the ample folds of the silk garment which fell from the shoulders on both sides, that she wore a breastplate. Upon closer examination it appeared the whole front of the body was covered with extremely sharp nails and small daggers or blades of knives with the points projecting outwards. The arms and hands had joints, and their motions were

*The reference is to John Huss, the Bohemian Protestant reformer who was burned at the stake in 1415 for rejecting the Pope's authority.

directed by machinery placed behind the partition. One of the servants of the Inquisition who was also present was ordered by the general to make the statue *manoeuvre* as he expressed it. As the statue extended its arms and gradually drew them back, as if she would affectionately embrace and press someone to her heart, the well-filled knapsack of a Polish grenadier supplied for this time the place of the poor victim. The statue pressed it closer and closer; and when, at the command of the general, the director of the machinery made it open its arms and return to its first position, the knapsack was pierced two or three inches deep, and remained hanging upon the nails and daggers of the murderous instrument.

(*The Percy Anecdotes*, Reuben and Sholto Percy, London 1820–23)

Jamaican Cart Whip
(see **Flagellation**)

Jeffreys, Judge George
Chief Justice of the King's Bench to James II of England, called 'Bloody Jeffreys' on account of the insane cruelty of his sentences while presiding over the Western Circuit court after Monmouth's rebellion had failed to overthrow James in 1685. The Bloody Assizes, as they were called, caused hundreds to be hanged and gibbeted and hundreds of others to be transported – a slower, but usually no less sure death.

As one might expect from such a formidable abolitionist as Mrs Violet Van Der Elst (*On the Gallows*), her words on George Jeffreys are less than benevolent:

We know of the malignancy of judges in the past. Judge Jeffreys was known to have a very handsome face, and at times he would look most benevolent and angelic; but there was no man living who had a blacker soul. He was created a judge at the time of

the Monmouth rising. I might mention that Miekle-
john in his *History* states that after the Monmouth
Rebellion, 'the pitch cauldron was constantly boiling
in the assize towns, and the heads and limbs preserved in it were distributed over the lonely western
country where, for years after, despite storms and
crows and foxes, they frightened the village labourer
as he passed to his cottage in the evening gloom'
(see also **Hanging in Chains**). Macaulay says, 'The
peasant who had consented to perform this hideous
office returned to his plough. But a mark like that
of Cain was upon him. He was known throughout
the village by the horrible name of William Boil-
man'. Innocent men too were hanged. There was
the case of Charles Lindell. He said that he had not
left his shop – in fact, he was arrested there. He had
never at any time assisted Monmouth's men; the
night he was supposed to be out he was sitting at
home with his mother and his sweetheart. All this
was told to Judge Jeffreys. With his most benevolent
smile he listened and seemed to sympathise. Then
his face was contorted into a horrible grimace as he
turned to the poor prisoner, who had thought that
he had a kind judge to hear the truth he was telling,
but now realised that he had a fiend to judge him,
and not a man. Judge Jeffreys told him that he
would be hanged by the neck, if only for the lies he
had told; he had taken God's name in vain when he
swore to such lies. This man was only one of
hundreds that the 'hanging judge' condemned to
death. He seemed to take a devilish delight in mocking and insulting poor unhappy men who were for
the most part innocent of what they were accused.
He suffered from kidney trouble, but one can hardly
believe that this complaint was the cause of the man
acting like the cruellest demon. He never let anyone
escape him. In the reign of James II, Judge Jeffreys
was handing out death and torture to all who came
before him. When he tried Titus Oates for perjury

at the Old Bailey, he sentenced him to be pilloried in Palace Yard, led round Westminster Hall with a description of his crime over his head, pilloried again in front of the Royal Exchange, tied to a cart and whipped from Aldgate to Newgate, and after two days whipped from Newgate to Tyburn. When he went to the Pillory people pelted him with refuse and nearly tore him to pieces. His first flogging, before a huge crowd, was very severe. For a long time he stood it without a murmur; then he gave way and his shrieks were terrible to hear. Although he continually fainted he was still whipped without mercy. When his bonds were loosed he appeared to be dead.

Two days later he was again brought out before the crowd assembled at Newgate, and as he could not stand he was dragged to Tyburn on a hurdle, where he again received hundreds of stripes, although he was unconscious. He was then taken back to Newgate and kept in irons for several months in a dark dungeon. One who was present said: 'He received upwards of two thousand lashes. Such a thing was never inflicted by any Jew, Turk or heathen, but by Jeffreys. Had they hanged him they had been more merciful; had they flayed him alive it is a question whether it would have been such a torture. When James II fled from Britain, Jeffreys tried to disguise himself as a seaman, but he was recognised and taken to the Tower [of London]. He died there of a malady which it is believed was stone in the kidney. Never before had died a more cruel or cold-blooded villain.

Justice and humanity, divorced from all party considerations, gained a great deal from the overthrow of James II and his Chief Justice. Judges ceased to be employable and removable at the whim of the Crown; trials began to be conducted with reasonable fairness and decency.

Cruelty and violence ceased, by and large, to be a weapon
in the arsenal of factional politics.

Jougs
(see **Scold's Bridle**)

Judicial Errors
One of the strongest arguments in the repertoire of capital
punishment's abolitionists has always been the possibility
of executing an innocent person. Certainly in the more
barbarous days of the seventeenth and eighteenth centuries, when justice at its best was rough, there are records
aplenty of the hanging of people whose crimes were subsequently attributed to others, or who were, quite simply,
innocent.

However, even in more recent times there have been
errors enough – or judgements which leave enough doubt
to constitute error – to make capital punishment a very
unreliable tool of justice. The problem with hanging is
that it is irreversible; it is the one mistake that can never
be rectified.

Thankfully – and despite public opinion still in its
favour – Britain has effectively abolished capital punishment, in line with all other civilised countries of the world
(see **Capital Punishment**). But lest we should be tempted
once again to make death the ultimate sanction, it would
be as well to remember just a few of those for whom it
was judicial murder:

William Shaw
Shaw was an upholsterer at Edinburgh in the year 1721,
and had a daughter, Catherine, who lived with him. She
encouraged the attentions of John Lawson, a jeweller,
to whom William Shaw declared the utmost objection,
alleging him to be a profligate young man, addicted to
every kind of dissipation. He was forbidden entry to the
house, but as the daughter persisted in seeing him clan-

destinely, the father, on this discovery, kept her strictly confined.

Shaw had for some time pressed his daughter to receive the addresses of a son of Alexander Robertson, a friend and neighbour. One evening, her father being very pressing with her on the matter, Catherine peremptorily refused, declaring that she preferred death to being young Robertson's wife. Shaw grew enraged and the daughter more stubborn, so that the most passionate expressions arose on both sides, and the words 'barbarity, cruelty and death' were frequently pronounced by the daughter. At length her father left the room, locking Catherine Shaw inside.

The greatest part of the buildings in Edinburgh were formed on the plan of the chambers in our Inns of Court, so that many families inhabited rooms on the same floor, having all one common staircase. William Shaw dwelt in one of these, and only a single partition divided his apartment from that of James Morrison, a watch-case maker. This man had indistinctly overheard the conversation and quarrel between Catherine and her father, but was particularly struck by the repetition of the above words. For some time after the father had gone out all was silent, but presently Morrison heard several groans from the daughter. Alarmed, he ran to some of his neighbours, and these, entering Morrison's room not only heard the groans, but distinctly heard Catherine Shaw faintly exclaim: 'Cruel father, thou art the cause of my death!' Struck with this they flew to the door of Shaw's apartment and knocked – no answer was given. The knocking was repeated – still no answer. Suspicions had before been aroused against the father; they were now confirmed. A constable was summoned and an entrance forced. Catherine was found weltering in her own blood, the fatal knife by her side. She was still alive, but speechless. On questioning her whether she owed her death to her father, she made an apparent affirmative motion with her head and expired.

Just at the critical moment William Shaw returned and

entered the room. All eyes were on him. He saw his neighbours and a constable in his apartment, and seemed much disordered thereat. But at the sight of his daughter he turned pale, trembled and was ready to sink. Initial surprise and subsequent horror left little doubt of his guilt in the minds of the onlookers, and even that was dispelled on the constable discovering blood on the shirt Shaw was wearing.

He was instantly hurried before a magistrate, and upon the depositions of all the parties, committed to prison on suspicion of murder. He was shortly brought to trial and in his defence acknowledged having confined his daughter to prevent her intercourse with Lawson; and admitted that he frequently insisted on her marrying Robertson. He told the court he had quarrelled with her on the evening she was found murdered, as Morrison had deposed, but he averred that he left his daughter unharmed and untouched, and that the blood on his shirt was there in consequence of him having cut himself some days before and the bandage come undone. These assertions did not weigh with the jury when compared to the strong circumstantial evidence of the daughter's expressions of 'barbarity, cruelty, death', and of 'cruel father, thou art the cause of my death' – together with the apparently affirmative motion of her head and of the blood found on the father's shirt. On these several concurring circumstances William Shaw was found guilty and executed, and was hanged in chains at Leith Walk in November, 1721.

In August 1722 a man who had become possessor of the late William Shaw's apartment was rummaging by chance in the chamber where Catherine Shaw died, and accidentally perceived a paper which had fallen into a cavity on one side of the chimney. It was folded as a letter which, on being opened, contained the following:

Barbarous Father, – Your cruelty in having put it out of my power ever to join my fate to that of the only man I could love, and tyrannically insisting upon my marrying one who I always hated, has made me form a resolution to put an end to an existence which is become a burden to me. I doubt not I shall find mercy in another world; for surely no benevolent being can require that I should any longer live in torment to myself! My death I lay to your charge; when you read this, consider yourself as the inhuman wretch that plunged the murderous knife into the bosom of this unhappy

Catherine Shaw.

The letter being shown, the handwriting was recognised and avowed by friends and relations to be Catherine Shaw's. The magistracy of Edinburgh, on a scrutiny, being convinced of its authenticity, ordered the body of William Shaw to be taken from the gibbet and given to his family for interment; and as the only reparation to his memory and the honour of his surviving relations, they caused a pair of colours to be flown over his grave, in token of his innocence.

(The Newgate Calendar)

Martin Clench and James Mackley

On Sunday 7 May 1797, Sydney Fryer, Esq, a gentleman of considerable property, called by appointment on his cousin, Miss Ann Fryer, who resided in Shepherd Street, in order to take a walk with her in the environs of London to visit their aunt. When they had proceeded across the fields to the back part of Islington Workhouse they heard, as they thought, a female voice in distress; upon which Mr Fryer, contrary to his cousin's advice, leaped over the hedge into the field whence the voice seemed to proceed. But instead of seeing a woman he met with three men who, upon him rashly drawing his tuck-stick (the sword of which fell out), fired and wounded him a little above the left eye, and he fell into a small pond. One of the villains took the watch out of his pocket and a purse from the lady, and another took her cloak. Mr Fryer died two hours later.

Several were taken up on suspicion and strictly examined in the presence of Miss Fryer, but dismissed for want of evidence. On 27 May the Worship Street officers apprehended Clench, Mackley and one Smith, a chip-hat maker; no criminality being detected in Smith he was discharged, and the other two fully committed.

The prisoners were most impartially tried by Mr Justice Grose. They had four eminent counsel, so that no effort was wanting to plead their case effectually to the jury. Indeed, there was no positive evidence except Miss Fryer's, who swore to the two prisoners' identities. The jury, having retired half an hour, returned with a verdict of guilty. The two men were accordingly executed and their bodies were publicly exposed in a stable in Little Bridge Street, near Apothecaries' Hall.

A short time before the white caps were drawn over their eyes on the scaffold, the platform, by some improper construction, suddenly went down with two clergymen, the executioner, and his assistant. The Catholic priest who attended Clench, being very lusty, suffered most. When the two men died, most of the people were of the opinion that their fate was just. But soon after, the confessions of three separate criminals, who could have had no interest in taking the crime upon themselves, threw a different light upon the transaction, and recalled to mind the strong assertions which Clench and Mackley had made of their innocence. Clench, upon leaving the dock, offered thanks to the court for the fairness of his trial but observed (not in a rough way) that, though they were condemned to die, and be teased afterwards (alluding to their dissection), they were no more guilty of murder than their prosecutors.

A man named Burton Wood, who was afterwards executed at Kennington Common, and another, while under sentence of death wrote a letter to Carpenter Smith, Esq, magistrate of Surrey, declaring the innocence of Clench and Mackley, for they were themselves, with another not then in custody, guilty of the murder. Not long after, the third man, named Timms, was executed at Reading for another offence, and made the same confession.

Elizabeth Fenning

Who in 1815, while employed as a cook in the Turner household, made the family a plate of dumplings which were later found to be heavily impregnated with arsenic. Though Elizabeth herself had partaken of the dumplings and suffered severely, as soon as she was recovered she was confined to Newgate Gaol and eventually brought to trial 'for administering Arsenic to Orlebar Turner, Robert Gregson Turner, and Charlotte Turner, with intent the said persons to kill and murder'. She pleaded not guilty, and after a trial remarkable for its bias and vindictiveness Elizabeth Fenning was convicted and sentenced to death. The Turner family themselves did not believe in Elizabeth's guilt, and Orlebar Turner as head of the house was more than willing to sign the petition for her reprieve – until he was advised by the judge that this may cast suspicion on the family. It transpired that two witnesses of impeccable character had already approached the judge and informed him that for some time Robert Turner had exhibited all the symptoms of mental derangement, and had visited them a little time previously in a most violent state and pleaded with them to have him confined to an asylum: 'Do so, for God's sake, for, if I'm at liberty I shall do some mischief; I shall destroy myself and my wife; I must and shall do it, unless all means of destruction are moved out of my way; therefore do, my good friends, have me put under some restraint; something from above tells me I must do it, and unless I am prevented I certainly shall.' It was also pointed out that it had been Robert who had bought a packet of white arsenic which had disappeared a fortnight before the incident of the dumplings. Elizabeth Fenning was duly hanged at Tyburn.

Job Cox

Job Cox was a postman in the service of the General Post Office, and was charged with removing a letter entrusted to him for delivery and stealing its contents. On the 18th of March 1833, a Mr Foreman of Grafton Street, Dublin, sent a letter containing a ten-pound bank-note to his brother, Mr H. Foreman, in Queen Street, London, which, however, never reached its destination. Inquiry was made at the post office, and Cox was found to have signed a book in the ordinary way as having received the letter. It was subsequently ascertained that he had paid the same bank-note to Mr Lott, a publican in Lambeth, who had given him change for it. Cox was taken into custody and at the ensuing sessions at the Old Bailey he was tried and convicted of the offence and on the 20th of May, 1833, he received sentence of death according to the requirements of the Act of Parliament. At this time it was the practice for the Recorder of London to report to His Majesty in Council the cases of the various prisoners in custody upon whom sentence of death had been passed. The case of Cox was reported, with others, and upon the return of the learned Recorder to London he made it known to the prisoner that his execution was directed to take place. The unhappy wretch had looked forward with confidence to a reprieve, and so received this news with deep dismay. He was told to prepare for death, and the reverend Ordinary of the jail proceeded to pay him those attentions usually expected at his hands.

However, a blunder of a most extraordinary nature was soon discovered to have been made, which was thus described in a newspaper of 23rd June:

On Thursday morning Sir Thomas Denman, Lord Chief Justice of the King's Bench, on casting his eyes on a newspaper saw it reported that Job Cox was ordered for execution on Tuesday. His Lordship thought the statement had been published from false information, and he adverted to the circumstances in the presence of one of his under-sheriffs, as of a very mischievous nature. The under-sheriff, in some surprise, observed to his Lordship that the paragraph was correct – that the Recorder's warrant had been received on Wednesday evening at Newgate and notice had been sent to the prisoner and to the sheriff and other officials. 'What!' said Sir Thomas, 'Cox ordered for execution! Impossible! I was myself one of the Privy Council present when the report was made, and I know that no warrant for the execution of anyone was ordered. Cox was ordered to be put into solitary confinement and kept to hard labour until he be transported for life – which was the sentence to which his judgement to die was commuted.' The under-sheriff repeated the extraordinary information to his Lordship, who instantly requested he apply to the Secretary of State's office where he would be reassured of the facts and receive an order of contradiction to the learned Recorder's warrant. It is needless to say that the under-sheriff, who was extremely glad to be the bearer of such good tidings to a poor unhappy fellow-creature, speedily went about his mission. Consequently, Lord Melbourne countermanded the warrant, and needless to say Cox, on learning of the mistake felt full relief of heart.

The Recorder, Mr Newman Knowlys, was immediately called upon to explain this very remarkable error into which he had fallen. And when they had heard his excuse, the honourable members of the Common Hall of the City of London 'resolved unanimously, with feelings of deepest horror and regret, that the life of Job Cox, a convict under sentence of death in Newgate, had well-nigh been sacrificed by the act of the Recorder in sending down a warrant for his execution, notwithstanding his Majesty had graciously exercised his Royal Prerogative of mercy'.

They also resolved that the Recorder must, in charity, be said to have acted under the influence of 'mental infirmity incident to his advanced age', but nevertheless it was the Common Hall's opinion that the Recorder 'ought forthwith to retire from an office which, from whatever cause, he was incompetent to discharge'. Thus, after serving the City for forty-seven years Mr Knowlys resigned the office of Recorder.

(The Newgate Calendar)

Serafino Pelizzioni

It was around Christmas time in 1856 that Pelizzioni became involved in a drunken brawl between some of his Italian compatriots and a group of Englishmen in the Golden Anchor in Great Saffron Hill, London. At the end of the fight two Englishmen were found to have been seriously stabbed, and one of them, Michael Harrington, died of his wounds the same night. Pelizzioni (who had in fact been trying to stop the trouble) was arraigned at the Old Bailey charged with murder; he was found guilty and sentenced to death. Meanwhile the real killer – a man named Gregorio Monghi – had been persuaded to give himself up, which he did at Kings Cross police station. The police, however, thought this to be a ruse to save Pelizzioni's life and refused to prosecute. Eventually a private prosecution was brought against Monghi, and his plea of self-defence in the matter of Harrington's stabbing was accepted. Pelizzioni was granted a stay of execution in order that he might be retried; after a gruelling three days in the dock of the Old Bailey he was finally found not guilty and released – a man who had had a very lucky escape! Baron Martin, the judge who had passed the original death sentence on Pelizzioni, stated: 'The evidence was about the clearest and most direct that, after a long course of experience of criminal justice, I have ever known.'

Oscar Slater

On 21 December 1908 Miss Marion Gilchrist was found battered to death in her flat at 14 Queen's Terrace, Glasgow; she had been robbed of a crescent-shaped diamond brooch. On Christmas Day the police were informed that a man by the name of Oscar Slater had been trying to sell a pawn ticket for a crescent-shaped diamond brooch. By this time Slater had emigrated to the United States and had to be extradited to face trial. It turned out that the diamond brooch in question was not the one that had belonged to Miss Gilchrist, and besides it had been pawned a month before her death. Nevertheless, on the flimsiest of identifications, Oscar Slater was convicted by a majority verdict and sentenced to death.

In the event his sentence was commuted and he was sent to Peterhead Gaol where he remained for the next eighteen years. During this time a tireless campaign was launched to secure his release, led by no less a popular figure than Sir Arthur Conan Doyle. Eventually a court of appeal quashed the sentence, and Oscar Slater was awarded £6,000 for wrongful imprisonment and the anguish suffered while under sentence of death.

Edith Thompson

Accused in 1922 with her young lover, Frederick Bywaters, of conspiring to murder her husband Percy. Although the killing was entirely Freddie's idea, and only Freddie carried out the attack, Edith Thompson – who, as an adultress, was popularly considered little better than a murderer – was convicted and executed.

Walter Graham Rowland

On the morning of Sunday, 20 October 1946, the body of Olive Balchin was found on a bomb site in Manchester's Deansgate; she had been bludgeoned about the head with a hammer. Subsequently, Rowland was taken into custody, tried and convicted of her murder. While Rowland awaited execution, David John Ware – a prisoner in Liverpool Gaol – claimed he had murdered Olive Balchin. A Home Office inquiry decided that there had been no miscarriage of justice, and Walter Rowland was executed on 27 February 1947. In November 1951 David Ware was arrested on a charge of attempted murder at Bristol. He told police: 'I have killed a woman. I keep having this urge to hit women on the head.' He was found guilty but insane.

Timothy John Evans

Accused in 1949 of the murder of his wife Beryl and their daughter Geraldine. Evans had confessed, but later retracted this confession, accusing John Christie (another resident of the soon to be notorious 10 Rillington Place) of killing his wife while performing an abortion. Tim Evans was found guilty and hanged on 9 March 1950. Three years later Christie was proved to have been responsible for the deaths of seven women, among them his wife and, on his own admission, Beryl Evans. John Christie was hanged at Pentonville on 15 July 1953. In 1966 Timothy Evans was granted a much overdue posthumous pardon.

Knout
(see **Flagellation**)

L

Lead Sprinkler

In a ghastly parody of the holy-water sprinkler beloved of High Church ceremony, this device was like a ball-shaped ladle, half of the cup being perforated with small holes. The undrilled half of the cup was then filled with molten lead, and with a flick of the wrist the executioner could release on to the bare body of his captive a shower of searing droplets that would burn their way into his flesh. Lead could be replaced – according to whim or inclination – by boiling oil, molten pitch or even boiling water.

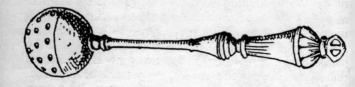

Lethal Injection

The conscience-salving quest for a 'humane' method of judicial execution led to the making of legal history in December 1982, when the first execution by 'lethal injection' was carried out (though the method had been officially adopted by the states of Oklahoma and Texas as early as 1977). The victim of this experiment was a 40-year-old black man named Charlie Brooks who had been convicted in 1976 of killing David Gregory, a secondhand-car salesman of Fort Worth.

Brooks was to be the first person executed in Texas for eighteen years, and the case caused widespread controversy both on legal and ethical grounds. Brooks's partner in the shooting, Woody Lourdres, had his original conviction and death sentence overturned as the result of a legal technicality – the jury had been incorrectly selected – and subsequently Lourdres plea-bargained himself a 40-year term of imprisonment. As it was unclear which of the men fired the fatal shot, there was an obvious unfairness in two different sentences for the same conviction on the same set of evidence.

The American medical profession was strongly opposed to the practice of doctors administering lethal injections and their Association issued a statement saying that 'The use of a lethal injection as a means of terminating the life of a convict is not the practice of medicine. A physician who accepts the task of performing an execution on behalf of the State obviously does not enhance the image of the medical profession . . . This is not an appropriate role for a physician.' In September 1981, the Secretary-General of the World Medical Association issued this statement as part of a press release: 'Acting as an executioner is not the practice of medicine and a physician's services are not required to carry out capital punishment even if the methodology utilizes pharmacologic agents or equipment that might otherwise be used in the practice of medicine. The physician's only role would be to certify death once the state had carried out the execution.' In the end it was 'medical technicians' from the staff of the Medical Director of the Texas Department of Corrections, overseen by a doctor, who performed the first 'operation'.

Strapped to a hospital trolley, Brooks was wheeled into the execution room (formerly a gas chamber) at Huntsville Prison. While the prisoner was awaiting execution, his lawyers had been appealing to a judge of the Fifth Circuit Court of Appeals to reverse its earlier refusal to grant a stay. After hastily convening a telephone jury, the court reconfirmed at a few minutes to midnight that it would not grant a stay.

Just after midnight the condemned man's arm was bound to a padded board and his veins examined by the

doctor to ensure that they were large enough to take the injection catheter. (This is a particular problem in subjects who have been habitual drug users, where veins may be weak and scarred, requiring surgery to expose a deeper vein.) The needle was inserted into his vein and attached to a rubber tube which went across the floor and through a hole in the wall to the executioner's chamber.

Among the witnesses in the death house was Brooks's girlfriend, 27-year-old nurse Vanessa Sapp. After the couple had exchanged some final affectionate words the condemned man was joined by two Islamic priests who accompanied him in a brief Muslim service.

At 12.07 a.m. a dose of the barbiturate drug sodium thiopental was added to the intravenous saline drip which had already been started to keep the vein open. Brooks was observed to clench his fist, raise his head and appear to yawn or gasp for breath before falling into unconsciousness. The second ingredient of the deadly cocktail was added – pancuronium bromide, a muscle relaxant used in sufficient quantity to paralyse the lungs; and then the third – potassium chloride to induce cardiac arrest. At 12.16 Charlie Brooks was pronounced dead.

The claim that lethal injection provided the state with a speedy and painless way of disposing of its condemned prisoners was met with a mixed reaction from the medical profession and interested laymen from the very beginning, and experience with upwards of forty prisoners since 1982 has done nothing to allay the fears of the abolitionist lobby. Death results from the injection into a vein of the arm of a succession of lethal drugs. The problem of finding a suitable vein in some inmates has already been mentioned and a case has been cited in Texas in 1985 where no less than 23 attempts were made to find a vein, taking forty minutes during which the condemned man was strapped to the trolley. Complications can also arise from the simple eventuality of the prisoner resenting his undignified end to such an extent as to struggle; in this case the poison could be injected into a main artery or into the muscle, causing considerable pain. In another instance reported by Amnesty International in its vital report *When the State Kills . . .* (London, 1989), during the execution by lethal injection of Raymond Landry in December 1988, the tube feeding the needle became detached and the poisonous mixture spurted across the room towards the witnesses. According to the Texas Attorney-General: 'There was more pressure in the hose than his veins could absorb.'

Although it is certainly the most 'modern' of all the official methods of judicial execution, the concept of lethal injection had been under serious discussion in America for almost a hundred years before its first use. In March 1888 the *Medico-Legal Journal* published an extensive paper by J. Mount Bleyer MD of New York entitled 'Best Method of Executing Criminals', the result of research undertaken on behalf of the then Governor of New York with the aim of 'rendering the infliction of the death penalty less offensive to the humane sentiments of the age':

Death by Morphine Injection
Equally painless is death by hypodermic injection of morphine; and in other respects this method of destroying life seems to be eminently suitable to be employed in capital executions. Hypodermic, or Subcutaneous Injection is a simple method of introducing into the circulation certain drugs, especially anodynes. The details of a capital execution by morphine injection would be as follows:

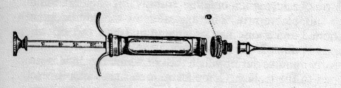

At the appointed time the sheriff, accompanied by two deputies and the citizens prescribed by statute, enters the cell of the convict, who is lying on a couch. The sheriff administers six grains of sulphate of morphine under the skin of the felon who, in a few moments, begins to be drowsy. Soon he is overpowered with sleep, and the officer, to make doubly secure, repeats the dose. Within half an hour the heart has ceased to beat and the man is dead, having passed away without pain, convulsion, struggle or consciousness. The advantages of this method are its certainty, its painlessness, the freedom from the chance of horrible displays, the reduction of the dramatic element to a minimum, and its inexpensiveness.
1. No one will dispute the certainty of the result. If anybody fears that the dose is too small, it can be repeated over and over again, so that the end may be greatly hastened. There is no possibility of the rejection of the poison.

2. No suffering is caused to the condemned man, for the slight sting of the hypodermic injection is unworthy to be called pain.

3. There are no convulsions, no decapitation, none of the hideous phenomena that often attend a hanging; the man simply goes to sleep never to wake.

4. Many of the criminals who are condemned to death, finding that a change of punishment is impossible, make the most of their situation and try to glorify themselves in the eyes of their friends by 'dying game' on the gallows, and carrying themselves jauntily on the threshold of eternity. The exclusion of the public from executions has greatly diminished the opportunities for spectacular display, but the quiet and seclusion of the cell in which the fatal dose of morphine is taken reduces these chances to their very lowest terms. A villain on the scaffold, in full possession of his faculties, anticipating instant extinction, may appear heroic; the same man submitting to the trivial puncture of a hypodermic, and presently becoming too stupid to keep his eyes open, is far less likely to consider himself, or be thought by others, a hero.

5. The cost of erecting the gallows is considerable; that of a hypodermic syringe and morphine insignificant. It may be a small matter to discuss, but after the State has been at the expense which a murder trial usually costs, generally paying the fees of the defendant's counsel as well as those of the prosecution, it is not improper to desire that the last act of the tragedy may be as inexpensive as possible.

And in post-war Britain there was a serious suggestion of combining both the injection and the inhalation of drugs. In the *British Medical Journal* of 27 December 1947,

Lieutenant-Colonel John Carrey IMS (Retd) wrote:
'. . . I cannot see why shooting, decapitation or electrocution should produce the required result more speedily.
If reform is required rather than abolition, the possibility
of intravenous injection of thiopentone followed by prolonged chloroform inhalation might be considered.'

Lynching

Despite the notional triumph of justice and equality
resulting from the success of the Union forces during the
American Civil War, Reconstruction brought with it a
heavy backlash, particularly from the Southern states,
where white supremacy began to be upheld by the increasingly desperate means of *ad hoc* illegal executions, or
lynchings. Between 1882, when the earliest records were
kept, and 1927, 4,951 people were lynched. Although the
majority of these summary executions – particularly those
that took place in the North and West of the Union –
were by simple hanging or shooting many of those in the
Southern states were characterised by a quite appalling
level of sadism and gratuitous cruelty. In 1893, for
example, a mob of upwards of ten thousand spectators
gathered at Paris, Texas, many travelling from miles
around to witness the lynching of a mentally retarded
black man accused of killing a small child. First red-hot
pokers were pushed into his body; then his eyes were
burned out, and flaming brands forced down his throat.
After almost an hour of this torture, the unfortunate man
was burned alive. Although the increasing urbanisation
of the South and the greater effectiveness of the National
Guard in controlling the savage mobs led to a gradual
decrease in unlawful executions in the first years of the
twentieth century, there are still sufficient records to show
that there were isolated pockets of the community where
lynch law continued to govern the relationships between
whites and blacks. In 1918, in a five-day orgy of mob
violence in Georgia, eight blacks were murdered, one of
them a pregnant woman who was slowly roasted alive and

her baby cut from her womb and trampled by the crowd; two others were burned to death for no greater crime than allegedly 'talking back' to whites. More terrible perhaps, was the news that as late as 1987 the scourge of lynching had still not been eradicated in the South. In February of that year an all-white Alabama jury awarded $7 million to the mother of Michael Donald, a nineteen-year-old black who had been beaten and strangled to death and his body left hanging from a tree by members of the local chapter of the Ku Klux Klan. In what may have been an overoptimistic assessment of the verdict, State Senator Mr Michael Figures was reported as saying: 'This is a landmark ruling which will make sure the Donald death was the last Klan lynching.' Sure enough, just three years later, in October 1990, an award was made for $2.5 million against a former Ku Klux Klan chief for allegedly inciting the killing of a black man in Portland, Oregon.

Lynching at Memphis
The following is an eye-witness account of a lynching that took place on 22 July 1893. It was written by Ida Wells-Barnett, who was editor of a black Memphis newspaper until she was herself driven out by the mob in 1892, and became a life-long public campaigner against lynching:

Memphis is one of the queen cities of the south, with a population of about seventy thousand souls – easily one of the twenty largest, most progressive and wealthiest cities of the United States. And yet in its streets there occurred a scene of such shocking savagery which would have disgraced the Congo. No woman was harmed, no serious indignity suffered. Two women driving to town in a wagon were suddenly accosted by Lee Walker. He claimed that he demanded something to eat. The women claimed that he attempted to assault them. They gave such an alarm that he ran away. At once the dispatches spread over the entire country that a big, burly

Negro had brutally assaulted two women. Crowds began to search for the alleged fiend. While hunting him they shot another Negro dead in his tracks for refusing to stop when ordered to do so. After a few days Lee Walker was found and put in jail in Memphis until the mob was ready for him.

The *Memphis Commercial* of Sunday, 23 July, contains a full account of the tragedy from which the following extracts are made:

At 12 o'clock last night, Lee Walker, who attempted to outrage Miss Mollie McCadden last Tuesday morning, was taken from the county jail and hanged to a telegraph pole just north of the prison. All day rumours were afloat that with nightfall an attack would be made upon the jail, and as everybody anticipated that a vigorous resistance would be made, a conflict between the mob and the authorities was feared.

At 10 o'clock Captain O'Haver, Sergeant Horan and several patrolmen were on hand, but they could do nothing with the crowd. An attack by the mob was made on the door in the south wall and it yielded. Sheriff McLendon and several of his men threw themselves into the breach, but two or three of the storming party shoved by. They were seized by the police but not subdued, the officers refraining from using their clubs. The entire mob might at first have been dispersed by ten policemen who would use their clubs, but the sheriff insisted that no violence be done.

The mob got an iron rail and used it as a battering ram against the lobby doors. Sheriff McLendon tried to stop them, and one of the mob knocked him down with a chair. Still he counselled moderation and would not order his deputies or the police to disperse the crowd by force. The pacific policy of the sheriff impressed the mob with the idea that the officers were afraid, or at least would do them no harm, and they redoubled their efforts, urged on by a big switchman. At 12 o'clock the door of the prison was broken in with the rail.

Walker made a desperate resistance. Two men entered his cell first and ordered him to come forth. He refused, and they failing to drag him out, others entered. He scratched and bit his assailants, wounding several of them severely with his teeth. The mob retaliated by striking and cutting him with fists and knives. When he reached the steps leading down to the door he made another stand and was stabbed again and again. By the time he reached the lobby his power to resist was gone, and he was shoved along through the mob of yelling, cursing men and boys, who beat, spat upon and slashed the wretch-like demon.

The mob proceeded north on Front Street with the victim, stopping at Sycamore Street to get a rope from the grocery. 'Take him to the iron bridge on Main Street,' yelled several men. The men who had hold of the Negro were in a hurry to finish the job, however, and when they reached the telephone pole at the corner of Front Street and the first alley north of Sycamore they stopped. A hastily improvised noose was slipped over the Negro's head, and several young men mounted a pile of lumber near the pole and threw the rope over one of the stepping pins. The Negro was lifted up until his feet were three feet above the ground, the rope was made taut, and a corpse dangled in midair. A big fellow who helped lead the mob pulled the Negro's legs until his neck cracked. The wretch's clothes had been torn off, and as he swung, the man who pulled his legs mutilated the corpse. One or two knife cuts more or less did not make much difference in the appearance of the dead rapist, however, for before the rope was around his neck his skin was cut almost to ribbons. One pistol shot was fired while the corpse was hanging. A dozen voices protested against the use of fire-arms, and there was no more shooting.

The body was permitted to hang for half an hour,
then it was cut down . . . The body fell in a ghastly
heap, and the crowd laughed at the sound and
crowded round the prostrate body, a few kicking
the inanimate carcass . . . Then someone raised the
cry of 'Burn him!' It was quickly taken up and soon
resounded from a hundred throats. Detective
Richardson, for a long time single-handed, stood
the crowd off. He talked and begged the men not
to bring disgrace on the city by burning the body,
arguing that all the vengeance possible had been
wrought.

While this was going on a small crowd was busy
starting a fire in the middle of the street. The
material was handy. Some bundles of staves were
taken from a nearby lumber yard for kindling. Heavier wood was obtained from the same source, and
coal oil from a neighboring grocery. Then the cries
of 'Burn him! Burn him!' were redoubled.

Half a dozen men seized the naked body. The
crowd cheered. They marched to the fire and, giving
the body a swing, it was landed in the middle of the
flames. There was a cry for more wood as the fire
had begun to die owing to the long delay. Willing
hands procured the wood, and it was piled up on
the Negro, almost for a time obscuring him from
view. The head was in plain view, as also were the
limbs, and one arm which stood out high above the
body, the elbow crooked – held in that position by
a stick of wood. In a few moments the hands began
to swell, then came great blisters all over the
exposed parts of the body; then in places the flesh
was burned away and the bones began to show
through. It was a horrible sight, one which perhaps
no one there had ever witnessed before. It proved
too much for a large part of the crowd, and the
majority of the mob left very shortly before the
burning began.

But a large number stayed, and were not a bit set

back by the sight of a human body being burned to ashes. Two or three white women, accompanied by their escorts, pushed to the front to obtain an unobstructed view, and looked on with astonishing coolness and nonchalance. One man and woman brought a little girl, not over twelve years old, apparently their daughter, to view a scene which was calculated to drive sleep from the child's eyes for many nights, if not produce a permanent injury to her nervous system. The comments of the crowd were varied. Some remarked on the efficacy of this style of cure for rapists, others rejoiced that men's wives and daughters were now safe from the wretch. Some laughed as the flesh cracked and blistered, and while a large number pronounced the burning of a dead body as a useless episode, not in all that throng was a word of sympathy for the wretch himself.

The rope that was used to hang the Negro, and also that which was used to lead him from the jail, were eagerly sought by relic hunters. They almost fought for a chance to cut off a piece of rope, and in an incredibly short time both ropes had disappeared and were scattered into the pockets of the crowd in sections of from one inch to six inches long. Others of the relic hunters remained until the ashes cooled sufficiently to obtain such ghastly relics as the teeth, nails and bits of charred skin of the immolated victim of his own lust. After burning the body the mob tied a rope around the charred trunk and dragged it down Main Street to the court house, where it was hanged to a center pole. The rope broke and the corpse dropped with a thud, but it was again hoisted, the charred legs barely touching the ground. The teeth were knocked out and the finger nails cut off as souvenirs. The crowd made so much noise that the police interfered. Undertaker Walsh was telephoned for, who took charge of the body and carried it to his establishment, where it was prepared for burial in the potter's field today.

Maiden

According to the historian Pennant, the Maiden, an early Scottish form of **guillotine**, was based on the design of the **Halifax Gibbet** 'introduced by the Regent Morton, who took a model of it as he passed through Halifax, and at length suffered by it himself. It is in the form of a painter's easel and about ten feet high; at four feet from the bottom is a cross bar on which the felon lays his head, which is kept down by another placed above. In the inner edges of the frame are grooves; in these is placed a sharp axe, with a vast weight of lead, supported at the very summit by a peg. To that peg is tied a cord which the executioner cutting, the axe falls and does the affair effectually, without suffering the unhappy criminal to undergo a repetition of strokes, as has been the case in the common method.'

James Douglas, fourth Earl of Morton, was Regent of Scotland for James VI between 1572 and 1580. A Protestant, Morton was at the hub of a series of conspiracies against Mary Queen of Scots, took part in the murder of her favourite, the Italian musician David Rizzio, and was involved in the death of Lord Darnley, Mary's Consort. The tables turned when a group of Scottish noblemen plotted his removal from the Regency, and Morton was forced to seize Stirling Castle and with it the young king. He was finally removed when he was convicted of the murder of Darnley and, ironically, executed on his own Maiden.

Sir Walter Scott recorded in his *History of Scotland* (1830): 'He met his death with the same determined courage that he had often displayed in battle; and it was remarked with interest by the common people that he suffered decapitation by a rude guillotine of the period which he himself during his administration had introduced into Scotland from Halifax.'

Mantles

The punishment for anti-social drunkenness was subject to many ingenious variations on the wearing of a 'barrel'. At its most prosaic, a hole was cut in one end of an actual barrel, and the bibber's head put through it, so that he might be paraded through the streets, wearing the barrel like a cloak, for all to witness his shame.

An elaborate refinement appeared as the Drunk's Mantle (sometimes called the 'Spanish' Mantle). In shape it was like a long barrel, slightly larger at the bottom than at the top, made of wood and metal. At the back there was a door, and at the top an iron-bound opening for the victim's head, over which a metal helmet was locked with a grille at the front.

The length of time that an offender was imprisoned in this heavy mantle varied with the seriousness of the crime. It has been observed that for a short man the punishment is really quite mild, requiring him merely to stand patiently until his imprisonment was over. But a tall person would be uncomfortably bowed down by the weight, causing painful pressure on the knees.

Similar cloaks, or mantles, have been recorded throughout Europe, and the historian John Evelyn recorded in 1641 that 'In the Delft Senate House hangs a weighty vessel of wood, not unlike a butter churn, which the adventurous woman that hath two husbands at one time is to wear on her shoulders, her head peeping out of the top only, and so is led about the town as a penance for her incontinence.' And according to the prison reformer John Howard, 'In Denmark some criminals of the lower sort such as watchmen, coachmen, etc., are punished by being led through the city in what is called the Spanish Mantle; this method of punishment is particularly dreaded, and is one reason why night robberies are never heard of in Copenhagen.'

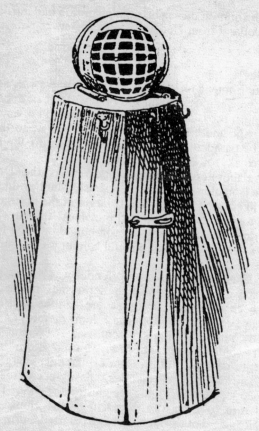

Spanish mantle

An intriguing theory has been advanced by the German historian F. T. Schulz that the infamous **Iron Maiden of Nuremberg** was originally an ordinary, if elaborate, 'mantle of infamy' to be used as a cloak of shame on drunken or promiscuous women; the spikes, Schulz suggests, were a later addition.

Masks of Shame

The public humiliation of those condemned as public nuisances took many forms, such as the **stocks** and the **pillory**, and the **scold's bridle**, but none were more imaginative

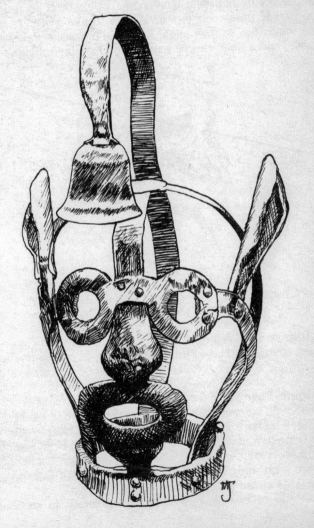

than the masks of shame. Rather after the style of the brank, these masks were designed to expose to ridicule those found guilty of boorish or quarrelsome behaviour, cheats and shrews, slanderers and cuckolds. For example, a man accused of swinish behaviour would be condemned to parade the streets in a mask shaped like a pig's head; an inquisitive woman might have had a mask with a long nose, and a quarrelsome one a large flapping tongue.

Mask worn by one reprieved from the death sentence

Military Punishments
(see **Roman Military Punishments**)

Mouth Pear

Although we may not entirely agree with one observer that 'Spaniards have always been noted for their cruelty', they do as a nation of torturers seem to have been prolific inventors of cruel devices. One of the most commonly used – not only in Spain but in other parts of Europe as well – was the mouth pear.

Made of iron, the 'pear' part was made in sections

cunningly hinged at the top so that when it was placed in
a prisoner's mouth and the end screw turned, the sections
opened out, forcing the victim's mouth open. Often it
would tear the lips and smash teeth, and some versions
contained an additional device within the pear for the
purpose of lacerating the tongue and throat.

Mudgett, Hermann Webster
(The Torture Doctor)

Born in New Hampshire in May 1860, Mudgett has been called America's worst mass killer. Whether or not he deserves this tribute, he was certainly one of that country's most prolific and inventive criminals.

Bigamist, swindler and multicide, the final total of Mudgett's killings will never be known; remains of as many as 200 corpses were found in the Chicago death-house known as 'Holmes Castle', though he had only got as far as detailing 27 of them before he was executed.

Hermann Mudgett studied medicine at Ann Arbor, and for a short while afterwards practised as a doctor in New York. After some misunderstanding with the law over the possession of corpses, Mudgett fled to Chicago where he entered employment with a drug company. The owner of the business, poor woman, disappeared mysteriously shortly after meeting Mudgett, and he repaid her memory by taking over the company. Actually, quite a lot of people whose paths crossed Hermann Mudgett's disappeared mysteriously – including a succession of mistresses and bigamous wives.

In 1891 the man now calling himself H. H. Holmes gave up the drug business and moved in to manage the bizarre hotel which he had commissioned to be built on a vacant lot on the corner of Chicago's 63rd Street. He had hired and fired his builders at such a rapid rate that none ever knew the exact layout of the building – which was how the labrynthine series of torture chambers remained a secret for so long. The hotel was visited by hundreds of guests, particularly during the period of the Chicago World's Fair, and many of them never checked out – at least not through the lobby. Particularly vulnerable were attractive young women, whom Holmes lured to his lair, seduced, and, after sexual intercourse, drugged and dispatched to the cellar via a specially constructed chute. Although the sequence varied according to whim or circumstance, most of the victims next found themselves in one of the air-tight gas chambers where they

Scenes from the life and crimes of Hermann Mudgett. Above: child victims beg piteously for mercy. Bottom: Mudgett arranges a tube attached to a gas supply into a hole in the top of the trunk

would choke their last breaths while Holmes watched through a glass panel. When they were dead, the girls were transported to the dissection room where the deadly doctor performed his 'experimental' surgery, disposing of the unwanted remains in one of the many acid baths, furnaces and quicklime pits.

It was, nevertheless, a careless insurance fraud committed in Texas that first drew official attention to H. H. Holmes (or H. M. Howard as he then was). Thanks to a crooked lawyer he was free once again, but by then he had come to the unwelcome notice of a tenacious detective named Geyer, who pursued his quarry through Pennsylvania, New Hampshire and Massachusetts. By this time Holmes had disposed of a former partner named Pitezel and the three Pitezel children, and run off with his wife. When the corpses were found in an Indianapolis rooming house, Holmes was taken into custody.

On 30 November 1895, Hermann Mudgett was sentenced to death for the murder of Benjamin Pitezel. Meanwhile, police had explored 'Torture Castle' and uncovered its grisly secrets. In the time that remained to him, Mudgett began a rambling memoir in which he was able to detail 27 of his murders before being executed on 27 May 1896. Contrary to the last, Mudgett retracted his confession at the foot of the gallows, claiming that his previous admissions were simply for the purpose of publicity – to give the newspapers a good story.

Necklacing

In the strife-torn east African nation of Mozambique in the 1990s, problems of daily life caused by a crumbling infrastructure have been compounded by its ill-fed, badly clothed and uncontrollable conscript army forming themselves into armed gangs which have been responsible for a huge escalation in urban crime. This in its turn has resulted in an unprecedentedly violent civilian backlash by residents who no longer have faith in their government's ability to control crime. Criminals – called 'ninjas' in local slang (after the popular martial arts films) – are summarily tried by *ad hoc* vigilante groups who also carry out death sentences. The most common punishment for convicted ninjas is 'necklacing', where a petrol-filled tyre is hung around a victim's neck and set on fire.

OPQ

Oakum Picking

A tedious and painful form of hard labour seemingly confined to the British prison system of the eighteenth and early nineteenth centuries. Oakum is the product of shredding 'junk', the name given to discarded lengths of tarred hemp from ships' cables and other ropes. During the days of Britain's mighty wooden-shipped navy, oakum was mixed with pitch to give the caulking that was pressed into the seams on the sides and decks of ships to seal them watertight. Vast quantities were used right up to the emergence of the first steel vessels.

At many prisons oakum picking was the sole means of employment for men, women and children, and vast oakum-picking sheds were attached to the penal buildings in which prisoners laboured hour after hour, their hands cut and bleeding from the coarse fibre and sharp fragments of tar. In Cold Bath Prison alone there was a shed capable of housing five hundred oakum pickers.

In his suite of engravings 'The Harlot's Progress' (1730), William Hogarth depicted his subject in Bridewell Prison beating 'junk' preparatory to picking. And more than a century later Mayhew and Binney (*Criminal Prisons of London*) described the scene in one gaol:

> On the side fitted with windows the dark forms of the warders are seen, each perched on a raised stool. The bright light shines on the faces of the criminals, and the officer keeps his eye rapidly moving in all directions to see that no talking takes place. The utter absence of noise struck us as absolutely terrible. The silence seems after a time almost intense enough to hear a flake of snow fall. Each picker has by his side his weighed quantity of old

rope, cut into lengths. Some of the pieces are white and sodden-looking as a washerwoman's hands, whilst others are hard and black with the tar upon them. The prisoner takes up a length of junk and untwists it, and when he has separated it into so many corkscrew strands he further unrolls them by sliding them backwards and forwards on his knee with the palm of his hand, until the meshes are loosened. Then the strand is further unravelled by placing it in the bend of a hook, fastened to the knees, and sawing it smartly to and fro, which soon removes the tar and grates the fibres apart. In this condition all that remains to be done is to loosen the hemp by pulling it out like cotton wool and the process is completed. By the rays of sunlight shining through the window you can see that the place is full of dust; the shoulders of the men, too, are covered with the brown dust almost as thickly as the shirt-front of a snuff-taker. A prisoner with a bright water-can is going the round, handing up drink to the warders, who gulp it down as if choked. As the day advanced, the pieces of old rope by the prisoners' sides disappeared bit by bit, and in their place the mound of treacle-brown oakum at their feet grew from the size of a scratch-wig to that of a large pumpkin. At length the men had all completed their tasks, and each sat holding on his knees his immense tar-covered ball, waiting his turn to go to the scales and have his pickings weighed.

Papal Inquisition
(see **Inquisition**)

Peine Forte et Dure
(see **Pressing to Death**)

Picketing

A punishment from the English army penal code, apparently confined to the artillery and cavalry. It was described by Captain Francis Grose in his *Military Antiquities* (1788):

A long post being driven into the ground, the delinquent was ordered to mount a stool near it, when his right hand was fastened to a hook in the post by

Picketing

a noose round his wrist drawn up as high as it could be stretched. A stump, the height of the stool, with its end cut to a round and blunt point, was then driven into the ground near the post before mentioned, and the stool being taken away, the bare heel of the sufferer was made to rest on this stump, which though it did not break the skin, put him to great torture.

The length of time that the victim was left in this perilous position was usually fifteen minutes, though this was frequently extended to suit either the seriousness of the offence or the sadistic temperament of individual officers. Indeed, so numerous were the injuries resulting from picketing that it was eventually abolished.

Pillie-Winkies
(see **Thumbscrew**)

Pillory
The exposure of nuisances and felons to public ridicule or vilification is one of humankind's oldest and most successful punishments. As with most forms of punishment which have evolved over the centuries, 'shaming' has undergone many variations and fashions. The categories that have been examined at length in this volume are **masks of shame**, **halters** and **mantles**, where the enforced wearing of a ridiculous mask or costume about the streets highlighted the prisoner's offence. **Branks** revealed the sharp-tongued and shrewish to the derision of neighbours, and a few hours of abuse in the **stocks** may well have persuaded many away from a continued career in petty crime. However, the most widely used device for painful and degrading exposure was the pillory, and although many other physical punishments such as **flagellation** have been associated with such captivity, it was primarily intended for the *display* of offenders.

The ancient Greeks had a special word for a pillory-type punishment, and the Romans may have had a similar device. Certainly in England the pillory predated the Norman Conquest, and the Anglo-Saxons had the word *healfang* ('stretch-neck') for it in at least the seventh century. The earliest form of pillory would have been a simple post, usually set up at a crossroads by the lord of the manor, who was obliged to provide and maintain the pillory. Attached to the post was a chain, and at the end of the chain a metal collar by which the offender was secured. An almost identical punishment survived in Scotland as the **jougs**. As the pillory evolved it lost the collar, and at the top of the post instead gained a cross-beam of wood – rather like a sign-board. This cross-piece was in two halves, the upper of which hinged open to admit the head and two wrists of the prisoner through carved holes. When he was thus installed, the upper board was lowered and padlocked, leaving the unhappy victim prey to the rabble who had gathered to enjoy his humiliation.

Originally the pillory was a punishment reserved almost exclusively for forgers, perjurers, fraudulent traders, etcetera. However, by the sixteenth century, in England at least, it had become a catch-all punishment applied to both men and women for any number of petty offences and nuisances. At this time it was often preceded by whipping, and sometimes combined with the wearing of **masks of shame** and **scold's bridles**, so that the victim could be presented in a public place for as long as the sentence was required to last. Less frequently other, more gruesome torments were added. It is known that in 1570, one Timothy Pendredd was convicted of counterfeiting the writs and seals of the Court of the Queen's Bench in order to have two people falsely arrested. The judgement against him was that he should be put into the Cheapside (London) pillory on two successive market days; on the first occasion his left ear was nailed to the pillory 'so that he be compelled by his own proper motion' to pull the ear from his head. The punishment was repeated on the next market day with Pendredd's right ear.

In the following century England would see a new and sinister use of the pillory as a tool for punishing religious and political dissent, and in particular the authors of inflamatory pamphlets. One of the most famous of this category was the creator of *Robinson Crusoe*. For publishing *The Shortest Way with the Dissenters* Daniel Defoe was sentenced in 1703 to be fined and exposed in the pillory on three separate occasions. Defoe was pilloried at Cheapside and at the Temple, but so great was his popularity with the common mob that instead of pelting him with filth, they garlanded Defoe with flowers, and drank his good health and long life while joining in a few choruses of 'Ode to the Pillory', which he had composed while in prison.

Not all victims of the pillory were so lucky, and when John Waller (also called John Trevor) was exposed in Seven Dials in 1732 it cost him his life. Waller had been convicted of falsely accusing innocent men of being highway robbers in order to secure the rewards for their capture. So despicable was this crime in the eyes of the assembled crowd that as Waller stood helpless they pelted him to death. Twenty years later four true highwaymen and murderers – James Egan, James Salmon, John Berry and Stephen M'Daniel – were sentenced to the pillory, ironically for the same crime of false accusation for reward. It must be remembered that at this time, 1752, there was no organised police force and only a rudimentary watch; Justices of the Peace and the general public relied on the professional 'thief-taker'. These men, among whom the most notorious was Jonathan Wilde, were almost always crooks themselves, and took dishonour among thieves to the level of a fine art, both blackmailing other criminals and falsely accusing innocent men. In the case of James Egan *et al*, the two young men they accused were convicted and sentenced to death. The gang were later taken up for their cynical crimes, tried, found guilty, and sentenced at the Old Bailey:

. . . to be punished in the following manner: Berry

and M'Daniel to stand in the pillory once at the end
of Hatton Garden, in Holborn, and once at the end
of King Street, in Cheapside; Salmon and Egan to
stand once in the middle of West Smithfield, and
the second time at the end of Fetter Lane, in Fleet
Street; and all to be imprisoned in Newgate for the

Egan and Salmon in the Smithfield pillory

space of seven years; and upon the expiration of that time not to be discharged without finding sureties to be bound in the penalties of a thousand pounds each for their good behaviour for the seven following years.

On the 5th of March, 1756, M'Daniel and Berry were set in the pillory at the end of Hatton Garden, and were so severely treated by the populace that their lives were thought to be in danger. Egan and Salmon were taken to Smithfield on Monday, the 8th of the same month, amidst a surprising concourse of people, who no sooner saw the offenders exposed in the pillory than they pelted them with stones, brickbats, potatoes, dead dogs and cats, and other things. The constables now interposed; but being soon overpowered, the offenders were left wholly to the mercy of an enraged mob. The blows they received caused their heads to swell to an enormous size; and by people hanging to the skirts of their clothes they were nearly strangled. They had been in the pillory about half-an-hour when a stone struck Egan on his head and he immediately expired. The sheriffs fearing that should the survivors be again exposed to the vengeance of an enraged people they would share the fate of their companion in iniquity, the remainder of the sentence of pillory was on that account remitted; but the length of their sentence of imprisonment, added to the great amount of the sureties for their good behaviour after the expiration thereof, might have been considered tantamount to imprisonment for life – a fate well suited to such mischievous, hard-hearted and unrelenting villains. They, however, soon died in Newgate.

(*The Newgate Calendar*)

At one stage there was hardly a village green or market square which did not boast its pillory; indeed, many can still be seen *in situ*, such as those at Wallingford and Coleshill. Others, for reasons of preservation, have been taken into the care of local museums, and fine examples can be seen at Brighton and Rye, in Sussex.

It was not until 1837 – the first year of Queen Victoria's reign – that the pillory was officially abolished, though it is thought that the last time the punishment was imposed was in 1830, on one Dr Bossy, for perjury.

In Germany and France there are ample records of the pillory, spreading in the twelfth and thirteenth centuries until it became as ubiquitous as in England. In the north of Germany the pillory was called the *katz*, and in the south and in Austria *prechel* or *schreialt*. The French called their pillories *pilori* and *carcan*. Although it was used as a punishment in most parts of Europe only for as long as it survived in England, there is evidence that the pillory was used at Flensburg as late as 1864.

The Trülle

This cage type of pillory is described in the entry on **whirligigs** but it also served the simpler function of dis-

The cage on London Bridge

playing prisoners to public scorn. What appears to be a unique type of 'cage' pillory is depicted in an early edition of Fox's *Book of Martyrs*, and shows a woman – no doubt a persecuted Protestant – in what is called 'the cage on London Bridge'. I have been unable to find any more detailed description, but it is interesting to see, beside the cage, the London Bridge stocks.

Finger Pillory

The finger pillory, or finger stocks, was designed to imprison a miscreant by the fingers only, but otherwise served the same purpose as the pillory itself. These devices were to be found in churches (the magnificent example in the parish church at Ashby-de-la-Zouche can still be seen) where they might be used to punish those failing to attend service, or perhaps falling asleep during the sermon. They were also used in schools to punish minor misdemeanours, and in large houses where unwilling or slovenly servants might be punished.

Finger pillories consisted of two hinged blocks of wood with grooves cut, into which the digits were fitted before the upper and lower blocks were padlocked together.

Pincers

Used to tear the flesh piecemeal from a victim's body, considerable ingenuity has been invested in the design of implements to cause maximum pain and physical devastation. One of the cruellest variations was the Spider which, although it was in use in antiquity, survived well into the Middle Ages and beyond. The Romans knew this instrument as the *ungula*, and the early Germanic tribes, among whom it was a firm favourite, called it *Ghlave* on account of its roughened, or teeth-like appearance.

The claws of this frightening tool, much resembling the legs of the Arachnida from which it takes its name, have sharpened edges and points which, when the handles are closed, lock around the prisoner's flesh and tears it from

The terrible 'Spider'

the body. Used in this way, such torture frequently proved fatal.

Special pincers were used for the excruciating business of tearing out finger and toe nails, and a popular refinement of the torture chamber was heating pincers in a brazier until they were red hot before tearing at the flesh.

Pressing to Death; or the Torture of *Peine Forte et Dure*

The punishment of *peine forte et dure*, or 'pressing to death', was first adopted in England around the year 1406, and although it fell into gradual disuse was not abolished until 1772. Indeed, the prevalence of this torture led to the Newgate exercise yard being given the name 'Press-Yard', as well as the so-called 'Press-Room' where the pressing was carried out.

The procedure was as simple as it was cruel, and the form was embodied in the words of the judge's sentence:

> That the prisoner shall be remanded to the place from whence he came, and be put in some low, dark room, and there laid on his back, without any covering except a cloth round his middle; and that as many weights shall be laid upon him as he can bear, and more; and that he shall have no more sustenance but the worst of bread and water, and that he shall not eat on the same day on which he drinks, nor drink on the same day on which he eats; and he shall so continue till he die.

This was later somewhat refined:

> That the prisoner shall be remanded to the place from whence he came, and put in some low, dark room, that he shall lie without any litter or anything under him, and that one arm shall be drawn to one quarter of the room with a cord, and the other to another, and that his feet shall be used in the same manner, and that as many weights shall be laid on him as he can bear, and more. That he shall have three morsels of barley bread a day, and that he shall have the water next the prison, so that it be not current, and that he shall not eat . . .

The punishment was originally developed to 'encourage' prisoners to plead. To understand this we must remember that until the time of its introduction a person could not be tried by a court until he had pleaded 'guilty' or 'not guilty' to the charge brought against him. This fact, combined with another – that the property of a convicted felon was forfeit to the state – made it not uncommon for a criminal to affect muteness in the hope of preserving the estate for his heirs. Though a majority of sufferers will clearly have been persuaded by pressing to talk, there are ample records of those who bore the torture unto death thus depriving the Crown of its 'booty'. There also exists tragic reports of the genuinely mute perishing under *peine forte et dure*:

At the Kilkenny Assizes, in 1740, one Matthew Ryan was tried for highway robbery. When he was apprehended, he pretended to be a lunatic, stripped himself in the jail, threw away his clothes, and could not be prevailed on to put them on again, but went as he was to the court to take his trial. He then affected to be dumb, and would not plead; on which the judges ordered a jury to be empanelled, to inquire and give their opinion, whether he was mute and lunatic by the will of God, or wilfully so. The jury returned in a short time, and brought in a verdict of 'wilful and affected dumbness and lunacy'. The judges on this desired the prisoner to plead; but he still pretended to be insensible to all that was said to him. The law now called for the *peine forte et dure*; but the judges compassionately deferred awarding it until a future day, in the hope that he might in the meantime acquire a juster sense of his situation. When again brought up, however, the criminal persisted in his refusal to plead; and the court at last pronounced the dreadful sentence, that he should be pressed to death. This sentence was accordingly executed upon him two days after, in the public market place of Kilkenny. As the weights were heaping on the wretched man, he earnestly supplicated to be hanged; but it being beyond the power of the sheriff to deviate from the mode of punishment prescribed in the sentence, even this was an indulgence which could no longer be granted to him.

(*The Terrific Register*, Edinburgh, 1825)

Mute of Malice
The nineteenth century saw a more enlightened approach to overcoming the difficulty of a prisoner refusing to plead. The original motivation for silence, it is true, had disappeared, but by reason of contempt, or a misinformed feeling that no plea means no trial, (and by some, it must be credited, 'mute by the visitation of God') an accused would periodically stand silent.

The law now required that a jury should first decide upon the question of ability to plead. The following example shows the recent formula in operation:

Friday, November 8, 1912
TITUS, Stephen (27, tailor) was indicted and charged on coroner's inquisition with the wilful murder of Esther May Towers. . . .

Mr Bodkin and Mr Perceval Clarke prosecuted.

Prisoner, called upon to plead, stood mute. A jury was sworn to try whether prisoner stood mute of malice.

Sidney Reginald DYER, principal medical officer Brixton Prison: 'Prisoner has been under my observation since September 28. I have had various conversations with him, and he has answered the questions I have put to him and understood the English language. He had no difficulty whatever in hearing and answered as a person would who heard and understood. I had a conversation with him last night. Now and again he has been in a morose condition. I saw him before he came to the Court this morning and he was in that condition then. He is in the same condition now, but he quite understands, and I think he is fit to plead and follow the course of the trial and give the necessary instructions for his defence.'

The jury found that the prisoner stood mute of malice.

Mr Justice Phillimore directed a plea of Not Guilty to be entered upon each indictment, and requested Mr Waldo Briggs to represent the prisoner.

(*Sessions Papers of Central Criminal Court*,
G. Walpole and Co.)

Major George Strangeways

At the death of his father, Major Strangeways was left in possession of the family farm, and his elder sister, Mabellah, was created executrix by the will. In simpler terms, everything passed into Mabellah's legal possession, including the title-deeds and bonds. George's reason in doing this was to avoid the unthinkable consequence of his lack of loyalty to Cromwell – the sequestration of his goods by the Commonwealth.

But all of a sudden the scene altered, and she, whom he thought sufficiently proof against all inclinations to matrimony, began to express some affection for Mr Fussel, a gentleman well esteemed at Blandford, the place of his residence, and of much repute for his eminent abilities in matters of law. Miss Strangeways made it now the least part of her care to disguise her sentiments concerning him; so it was not long before her brother came to a perfect knowledge of their mutual resolutions.

No sooner had he heard of the proposal of marriage – and the consequent transfer of his inheritance to the suitor – than George Strangeways spoke absolutely against it, and lost no opportunity in telling his sister of his disapproval. Just as often, and just as stubbornly, Miss Mabellah affirmed the steadfastness of her purpose.

Soon afterwards, the wedding took place; succeeded by a challenge to combat by Strangeways; followed by a lawsuit commenced by Fussel, for which purpose both men were present in the city of London.

Mr Fussel lodged at the sign of the George and Half

Moon, opposite a pewterer's shop. He came in one evening between nine and ten, and retired to his study, which fronted the street, sitting behind a desk, with his face towards the window. In this manner he had not sat above a quarter of an hour before two bullets shot from a carbine struck him, the one through the forehead and the other in about his mouth.

He dropped down upon his desk without so much as a groan, so that his clerk, who was in the room at the same time, did not apprehend anything of what was done; till at last, perceiving him to lean his head, and knowing him not apt to fall asleep as he wrote, he imagined something more than ordinary was the matter. Upon this he drew near, to be satisfied, when he was suddenly struck with such horror and amazement at the unexpected sight of blood that, for the present, he was utterly incapable of action. As soon as he had recollected himself, he called up some of the family . . . Instantly they all ran into the street, but could see nothing, everything appearing more silent and still than is usual at this time of night in the public parts of the city.

By the time the watchmen had carried out a fruitless search, Fussel's son (by a previous marriage) had recalled to mind the bitter quarrel that had for some time existed between his father and Uncle George Strangeways, and suggested that the officers might like to apprehend him; which action they in general approved of.

Thus George Strangeways found himself, at two-thirty in the morning, dragged from his lodging in Bull Inn Court and before Mr Justice Blake; the latter listening dispassionately to his denials before committing him to Newgate where remaining till next morning, he was then conveyed to the place where Mr Fussel's body was. When he came there, he was commanded to take his dead brother-in-law by the hand, and touch his wounds before the coroner's inquest.* As this piece of hocus-pocus failed

*It was in earlier times customary to oblige those persons suspected of murder to touch the victim's body as a test of their

to produce any positive result, the problem was remanded back to the jury for further inquiry.

On the 24th of February, 1685, Major George Strangeways was brought to his trial at the sessions house in the Old Bailey; where, his indictment being read, and he being commanded to plead, he absolutely refused to comply with the method of the Court unless, he said, he might be permitted, when he was condemned, to die in the same manner as his brother-in-law [that is, by shooting, which in his eyes meant the firing squad as a military 'honour']. If they refused this, he told them, he would continue in his contempt of the Court, that he might preserve his estate, which would be forfeited on his conviction, in order to bestow it on such friends as he had most affection for, as well as to free himself from the ignominious death of a public gibbet.

Many arguments were urged by Cromwell's Lord Chief Justice, Mr Serjeant Glyn, and the rest of the bench, to induce him to plead; particularly the terror of the death which his obstinate silence would oblige them to inflict upon him. But still he remained immovable, refusing either to plead or to discover who it was that fired the

---

guilt or innocence. This method of discovering murderers was first practised in Denmark under King Christian II, and its origin was as follows. Certain gentlemen were drinking together one evening in a 'stove', or tavern, when they quarrelled and began to brawl amongst themselves. During the fighting the candles were knocked out and in the darkness one of the men was fatally stabbed. As the murderer was not known owing to the darkness, the king caused all those involved to stand in a circle around the body, approaching in turn and laying their right hand on the victim's naked breast at the same time swearing that they had not killed him. The last of all was one of the king's own pursuivants, and as soon as he laid his hand upon the corpse, blood gushed from his wounds and from his nostrils. The killer, in mortal terror, confessed and was beheaded. The custom of 'touching the corpse' became common throughout Europe.

gun; only affirming that, whoever did it, it was done by his direction.

When it was clear that no argument would alter his resolution the Lord Chief Justice passed on Major Strangeways the terrible sentence of *peine forte et dure* to be his punishment until death.

On the last day of February – a Monday – at eleven o'clock in the morning, the Sheriffs of London and Middlesex, accompanied by several of their officers, met at the Press-Yard in Newgate . . .

After a short stay, Major Strangeways was guarded down, clothed all in white – waistcoat, stockings, drawers and cap, over which was cast a long mourning cloak. From whence he was conducted to the dungeon, the dismal place of execution . . .

He took his solemn last leave of all his lamenting friends, and prepared himself for the dreadful assault of Death, with whom he was speedily to encounter. He desired his friends, when he gave the signal, to lay on the weights, and they placed themselves at the corners of the press for that purpose. His arms and legs were extended, according to the sentence, in which action he cried out, 'Thus were the sacred limbs of my ever blessed Saviour stretched forth on the cross, when He suffered to free the sin-polluted world from an eternal curse.' Then crying with a sprightly voice, 'Lord Jesus receive my soul,' which were the words he had told them, his mournful attendants performed their dreadful task. They soon perceived that the weight they laid on was not sufficient to put him suddenly out of pain, so several of them added their own weight, that they might the sooner release his soul. While he was dying, it was horrible to all who stood by, as well as dreadful to himself, to see the agonies he was put into, and hear his loud and doleful groans. But this dismal scene was over in about eight or ten minutes, when all his spirit departed, and left her tortured mansion, till the great day that shall unite them again . . . His body having laid some time in the press, was brought forth and exposed to the public view, so that a great many people beheld the bruises made by the press, one angle of which being purposely placed over his heart, he was the sooner deprived of life, though he was denied what is usual in these cases, to have a sharp piece of timber under his back to hasten execution. The body appeared void of scars, and not deformed with blood, save where the extremities of the press came on the breasts and the upper part of the belly. The face was bloody, not from any external injury, but the violent forcing of the blood from the larger vessels into the veins of the face and eyes. After the dead corpse had been thus examined it was put into a coffin, and in a cart that attended at the prison door conveyed to Christ Church, where it was interred.

(*The Newgate Calendar*)

Pricking

Although the comparatively short vogue for witch-hunting in Britain was not characterised by such excesses of torture as were practised on the mainland of Europe, the method known as pricking was extensively employed in the discovery of witches.

The fundamental principle was that all witches had been marked, or 'branded', by the devil as his own, and that the flesh of these marks was dead and incapable of bleeding. Suspected witches were stripped and then shaved of hair lest it conceal a telltale blemish. Any obvious imperfection such as a mole, wart, or birthmark was taken to identify the suspect as a sorceress. However, if no marks were found the victim was 'pricked', lest as part of their cunning pact Satan had disguised his mark; if a spot was found which did not cause pain when pierced and did not bleed, then the devil's mark had been revealed. This

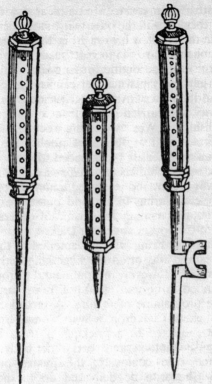

The two bodkins on the left are 'false prickers'; the one on the right is genuine. The example in the centre shows a retractable point

preposterous theory did not take account of the fact that most people when jabbed with a sharp metal point will both shout and bleed, which led to the witch-finders – who were paid by results – employing 'cheating pricks', the points of which retracted into the handle so that they appeared to pierce the flesh without obvious effect.

Pricking was carried out with devastating effect by Matthew Hopkins, the so-called Witch Finder-General of England, and his assistant John Stearne who, according to Notestein*, 'In fourteen months sent to the gallows more witches than all the other witch hunters in England.' Hopkins was a failed lawyer from Manningtree, Essex, who during the year 1645 to 1646 became the most feared man in the eastern counties of England. Although Hopkins himself and the witch persecutions in general have generated their own mythology, it should be added that the activity was carried out in front of the backcloth of the English Civil War, where the existing psychology of persecution aimed at Roman Catholics by Cromwell's Puritanism could easily be extended to other 'heretics'.

According to Robbins (*Encyclopedia of Witchcraft and Demonology*) Scotland produced a number of celebrated witch-prickers during the second quarter of the seventeenth century, naming John Kincaid of Tranent, John Balfour of Corhouse, and John Dick.

In Britain, pricking was fundamental to the discovery of witches and was often the beginning and end of the 'examination'. However, in Continental Europe the technique tended to be used gratuitously as part of a more extensive programme of torture. A record exists of the fate of Michelle Chaudron, a Swiss woman from Geneva, who was subjected to a pricking in 1652. Having had needles pushed into various parts of her body, and having yelled and bled copiously, the judges ordered that Madame Chaudron be delivered up to the torturers, under whose cruelty she readily confessed to everything that was demanded of her. After this the physicians once again searched her body for a mark and this time were rewarded by finding a small black spot on the woman's left thigh. So exhausted was she following the torture, that when the spot was pricked, Michelle Chaudron did not have the strength to cry out. This was taken as clear evidence to confirm her confession and the unfortunate victim was ordered to be strangled and burned.

History of Witchcraft in England from 1558 to 1718, Wallace Notestein, Washington, 1911.

Prison Hulks

These texts have been adapted from the researches of Henry Mayhew and John Binney, the eminent nineteenth-century social historians, who published in 1862 *The Criminal Prisons of London*.

History of the Hulks

The idea of converting old ships into prisons arose when the transportation of convicts to Britain's transatlantic possessions became impossible due to the outbreak of the American War of Independence. An Act of George III (19th Geo. III, cap. 74), had already laid down that

> . . . for the more severe and effectual punishment of atrocious and daring offenders, be it further enacted that, from and after the First Day of July, one thousand seven hundred and seventy-nine, where any male person . . . shall be lawfully convicted of Grand Larceny, or any other crime, except Petty Larceny, for which he shall be liable by law to be transported to any Parts beyond the seas, it shall and may be lawful for the Court . . . to order and adjudge that such Person . . . shall be punished by being kept on Board Ships or Vessels properly accommodated for the Security, Employment, and Health of the Persons to be confined therein, and by being employed in Hard Labour in the raising of Sand, Soil, and Gravel from, and cleansing, the River Thames, or any other River navigable for Ships of Burthen . . .

The *Justitia*, an old Indiaman, and the *Censor*, a frigate, were the first floating prisons in England, and by January 1841 there were 3,552 convicts on board the various hulks. Some idea of the sanitary condition of these establishments may be gathered from the report of Mr Peter Bossy, surgeon of the *Warrior* hulk, which shows that in the year 1841, among 638 convicts on board, there were no less than 400 cases of admission to hospital, and 38 deaths. At this period there were no less than 11 ships used by the British Government for the purposes of penal discipline (including those stationed at Bermuda) . . . 'we were assured by one of the warders who had served under the old hulk regime, that he well remembers seeing the shirts of the prisoners, when hung out upon the rigging, so black with vermin that the linen positively appeared to have been sprinkled over with pepper; and that when the cholera broke out on board the convict vessels for the first time the Chaplain refused to bury the dead until there were several corpses aboard, so that the coffins were taken to the marshes by half-dozen at a time, and there interred at a given signal from the clergyman; his reverence remaining behind on the poop of the vessel, afraid to accompany the bodies, reading the burial service at the distance of a mile from the grave, and letting fall a handkerchief when he came to "ashes to ashes and dust to dust", as the sign that they were to lower the bodies.'

It was impossible that a state of affairs so scandalous could last; and the successive reports of the directors of convict prisons are evidence of the anxiety with which they urged upon the government the reform – if not the abandonment – of the hulk system; for, to the disadvantage inseparable from the conduct of prison discipline on board ship, the governors of hulks were forced to add the rottenness of the vessels entrusted to them . . . 'The *Warrior*,' they said, 'is patched up as well as her unsoundness will permit, but there is no knowing how soon she may become quite unfit for further use, and it will be advisable to take the earliest opportunity that offers of transferring the prisoners to some more suitable place of confinement, as any serious repairs would be quite thrown away on so decayed a hulk. She is rotten and unsound from stem to stern.' Still the *Warrior* remained, with canvas drawn over her leakages, to keep the damp from the wards, moored off the Woolwich dockyard, with 436 convicts between her crumbling ribs.

The hulk system, condemned, as we have already observed, from the date of its origin to the present time, was the despair of all penal reformers. Originally adopted as a makeshift under pressing circumstances, these old men-of-war remained during nearly half a century the receptacles of the worst class of prisoners from all the gaols of the United Kingdom – a striking instance of the inertness of government, as well as of its utter callousness as to the fate or reformation of the criminal.

Convict Labour at Woolwich

This labour was of the description called 'hard'; that is to say, the exercise of irksome brute force, rather than the application of self-gratifying skill . . . The directors stated that the kind of work performed by the convicts was chiefly labourers' work, such as loading and unloading vessels, moving timber and other materials, and stores, cleaning out ships, etc., whilst at the Royal Arsenal the prisoners were employed at jobs of a similar description, with the addition of cleaning guns and shot, and excavating the ground for the engineer department.

Another report (dated as early as 15 July 1776) described in greater detail the principles prevailing on the hulks almost a century before the publication of Mayhew and Binney:

The law for sentencing the convicts to work upon the Thames is indeed severe, but we trust it will be salutary. They are to be employed in as much labour as they can sustain, to be fed with legs and shins of beef, ox cheek, and such other coarse food; to have nothing for drink but water or small beer; to be clad in some squalid uniform; never to be visited without the consent of the overseers; and whoever gives them the smallest relief incurs a penalty of forty shillings. The expense of keeping and maintaining them is to be paid by the Government, and not out of the county rates.

The first vessel launched for the above purpose was constructed on a plan approved by His Majesty in council. It cannot be called a ship or tender,

THE DAILY DISTRIBUTION OF TIME ON BOARD THE "DEFENCE" HULK.

Occupation.	In Summer (longest day).			In Winter (shortest day).		
	(In intermediate seasons, the hours vary according to light).					
	A.M.	A.M.	Hrs. Min.	A.M.	A.M.	Hrs. Min.
Prisoners rise, wash, and roll up hammocks	5 30	6 0	= 0 30	5 30	6 0	= 0 30
Breakfast (officers and servants)	6 0	6 30	= 0 30	6 0	6 30	= 0 30
Cleaning classes	6 30	7 15	= 0 45	6 30	7 15	= 0 45
In readiness to turn out to work (preparing the boats, &c.)	7 15	7 30	= 0 15	7 15	7 30	= 0 15
Labour, including landing and marching to and from working ground	7 30	12 noon	= 4 30	7 30	12 noon	= 4 30
Dinner for officers and prisoners	12 noon	1 P.M.	= 1 0	12 noon	1 P.M.	= 1 0
Labour, including mustering and marching to and from working ground	1 P.M.	5 30	= 4 30	1 P.M.	4 0	= 3 0
Prisoners are mustered, wash, and prepare for supper	5 30	6 0	= 0 30	4 0	4 45	= 0 45
Supper, washing-up, &c.	6 0	6 45	= 0 45	4 45	5 30	= 0 45
Evening prayers, school, and those not at school repairing clothing, &c., mustered intermediately	6 45	8 30	= 1 45	5 30	7 30	= 2 0
Sling hammocks	8 30	9 0	= 0 30	7 30	8 0	= 0 30
All in bed	9 0			8 0		
	Total from 5.30 A.M. to 8.0 P.M.		15 30	Total from 5.30 A.M. to 8.0 P.M.		14 30

ABSTRACT OF THE ABOVE.

Meals		2 15			2 15
Labour, including mustering, and moving to and from		9 0			7 30
In-door occupation, evening instruction, &c., &c.		4 15			4 45
	In Summer	15 30	In Winter		14 30

neither is it so flat or open as a lighter; it is calculated to hold twenty-seven tons of ballast. On the larboard side the gunwale is considerably broader than in the common lighters; on the starboard side is a flooring about three feet broad for the men to walk on, and a machine called a david [or 'davit'] with a windlass for raising the ballast. Part of the vessel is decked in abaft for the convicts to sleep in, and another in the forecastle is formed into a kind of cabin for the overseer. Her outward appearance differs very little from that of a common lighter. On the 5th of

August, the convicts chained by the leg, two and two, began to work in her, about two miles below Barking Creek under the direction of Duncan Campbell Esq., who has been appointed the governor of this new kind of Bridewell. Their behaviour, in general, since they came on board her and other lighters employed in the same service, has been very becoming. The clause in the Act which says that the time for which they were sentenced to work may be shortened, on a representation of their good behaviour, having operated very powerfully. A few of them, indeed, employed a little below Woolwich, attempted to get off their chains, and were guilty of some slight outrages to their commander, when a severe flagellation ensued on their being properly secured.

Eight others, a short time after, found means to seize on the arms-chest, and presenting pistols at the heads of their keepers threatened to blow their brains out if they did not immediately go down into the hold – which they were obliged to comply with. Upon which the villains jumped into a boat which had been designedly brought alongside by some of their friends and got clear off.

Badges

A distinctive portion of the discipline carried on at Woolwich consisted in the badges worn by the prisoners on the left arm, and the rings worn on the right. These badges were made of black leather, with an edge of red cloth, with white and black letters and figures upon it:

We advanced towards some convicts who were hauling up linen to the mast to dry, and who wore both rings and badges. The first badge we examined was marked thus:

The 7 meant that the prisoner had been sentenced to seven years' transportation; the 8 that he had been in the hulk for that number of months, and the V.G., that his conduct had been very good all the time he had been there. Another wore a differently marked badge; this denoted that the prisoner was suffering four years' penal servitude; that his conduct had been good during six months, and that he had been on board the hulk eight months.

The badges are collected once in every month, and conveyed to the governor's office. The character-book, as filled up from the weekly reports of the warders, is gone over in each case and at the same time, if the prisoner has behaved badly, his badge is altered, and he loses some of the advantages of his previous good conduct. Three months' good report in the character-book constitutes a V.G., or very good, and advances the wearer three months towards the second stage of penal servitude.

But the first man whose badge we noticed upon his left arm, had also upon his right arm a blue and two red rings. The blue ring denotes the second stage of penal servitude, and the red rings that he is a first-class convict. One red ring upon the right arm makes a second-class convict; and the third-class prisoner is known by the absence of all rings from the arm. By this system we are assured that it is almost impossible that a prisoner can be unjustly dealt with.

SCALE OF DIET
(Per man)

BREAKFAST
12 oz. Bread
1 pt. Cocoa

DINNER
6 oz. Meat
1 lb. Potatoes
9 oz. Bread

SUPPER
1 pt. Gruel
6 oz. Bread

ON SOUP DAYS
(Monday, Wednesday, Friday)
DINNER
1 pt. Soup
5 oz. Meat
1 lb. Potatoes
9 oz. Bread

GRUEL DIET
(served when on sick list)
BREAKFAST, DINNER, SUPPER
1 pt. Gruel
9 oz. Bread

PUNISHMENT DIET
1 lb. Bread per day
Water

The Convicts' Burial Ground

We approached a low piece of ground – in no way marked off from the rest of the marsh – in no way distinguishable from any section of the dreary expanse, save that the long rank grass had been turned in one place lately, and that there was an upset barrow lying not far off. Heavy, leaden clouds were rolling overhead, and some heavy drops of rain pattered upon our faces as we stood there. We thought it was one of the dreariest spots we had ever seen.

'This,' said the Governor, 'is the Convicts' Burial Ground.'

We could just trace the rough outline of disturbed ground at our feet. Beyond this was a shed, where cattle found shelter in bad weather; and on the right the land shelved up between the marsh and the river. There was not even a number over the graves; the last, and it was only a month old, was disappearing. In a few months the rank grass will have closed over it, as over the story of its inmate. And it is, perhaps, well to leave the names of the unfortunate men, whose bones lie in the clay of this dreary marsh, unregistered and unknown. But the feeling with which we look upon its desolation is irrepressible.

Then there is a legend – an old, old, legend, that has passed down to the present time – about a little pale-blue flower, with purple leaves – the Rubrum lamium – which, it is said, grows only over the convict's grave – a flower, tender and unobtrusive as the kindness for which legend gives it credit.

Quaker Persecutions

It was in England in 1647 that George Fox began preaching the principles which would, over the next decade, become the foundation of the Society of Friends; according to Fox, 'Justice Bennet of Darby was the first to call us Quakers [in 1650], because I bid them tremble at the Word of the Lord'. The sect had no definite creed apart from total pacifism, and no regular ministry. However, the Quakers became so successful as a 'religion' that, sensing a threat to orthodoxy, the established Church launched a programme of persecutions, as a result of which members of the Society were imprisoned, had their possessions confiscated and, though none were reportedly killed, subjected to all manner of tortures. It was this shameful treatment that led many of the sect's leaders to embark on their pilgrimage to America. Here they found themselves even less welcome, and fell prey to vicious persecution by the New England Puritans among whom they had landed in Boston, Massachusetts. Whipping was the most common lot of the Quakers, though some were sold straight off their ships into slavery on the plantations. The extent of the barbarous way in which these most gentle people were treated can be summed up by this description of the **flagellation** of William Brend:

The gaoler put him into irons, neck and heels, locked so close together as there was no more room between each than for the horse-lock that fastened them on; and so kept him in irons for the space of sixteen hours for not working; and all this without meat while his back was torn with whipping the day before, which did not satisfy the bloodthirsty gaoler, but as a man resolved to have his life, and by cruelties to kill him, he had him down again next morning to work, though so many days without meat, long together, because he could not bow to his will; yet laid on him with a pitch'd rope twenty blows over his back and arms, with as much force as he could drive, so that with the fierceness of the blows the rope untwisted and his arms were swollen with it. Presently after this, the gaoler having either mended his old, or got a new rope, came in again; and having hauled him downstairs with greater fury and violence than before, gave his broken, bruised and weak body four-score and seventeen blows more, foaming at the mouth like a madman and tormented with rage. Unto which great number he would have added more blows had not his strength and rope failed him, for now he cared not what he did. And all this because he would not work for him, which he could not do being unable in body and unfree in mind. So he gave him in all 117 blows with a pitch'd rope, so that his flesh was beaten black, and as into a jelly, and under his arms the bruised flesh and blood hung down, clodded as it were in bags, and so into one was it beaten that the sign of one particular blow could not be seen.

(*New England Judged by the Spirit of the Lord*, George Bishop, 1703)

Quartering Alive

This punishment should be distinguished from **drawing and quartering**, where the already dead body of a traitor

Execution by quartering of Francis Ravilliack in 1610;
Ravilliack had been convicted of the parricide of Henry VI of
France

was cut into quarters to be displayed above individual city
gates or in different towns.

Quartering alive was at one time achieved by much the
same means as quartering dead – that is, the prisoner
was simply chopped into pieces with an axe. An early
refinement, however, is described by the sixth-century
ecclesiastic and historian, Gregory of Tours, in his *Gesta
Francorum*. Here he tells how Queen Brunehild was
quartered by having her limbs tied to the tails of four
horses, the horses being driven slowly apart, rending her
body in pieces. Gregory also records the mass killing of
two hundred Frankish women by the Thuringians in the
same manner. The Dutch master Lucas van Leyden made
a drawing, 'Woman being pulled to pieces by horses',
dated c. 1530, which is likely to have been based on personal observation.

In 1757 a most spectacular demonstration took place in
Paris. The occasion was the execution of Robert Francois
Daumiens, who had been convicted of the attempted regi-

cide of Louis XV. As a preliminary to the main event of the day, it was ordered that Daumiens be taken to 'a scaffold erected for the purpose, and that his chest, arms, thighs, and calves be burnt with pincers; his offending right arm burnt in hot sulphur; then that boiling oil, melted lead, resin, and wax mixed with sulphur be poured into his wounds'.

After that Daumiens suffered the boot and further burning: 'When the flame touched his skin, Daumiens uttered a frightful shriek and pulled at his bonds. When the initial pain had passed, he raised his head and stared at his burning hand with no emotion save the grinding of his teeth.' Finally his arms and legs were each bound to a horse, and Daumiens was further tortured by the animals being encouraged to give short jerks, thus tearing at his limbs for some time before the horses were urged on to complete their job. Even so, the sinews proved so tough that the executioner was required to finish the job with a knife.

Quartering alive by this method was, as far as can be ascertained, unknown as a punishment in Britain.

R

Rack

The rack was in extensive use in classical times, notably during the Roman Empire, where the *equuleus* was at first one of the legal punishments for slaves and felons, and later, during the first few centuries AD, as a frequent torture used against the early Christians (it is ironic that later it would be used by Christians against Christians).

In the year 305 a young mother named Julietta, a Lyconian, was brought before Alexander, Governor of Tarsus, accused of being a Christian. To this charge Julietta proudly confessed, and for her honesty was put to the rack. While the unhappy woman was suffering, her small child, Cyricus, was heard to burble 'I am a Christian,' upon which Alexander took the mite up and dashed out his brains upon the stone floor. Julietta's punishment on the rack continued with having boiling pitch poured on her feet and being torn with hooks; she was finally beheaded, and in the course of time became Saint Julietta.

Racking was ubiquitous as a means of punishment throughout Europe in the Middle Ages, and became the most familiar instrument of terror during the various incarnations of the Inquisition. In France the machine was known as the 'Banc de Torture', and was in use until the late eighteenth century.

The Duke's Daughter

It has been claimed that the rack was introduced into England in 1447 by John Holland, fourth Duke of Exeter, while he was holding the office of Constable of the Tower of London; it thus became known as the 'Duke of Exeter's Daughter', and its clients were said to be 'marrying the Duke's Daughter'.

The English rack was described as being 'A large open

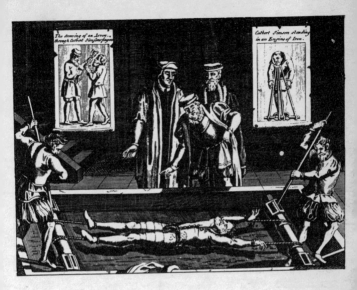

frame of oak, raised three feet from the ground. The prisoner was laid under it, his back on the floor. His wrists and ankles were attached by cords to two collars at the end of the frame which were then moved by levers in opposite directions till the body rose level with the frame. Questions were then put, and, if the answers did not prove satisfactory the sufferer was stretched more and more till the bones started from their sockets.' (*The Penny Magazine*, 1832).

During the period of its use at the Tower, the rack saw many celebrated victims, the best known of whom was Guy Fawkes. Fawkes was the Roman Catholic convert who, as part of a conspiracy known as the Gunpowder Plot, made an abortive attempt to blow up King James I and both Houses of Parliament. The conspirators were arrested in the cellars beneath Parliament on 4 November 1605. So severe was the torture inflicted on Fawkes in order to secure a confession that when he eventually agreed to sign he was incapable of scrawling more than 'Guido' before losing his feeble grip on the pen. And so badly had the rack distorted his limbs that he had to be carried on to the scaffold.

The signature of Guy Fawkes before, during and after torture; it can clearly be seen to deteriorate

The Nuremberg Rack

German torturers had a particular affection for the rack, and added several refinements of their own. The rack once in use in the city of Nuremberg had several sophisticated features missing from earlier, simpler versions:

It is constructed of wood, just over ten feet long, the windlass arrangement at one end being particularly powerful. The victim was laid naked, face down on the bed of the rack, his arms were securely bound at the wrists to the bar at one end, while his legs and ankles were equally well fastened to the roller at the other. The limbs were spread apart as far as possible and when the executioner had satisfied himself that the machine would have full play, he and an assistant took their stand at the handles, and the torture began. Creak, creak, creak the roller went as it turned cumbrously in its socket, and for a few moments that would be the only sound. Then as the unfortunate sufferer felt the first effects of the stretching process, a suppressed groan would break from him. Creak! Another turn, and this time a shriek from the poor soul whose muscles were cracking under the strain. Slowly now goes the roller, for, besides having to exert their strength, the executioners know that the slightest forward movement means an increase in the tortured one's agony. Close by stands an official whose signal to stop the torture is speedily obeyed. A few questions to the man on the machine, which brings forth a refusal, and again at his command the handles move round, the grinding noise of the spindles in their sockets being drowned by the anguished cries of the sufferer, whose every joint was by this time dislocated . . .

Spiked Hare

In the centre of the Nuremberg rack was an optional second roller, studded with pieces of iron. This is one version of the Spiked Hare (sometimes it was covered with sharp spikes instead of blunt ones, and some rollers were sharply corrugated). This instrument was brought into use as soon as the person on the rack was stretched out and before he had felt the excruciating pain which a further turn of the windlass would have given him. The

Hare was rolled over his body, every spike touching him piercing the flesh to a depth of an inch or more. At other times the victim was rolled over the spikes and, when the torture was intended to kill him, the Hare placed between his abdomen and the bed of the rack, every movement driving the nails deeper into his body.

Austrian Ladder

The Ladder employed the same principle as the rack, but was capable of inflicting even greater suffering. The wide Ladder was fixed to the ground and set at an angle of forty degrees to a wall. There was a moveable bar similar to that on a conventional rack at the foot of the Ladder. The victim was placed with his back against the device with his wrists tied behind him to one of the rungs; his ankles were then attached to a rope going down to the moveable bar. The bar, turned by the executioner, pulled the prisoner downwards and twisted his arms upwards and backwards until his shoulders were dislocated. In fact, the Ladder was not Austrian but German.

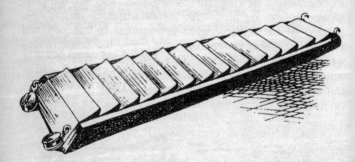

Rack and Cords

Although the rack was most commonly used as a torture in its own right, the opportunities presented by having a completely helpless captive occasionally proved too great a temptation for the executioners to resist, and any number of additions were made to the poor victim's suffering. A 'water torture' similar to the **Wooden Horse** was often used. Another variant was the simultaneous use of cords binding the limbs to the sides of the rack. The cords were wound around three times, and a rod inserted so that when it was twisted, the cords bit deeply into the flesh.

This method of torture, carried out on an unusual design of vertical rack, was suffered by the Scotsman William Lithgow, who was arrested as a spy in Malaga in 1620, found himself in the grasp of the Inquisition and, unusually, survived.

I was by the executioner stripped to the skin, brought to the rack, and then mounted by him on the top of it, where soon after I was hung by the bare shoulders with two small cords, which went under both my arms, running on two rings of iron that were fixed in the wall above my head. Thus being hoisted to the appointed height, the tormentor descended below, and drawing down my legs through the two sides of the three-planked rack, he tied a cord about each of my ankles and then ascending upon the rack he drew the cords upward, and bending forward with main force my two knees against the two planks, the sinews of my hams burst asunder and the lids of my knees being crushed, and the cords made fast, I hung so demained for a large hour.

. . . Now was I to receive my main torments. But what of this *Pottaro*, or rack: It stood by the wall, of timber, the uppermost end whereof is larger than a full stride, the lower end being narrow, and the three planks joining together are made conformable to a man's shoulders; in the downmost end of the middle plank there was a hole, wherein my head was laid. In length it is longer than a man, being interlaced with small cords from plank to plank which divided my supported thighs from the middle plank. Through the sides of the exterior planks there

A variant of the rack and cord procedure

were three distant holes in every one of them – the
use whereof you shall presently hear.

First the executioner laid a cord over the calf of
my leg, then another on the middle of my thigh,
and the third cord over the lower arm, which was
done on both sides of my body, receiving the ends

of the cords in the outward planks, which were fastened to pins, and the pins made fast with a device . . . And in every one of these six parts of my body was I to receive several tortures, each torture consisting of three winding throws of every pin, which amounted to twenty-one throws in every one of these six parts . . .

Thus I lay six hours upon the rack, between four o'clock in the afternoon and ten at night, having had inflicted on me these sixty several torments. Nevertheless they continued me a large half-hour at the full bending, where my body being all begored with blood and cut through in every part, to the crushed and bruised bones, I pitifully remained, still roaring, howling, foaming, bellowing and gnashing my teeth, with insupportable cries, before the pins were undone, and my body loosed.

Rats

Though it is one of the most appalling of all punishments, there are few reliable references to the Torture of the Rats. It is claimed that the practice was confined to the Inquisitorial period in the Netherlands, and there is an engraving depicting the torture of a 'heretic' in the treatise *Theatrum Crudelitatum Haereticorum* of 1592. The victim is disrobed and bound face up on a table (or spread-eagled to stakes in the ground). A metal bowl containing the rats is turned upside down on the prisoner's naked stomach and a fire lit on the top of it. Tormented by the heat, the enraged vermin seek escape by gnawing their way downwards through the soft flesh of the victim's body.

A less elaborate but equally revolting rat torture was a favourite of the Roman emperor Nero. Victims, usually Christians, were bound and put into a large barrel into which were tipped a couple of dozen starving rats which proceeded to eat the victims alive. So that the torture did not end prematurely, once one batch of rodents had eaten their fill of human flesh, they were removed and replaced by a further batch of hungry ones.

Torture of the rats

Revivals After Execution

[The following text is derived from *A Book of Oddities*.] The annals of crime have furnished the historian with many interesting chapters, the romance writer with innumerable suggestions, and themes for the poet. The numerous examples of persons who have returned to life after execution form a most remarkable chapter in criminal literature. It will be found from our notes that the hangmen employed by our forefathers did not do their work so thoroughly as the executioners of our own time. Our information is drawn from most reliable authorities, and cases that are not supported by historic evidence are not included in this paper.

'Half-hanged Smith'

We propose first to give some notice of a native of the East Riding of Yorkshire, whose eventful career obtained for him the title 'Half-hanged Smith', a place in *Remarkable Trials*, and a niche in the *Celebrities of the Yorkshire Wolds*. John Smith was born at Malton, the son of a farmer of that place. He was apprenticed to a packer in London, and after he had served his time to his trade he engaged for some time as a journeyman. He next went to sea in a merchantman, and afterwards volunteered into a man-o'-war, and in 1702 was in the glorious victory over the Spanish and French fleets by Rooke at Vigo, after this event obtaining his discharge.

Shortly after quitting the navy he joined the army, enlisting in a regiment of guards, but getting into bad company, he deserted and commenced the career of a burglar. He was soon caught, for we find on the 5th of December, 1705, he was arraigned on four different indictments, on two of which he was convicted, and received sentence of death. His execution was fixed for the 24th of the same month. On the appointed day he was conveyed to Tyburn, where he performed his devotions, and was hanged in the usual manner; but when he had been suspended about a quarter of an hour, the people present cried out: 'A reprieve! A reprieve!', which turned out to be correct. The malefactor was quickly cut down, and carried to a house in the neighbourhood. After undergoing bleeding and other applications he soon recovered. He was requested to describe his feelings at the time of the execution, and the substance of his reply was as follows: 'That when he was turned off he for some time was sensible of very great pain, occasioned by the weight of his body, and felt his spirits in a strange commotion, violently pressing upwards; that having forced their way to his head, he, as it were, saw a great blaze, or glaring light, which seemed to go out at his eyes with a flash, and then he lost all sense of pain. That after he was cut down, and began to come to himself, the blood and spirits forcing themselves into their former channels put him, by a sort of pricking or shooting, to such intolerable pain, that he could have wished those hanged who had cut him down.'

After his narrow escape from the grave, he received his pardon, and being discharged, bore ever after the name 'Half-hanged Smith'. Instead of reforming he followed his evil practices, and being apprehended was tried at the Old Bailey for house-breaking. But on account of some difficulty arising in the case, the jury brought in a special verdict, in consequence of which the affair was left to the opinion of the twelve judges, who determined in favour of the prisoner. Having twice escaped, he was again indicted, but the prosecutor dying the day before the trial he for a third time cheated the gallows.

John Bartendale

Another notable Yorkshire case is that of John Bartendale, the piper, who was tried at the York Assizes in 1634 for felony, and condemned to die. On the 27th of March he was hanged on the gallows erected outside Mickelgate Bar, York. At that period there were no houses built on the land, it being open country. The poor strolling musician was swinging for about three quarters of an hour, and appeared to be dead. He was cut down and buried near the gallows. The officers of justice had performed their task in a careless manner both as regards hanging and interring, for it afterwards transpired that he had not been efficiently executed nor properly buried. We are told that earth has a peculiarly invigorating and restorative effect, as has been discovered; and patients suffering from debility are by some medical men placed in earth baths, with the most salutary effects. In the case of gangrened wounds a little earth has been found efficacious in promoting a healthy action of the skin. The unfortunate piper experienced the advantages of an earth bath.

Shortly after he had been buried, one of the Vavasours of Hazelwood was riding by the place, and observed the movement of the earth. He and his servant dismounted, and unearthed Bartendale. He was discovered to be alive, and opening his eyes he sat up and enquired how he had got there. A conveyance was obtained and, covered with Mr Vavasour's cloak – for he had been stripped by the executioner before interment – he was again removed to York Castle. At the next Assize the poor fellow was brought up again. The Reverend S. Baring-Gould, who has paid some attention to this case, observes: 'It was a nice point of law whether the man could be sentenced to execution again, after the Sheriff had signed his affidavit that the man had been hanged till he was dead. Mr Vavasour was naturally reluctant to supply the one link in the chain of evidence which established the identity of the prisoner with the piper who had been hanged for felony and buried as dead. He made intercession that the poor fellow might be reprieved, popular sympathy was on his side, the judge was disposed to mercy, and Bartendale was accorded a full and free pardon, the judge remarking that the case was one in which the Almighty seemed to have interfered in mercy to frustrate the ends of human justice, and that, therefore, he was not disposed to reverse the decree of Providence, according to the piper a prolongation of his days on earth.'

Drunken Barnaby, the noted rhymster, in his *Book of Travels*, alludes to Bartendale when he stops at York:

Here a piper apprehended,
Was found guilty and suspended;
Being led t'fatal gallows,
Boys did cry, 'Where is thy bellows?
Ever must thou cease thy tuning.'
Answered he: 'For all your cunning;
You may fail in your prediction.'
Which did happen without fiction!
For cut down and quick [alive] interred,
Earth rejected what was buried;
Half alive or dead he rises.
Got a pardon next Assizes;
And at York continued blowing –
Yet a sense of goodness showing.

After his wonderful escape the poor fellow obtained an honest livelihood by following the occupation of an hostler. When desired to describe his sensations on being executed, he said that when he was turned off flashes of fire seemed to dark before his eyes, succeeded by darkness and a state of insensibility.

Anne Green

Dr Plot, one of the most painstaking antiquaries of his day, professor of Chemistry at Oxford, and Keeper of the Ashmolean Museum, furnishes in his works several instances of resuscitations of women after execution, and observes that this revival of life appears to happen more frequently in the female sex. In his *Natural History of Oxfordshire* (1677), he relates the following singular circumstance: 'In the year 1650, Anne Green, a servant of Sir Thomas Read, was tried for the murder of her new-born child, and found guilty. She was executed in the Castle-yard at Oxford, where, when they opened the coffin, notwithstanding the rope still remained unloosed and straight about her neck, they perceived her breast to rise; whereupon one Mason, a tailor, intending only as an act of charity, set his foot upon her; and, as some say, one Orum, a soldier, struck her again with the butt of his musket. Notwithstanding all this, when the learned and ingenious Sir William Petty, ancestor of the present Marquis of Lansdowne, then anatomy professor of the University, Dr William, and Dr Clarke, then president of Magdalen College, and vice-chancellor of the University, came to prepare the body for dissection, they perceived some small rattling in her throat; hereupon desisting from their former purpose, they presently used means for her recovery, by opening a vein, laying her in a warm bed, and also using divers remedies respecting her senselessness, insomuch that within fourteen hours she began to speak, and the next day talked and prayed very heartily. During this, the time of her recovery, the officers concerned in her execution would needs have had her away again to have completed it on her, but by the mediation of the worthy doctors and some other friends, with the Governor of the City, Colonel Kelsey, there was a guard set upon her to hinder all further disturbance until he had sued out her pardon from the government. Much doubt indeed arose as to the actual guilt. Thousands of people came in the meantime to see her, and many asserted that it must be the providence of God who would thus assert her innocence.

After some time, Dr Petty, hearing that she had discoursed with those about her, and suspecting that the women might suggest unto her to relate something of the strange visions and apparitions she had seen during the time she seemed to be dead (which they had already begun to do, she having said that she had been in a fine green meadow, having a river running round it, and all things there glittered like silver and gold), he caused all to depart from the room except the gentlemen of the faculty who were to have been at the dissection, and asked her concerning her sense and apprehensions during the time she was hanged, to which she answered that she neither remembered how the fetters were knocked off; how she went out of the prison; when she was turned off the ladder; whether any psalm was sung or not; nor was she sensible of any pains that she could remember. She came to herself as if she had wakened from a sleep, not recovering the use of her speech by slow degrees, but in a manner altogether, beginning to speak just where she left off on the gallows.

Being thus at length perfectly recovered, after thanks given to God and the persons instrumental in bringing her to life, and procuring her an immunity from further punishment, she retired to the country to her friends at Steeple Barton, where she was afterwards married, and lived in good repute among her neighbours, having three children, and not dying until 1659.

Dr Plot furnished a notice of a second malefactor, the servant of a Mrs Cope, at Oxford. She was executed in 1658, and kept suspended an unusually long time to make certain life was extinct; after which, being cut down, her body was allowed to fall to the ground with a violence that might have killed many unhanged persons. Yet she revived. In this instance the authorities next day completed their imperfectly performed duty.

The same author names a third case, that of Marjory Mausole, of Arley, in Staffordshire, but does not give any other particulars.

Walter Wynkeburn
Two instances of criminals being restored to life after being hanged are recorded, on good authority, to have occurred in the town of Leicester. Henry of Knighton (who was a Canon of Leicester Abbey) related in his *Chronicle* for the year 1363 that 'One Walter Wynkeburn, having been hanged at Leicester on the prosecution of Brother John Dingley, Master of Dalby, of the Order of Knights Hospitallers, after having been taken down from the gallows as a dead man, was being carried to the cemetery of Holy Sepulchre, Leicester, to be buried, began to revive in the cart, and was taken into the church of the Holy Sepulchre by an ecclesiastic, and there diligently guarded to prevent him being seized for the purpose of being hanged a second time. To this man King Edward granted pardon in Leicester Abbey, and gave him a charter of pardon . . .'

We learn on the authority of a contemporary record, preserved in the archives of the same town, and quoted in Thompson's *History of Leicester*, that in June 1313 'Matthew of Enderby, a thief, was apprehended and imprisoned in the King's gaol at Leicester, and that being afterwards convicted, he was sentenced by Sir John Digbe and Sir John Daungerville, the King's justices, to be hanged; that he was led to the gallows by the frankpledges of Birstall and Belgrave, and by them suspended; but, on his body being taken down and carried to the cemetery of St John's Hospital for interment, he revived, and was subsequently exiled.'

Patrick Redmond

We find particulars of this example in the *Gentleman's Magazine* of February 1767 as follows: 'One Patrick Redmond having been condemned in Cork, in Ireland, to be hanged for a street robbery, he was accordingly executed, and hung upwards of twenty-eight minutes, when the mob carried off the body to a place appointed, where he was, after five or six hours, actually recovered by a surgeon who made an incision in his windpipe called bronchotomy, which produced the desired effect. The poor fellow has since received his pardon, and a genteel collection has been made for him. It is recorded that the man had the hardihood to go to the theatre the same evening.'

It is stated that a person named William Brodie, hanged in Edinburgh, October 1788, for robbing the excise-office, had an arrangement made similar to the Cork malefactor for his recovery. His design was frustrated on account of having a greater fall than he had bargained for with the hangman.

Roasting Alive
(see **Gridiron**)

Rogers, Captain Henry

Captain Henry Rogers, of the *Martha and Jane*, was indicted at the Liverpool Assizes, along with his two mates, for the murder of a seaman named Andrew Rose under circumstances, according to the evidence given by the crew, of horrible cruelty.

The serious nature of the charge was emphasised by prosecuting counsel, who confirmed that the Crown had undertaken the proceedings in order to show that British subjects were never beyond the reach of British justice, and that seamen were to be protected from such barbarous abuse.

The case against Rogers, William Miles, and Charles

Edward Seymour opened before Mr Baron Watson on 1
August 1857. The prosecution was led by the Attorne·
General, Mr Bliss QC; counsel for the prisoner were M
Monk QC, and Mr Aspinall.

For the benefit of the court the Attorney-Gener·
opened the case with a dramatic reconstruction of th
prisoners' catalogue of crimes against the unfortunat
seaman Rose, which resulted eventually in his death:

The Attorney-General's Reconstruction of the Crime
'Gentlemen of the jury, the three prisoners at the b·
stand indicted of feloniously and of their malice afor·
thought killing one Andrew Rose. This offence was con
mitted on the high seas, between 11th May and 5th Jun
[1857]. The prisoner Henry Rogers was Master of the shi
Martha and Jane; the prisoner Miles was the chief mat·
and Charles Edward Seymour, the second mate. Andre
Rose, the deceased, was an able seaman on board, an
the means of death a series of violences and outrage
committed by the prisoners upon the deceased, by beatin
and ill-treating him. The *Martha and Jane* is a Britis
ship, owned at Sunderland, and it sailed from Hartlepo·
last year to Calcutta, where there was a change of Mas
ers. From Calcutta it came to Demerara, and fro
Demerara to Barbadoes, where Henry Rogers becam
the Master, and Andrew Rose entered on board ship. H
entered on the 29th of April as an able seaman, an
signed articles which stipulated, among other things, f·
a certain allowance of provisions. When he came on boar
he was put to some duty by the second mate, Seymou·
who found fault with him and beat him so severely th·
Rose was advised by some of the crew to leave the shi
and he ran away. About the 9th or 10th of May he w·
brought back by the police and was put in irons. Th
vessel sailed on the 11th May. The day after the vess·
sailed he was again beaten by Seymour; the chief mat·
also, and the Captain also beat him on the same day.

'From that day until the last outrage, about two ·
three days before his death, he was beaten by the pri·

oners almost every day with a rope and a whip, when in irons and out of irons. It is difficult to get the precise dates; but they all occurred after the sailing of the ship and before the death of the deceased. When he came on board he was apparently an able seaman and in good health; his hair was close cropped, and there is reason from that and his conduct to surmise that his intellect had been deranged. He was fond of singing, and he sang "Oh, be joyful". One Sunday morning the Captain bade him be silent, and said, "I'll make you sorrowful," and forced an iron bolt of considerable size into his mouth, and the other two prisoners tied it with a rope behind his head, and he was kept with that gag in his mouth for about an hour and a half. The Captain had a dog on board, and he taught that dog to bite the deceased. He first set him on with a command to "Bite that man", and afterwards, whenever the Captain came forward with his whip, the dog would fly at Rose and bite him. Upon some occasions the blood spurted out. The dog bit out a piece of the flesh, and as the deceased put out his hands to protect himself, the dog bit them too. Upon another occasion, when the deceased was sent aloft to furl the sail, he was naked and went up with a bucket of water probably for a cause to which I shall allude presently. The chief mate followed him up, and whipped him so severely that the blood ran in several places. Upon another occasion, when the deceased was in irons, he asked to be allowed to go to the bows to do a necessary act. And I must here mention that the deceased laboured under such an infirmity which prevented him containing his excrement, which came from him involuntarily. When he was in irons he asked leave to go forward for that purpose. He was refused, upon which he relieved himself upon the deck. The mate and the Captain then beat him, and the latter ordered two men to hold the deceased upon his back, and called for a spoon. He took a 'fid' – a wooden pin – with which he forced the excrement of the deceased into his mouth, and up his nose, saying, "Isn't it nice?" and "You shall have more of it," until those who were called to

assist shrunk away, unable to bear it longer. A day or
two after, this was repeated several times.

'The Captain ordered the carpenter to knock the head
out of a water-cask; but as he was not quick enough, the
captain and mates did it themselves. It was the smallest
of the water-casks on board the ship; they brought Rose
to the cask and put him in. They then rolled the cask
backwards and forwards several times over the deck, the
only means of getting air being through the bung-hole,
which was on the bilge. They lashed the cask to the side
of the ship, and there the deceased remained from twelve
at noon till twelve at night. While there he begged for
water, and uttered great cries of distress. One of the men
gave him a little pea soup – poured it into his mouth, at
which the Captain was very angry, demanding who had
done it, and threatened to serve him the same. Another
seaman gave him a little water, when he complained of
suffocation and excessive heat. The last act, which terminated the cruelties was upon the occasion the deceased was
told by the Captain – "Rose, I wish you would either
drown or hang yourself," to which Rose answered, "I
wish you would do it for me." The Captain and the two
mates then took him to the mainmast. They got a rope
and made what was called a "timber hitch". They put it
over his neck and hoisted him up, his feet being from one
to three feet from the deck. He remained suspended by
the neck for about two minutes. His face became black,
his eyes protruded from the sockets, and froth came out
of his mouth, and they then let him down. The moment
his feet touched the deck he fell flat, as if lifeless, and
the Captain was heard to say that, had they kept him
there half a minute longer he would have been dead. This
seems to have been the last outrage he had to endure.

'After this his body and mind both gave way. The crew
got him down to the forecastle, but he was so crazy they
were obliged to tie his hands. He remained in the forecastle a day or two, but on the morning of the 5th June
– two or three days after the hanging – they got him up
on the deck to wash himself. He could scarcely crawl. He

lay down on the deck, with his head towards the forward hatch, and the water came in over his legs, but not over his head, and he died. An hour or two after they came to remove him and found him dead. He had wounds all over his body from the biting of the dog and the whipping. These wounds had festered. There were maggots in some of them, and he was in such a state that the crew were loth to touch him. They dragged him with a rope aft, and in an hour after that, by order of the Captain he was thrown overboard. The ship made land the next morning, and arrived in Liverpool on the 9th of June. Information was given and the Captain and mates arrested . . .'

Such was the weight of evidence and the feeling of revulsion among the general public that the prisoners were necessarily found guilty, though with a recommendation to mercy from the jury on account of previous good behaviour. The passions of the mob had been excited by the revolting disclosures of the crew, and the verdict was received with vociferous cheering by the crowds which thronged the streets around the court. It is said that the verdict took all the professional men engaged in the trial by surprise, and it was supposed that upon the recommendation of the jury the obligatory sentence of death would have been commuted. This was done in the case of the two mates, but the captain was left to the extreme sentence of the law, and was executed at Kirkdale (now Walton Gaol) on 12 September.

When public indignation had time to cool it began to be felt that the grounds for convictions were of a very ambiguous nature. The crew, it was noted, had been almost in a state of mutiny during the voyage, and bore a violent prejudice against the captain. The fact that the two mates were indicted along with the captain – and so unable to offer evidence in his defence – deprived Rogers of all means of rebutting the charges. In such a case a conspiracy to exaggerate, if not to falsify, evidence was not difficult to achieve. Outside pressures had a good deal

to do with the verdicts, there having been reported a
great number of atrocious acts of cruelty perpetrated at
sea, especially on board American vessels. A remon-
strance made by the English to the American government
on this subject was met by the curt rejoinder of Mr Secretary Marcy 'that we might look at home'. Our government then would have been placed in a most awkward
position if, in the very first instance in which a capital
conviction had been obtained, the royal prerogative had
been exercised to screen the culprit. There can be little
doubt that Captain Rogers was executed to allay the
popular thirst for vengeance, and to vindicate the determi-
nation of the government.

In a solitary gesture of selfless generosity, a public sub-
scription was set up for Rogers's widow, which raised the
sum of £670.

Roman Circus

The Colosseum is without doubt the most celebrated
Roman architectural antiquity to survive that most
remarkable civilisation. Even in its decimated state it
remains a breathtaking sight. The three tiers surrounding
the arena could hold as many as 50,000 spectators and
were always packed with appreciative crowds on the
occasion of the regular 'circuses' and gladiatorial games.
The structure dates from the imperial period, more precisely from AD 70, and was more correctly called the
Flavian Amphitheatre. The name Colosseum almost certainly derived from the colossal bronze statue of the
emperor Nero which stood nearby. Nero's period as
emperor predated the Colosseum itself, but the entertainment of the circus was already well established and several
arenas existed – Nero himself had a wooden theatre built
near to the Campus Martius, and ironically in view of his
later iniquities, it was Nero's rule that nobody – even
criminals – were to be killed at his games.

Although the arenas were used for more traditional
theatrical and musical productions, it was the cruelty of

its great spectacles that drew the crowds. Successive generations of popular writers and film makers have so romanticised the context of the gladiatorial games that one could be forgiven for thinking of them as an early form of professional wrestling – a kind of glamorous burlesque enjoyed by all. In reality it was far from being an ancient form of *Jeux sans Frontières*, but a lethal combat of often indescribable barbarity. The ranks of the gladiators were not swelled by eager young men anxious to exhibit their prowess in the ring, eager for fame and fortune; there was no fame, no fortune, only certain death. On the whole, gladiators would have preferred to be anywhere *but* participating in the games – in fact many committed suicide rather than face the horrors that awaited them. For the most part the gladiators were prisoners of war, convicted criminals, slaves, and more latterly Christians – men and women. Death was the one thing that was sure – it was a Hollywood myth that survivors, people who had fought courageously and well, were granted freedom; they were not. And the ingenuity with which their ends were engineered often bordered on insane genius. Nero, for example, recreated huge and lavish battle scenes in the arena, in which armies of unwilling 'soldiers' fought to the death. There were great sea battles too, and visitors to the Colosseum at Rome can still marvel at the system of conduits and sluices by means of which the arena could become a lake.

With the arrival of the early Christians there was new blood to mingle with the sand, and those who did not fight (and understandably there were many who would not) met death in other ways. Some, in a hideous mockery of Christ's execution, were nailed to crosses set up in the arena, there to be torn to shreds by wolves and wild dogs. Others were dressed up in the skins of animals and thrown to the dogs.

The 'games' often went on until long after nightfall and it was one of Nero's eccentricities to have the arena encircled by Christian captives tied to posts, daubed with pitch and set on fire to provide human torches.

There were exotic animals too – wild beasts that had been collected the length and breadth of the Roman Empire for the amusement of the emperor and his blood-thirsty subjects. As there were mock battles, so there were wild animal 'hunts' where the creatures were the hunters and the prisoners the hunted. Lions, tigers, bears and bulls roamed artificial jungles, savaging their terrified prey; and always their screams were mingled with the jeering of the hostile rabble packing the seats of the amphitheatre. The emperor Nero was particularly fond of these spectacles, as was Caligula, who kept his collection of animals purposely short of food so that they might provide good sport in the arena. Suetonius (*The Twelve Caesars*) recorded that Caligula, finding butchers' meat too expensive, fed his beasts on the flesh of criminals, on one occasion not even bothering to check which were condemned to death, but lining them up and ordering: 'Kill every man between that bald head and the other one over there.'

The Martyrdom of SS Perpetua and Felicitas

For the females, the devil had purposely provided the unusual torture of a most ferocious wild cow, as if out of some mock consideration for their sex. They were stripped and wrapped around the waist with a net, and in this guise were produced before the people; but as the populace expressed their horror at seeing two delicate ladies thus exposed, they were recalled and clothed in a loose dress. Perpetua was the first to be brought forward, when she was tossed in the air and fell on her loins. When she observed her tunic torn from her side, mindful more of modesty than of pain, she gathered it around her.

Roman Military Punishments

Throughout this book references will be found to the ingenious punishments devised by the Romans to meet all eventualities – whether in the service of the civil law, the military code, or simply the persecution of minority groups such as the early Christians.

The civil law developed by the Romans became the envy of the world. First codified in 450 BC, and finalised under the Byzantine emperor Justinian I between 534–528 BC, it grew with the relentless spread of the Roman Empire to become the overall system of international law. Strengthened by the spread of the Roman Church, the

Codex Justinianus still underpins much of the world's legal system.*

Just as they have in all civilisations and times, different laws apply in times of war and within the armed services. Indeed, there are usually an entirely different set of offences and punishments – for example, for the British soldier in the trenches during World War I, leaving his post was an offence punishable by death in front of a firing squad, a crime and means of execution unknown under civilian law. The Romans were more adventurous.

In 1725 a small quarto book, privately printed, was published under the title *The Roman Military Punishments*; it was written by the historian John Beaver, and in this edition was illustrated by William Hogarth. Beaver took as his main period republican Rome and sought to show how, under the emperors, a practical system of punishments inflicted in the interest of loyalty and discipline degenerated into wanton cruelty. Hogarth illustrated thirteen chapters, each dealing with a different central punishment, though some engravings depict other tortures as well.

Fustigatio Beating to death with cudgels and sticks; as distinct from *castigatio* – beating with rods and scourges (see also **Flagellation**).

Decimation A punishment exercised when there were a mass of offenders, every tenth man was executed (usually by **beheading**) and the others were fed on barley instead of wheat (see below).

Beheading For Romans this was the most honourable death, though generally preceded by beating with rods or scourges (*castigatio*).

Crucifixion A common Roman means of execution, but in military law reserved for deserters. Also depicted are two other punishments discussed by Beaver – precipi-

---

*This includes to a great extent Scottish law, though the English system, and by early association that of America, owes more to the influence of Anglo-Saxon tribal practice.

tation, or 'throwing from a height'; and being put to the wild animals.

Dismemberment Not dissimilar from **quartering alive** with horses; the prisoner's feet were tied to the tops of two tree branches which had been bent down; when they were let go and sprang back into position, they tore the man in two.

Freemen degraded and sold into slavery Inflicted on freemen who contrived to evade military service – the ancient world's equivalent of 'draft dodgers'.

Banishment Sometimes from a city or district, but in more severe cases to another country.

Breaking the legs Usually inflicted only on slaves, in this punishment the legs are broken with a club in a similar manner to **breaking on the wheel** and **breaking on the cross**. The punishment of 'blood-letting' was also inflicted; this was described by Beaver as 'for those that were o'erstocked with blood, or in any way lethargically inclined'.

Fustium admonitio A lighter punishment than Fustigatio, inflicted for general negligence and failure to obey orders.

Shameful discharge Much as in the modern armies of the world a major infringement of orders, or bad conduct, results in 'dishonourable discharge'.

Taking away the military belt, or girdle Presumably having the same dishonourable associations as Shameful Discharge, above.

Degrading punishments Another means of inflicting disgrace, prisoners' spears are broken, and they are obliged to march with the baggage wagons and captives.

Issued barley instead of wheat For the serious offences of cowardice, stealing from fellow soldiers, and displaying unnecessary cruelty, the punishment was to be degraded to the status of beasts of burden, symbolically achieved by being fed barley instead of wheat.

Rosary
(see **Halters**)

S

Scalping

Although it is a form of mutilation which usually results in death for the victim – so making it suitable as a punishment – the practice of scalping was more often carried out for ceremonial purposes and for reward.

For example, in his *Histories*, Herodotus (485–425 BC) tells us:

> In the matter of war it is the custom of the Scythians for every soldier to drink the blood of the first man he kills. The heads of all enemies killed in battle are taken to the king, a head represents a 'ticket' which entitles the soldier to a share in the booty – no head, no booty. He strips the skin off the head by making a circular cut round the ears and shaking out the skull; then he scrapes the flesh off the skin with an ox's rib, and when it is clean works it supple with his fingers. He hangs these trophies on the bridle of his horse like handkerchiefs and is very proud of them. The finest warrior is he who has the most scalps. Many Scythians sew scalps together to make cloaks and wear them after the fashion of the peasants.

Among other civilisations, by a process of 'sympathetic magic' it was believed that taking the scalp of a powerful enemy endowed its new owner with the same strengths as the victim.

Although generations misinformed by Hollywood Westerns have come to associate scalping with the native tribes of North America – the so-called 'Indians' – it was the white settlers who were responsible for spreading this appalling habit. For the whites there was no mystical or ritual purpose in taking scalps – they were simply paid a bounty for every native they slaughtered, and a scalp became recognised proof of the deed. It is thought that this systematic attempt at genocide originated in an order made by Governor Kieft in 1641, and continued relentlessly over the following couple of decades.

The native Americans did adopt scalping, but regarded their collection as trophies. According to one account, they removed only the section on the crown of the head, lifting and pulling the hair while cutting around the skin.

Scavenger's Daughter
Invented, so it is recorded, by Sir William Skeffington (or Skevington) during his period of office as Henry VIII's Lieutenant of the Tower of London. Officially named Skeffington's Gyves, the apparatus became known as the Scavenger's Daughter from a corruption of the inventor's name.

A form of restraint far more painful than one would imagine, a prisoner's legs were passed through the lower fetters and, with the executioner's weight on his shoulders, he was bent double so that his arms and head could be forced through the other apertures. The instrument was much favoured by torturers during the religious persecutions of the seventeenth century, and the Jesuit Matthew Tanner wrote that '. . . by the cruel torture, more dreadful and more complete than the rack, by the cruelty of which the whole body is so bent that with some the blood exudes from the tips of the hands and feet, with others, the box of the chest being burst, a quantity of blood is expelled from the mouth and nostrils.'

Shame Boards
(see **Halters**)

Shame Flute
(see **Halters**)

Shame Masks
(see **Masks of Shame**)

Scold's Bridle, or Brank
More effective in reforming shrews, we hear, than even
the **ducking stool**, these popular icons of bygone English
village life were in use between the seventeenth century
and the first half of the nineteenth. Although there were
limitless refinements, bridles were basically a framework
of iron bands enclosing the head and neck and opening
by means of hinges at the sides and could be padlocked
or stapled shut over the unfortunate victim's head. On
the inside of the band which passed over the face an iron
plate was attached which projected inwards and while in
use was forced into the mouth of the sufferer, pressing
down on the tongue and effectively preventing speech.
On the more vicious designs, this mouthpiece had sharp
ridges or spikes which lacerated the tongue and mouth.
To add to her humiliation, the scold was paraded through
the streets, the hideous bridle round her head, to be
pelted with whatever filth the jeering mob had to hand;
sometimes she would be thus chained to the village cross
or whipping post.

Among the large number of scold's bridles that have
survived to the present time is the one at Congleton, in
Cheshire, about which one local historian has written: 'It
was formerly in the hands of the town gaoler, whose
services were not infrequently called into requisition. In
the old-fashioned half-timbered houses in the borough
there was generally fixed on one side of the large open
fireplace a hook, so that, when a man's wife indulged in
her scolding propensities, the husband sent for the town
gaoler to bring the bridle, and had her bridled and chained
to the hook until she promised to behave herself.' Popular

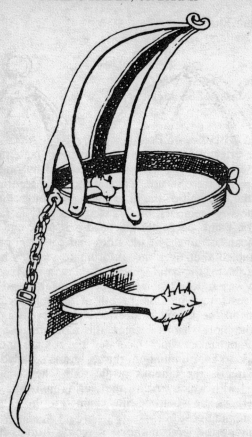

The Stockport brank showing spiked mouthpiece

folklore tells that the Congleton Bridle was last used in public in 1824 on a woman named Ann Runcom who had been abusive to the churchwarden for carrying out his duty of ensuring that public houses were closed during Sunday's divine services. Brought before the mayor, he told her: 'It is the unanimous decision of the mayor and justices that the prisoner there and then shall have the town's bridle for scolding women put upon her, and that

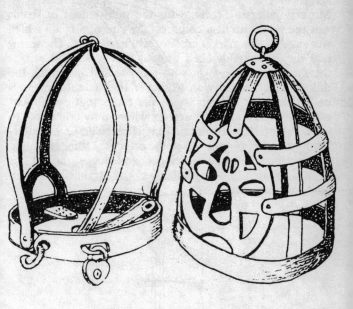

she be led by the magistrate's clerk through every street in town as the example to all scolding women, and that the mayor and magistrates were much obliged to the churchwarden for trying the case before them.'

For what it may offer as an insight into that country's treatment of its offenders, bridling scolds in Scotland dates from as early as 1567 (Edinburgh) – decades before its use south of the border. England's first recorded bridling was ordered by the Macclesfield Sessions in 1623. Like most of these old punishments, it is all but impossible to trace the last use of the scold's bridle, but it is claimed that the device at Bolton-le-Moore, Lancashire was still in use in 1856.

Jougs

More popular in Scotland for the punishment of scolds was the jougs, an iron collar on the end of a chain which was stapled to a market cross or whipping post. The shrew had the collar padlocked around her neck, and was at the mercy of the crowd, who took delight in pelting the unfortunate woman with whatever they could lay hands on. Such was the brutality of the times that even rocks were thrown, and many women whose only crime was to have a sharp or quarrelsome tongue received severe injuries quite out of proportion to the offence. Other coloquial variants on the name are 'joggs' and 'juggs', and it has been suggested that this latter was the origin of the term 'jug', meaning prison.

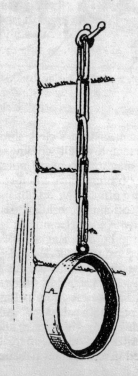

Skeffington's Gyves
(see **Scavenger's Daughter**)

Slander Stone
(see **Halters**)

Smithfield

Well known in the Middle Ages as a horse market and later for trading in sheep, cattle, and pigs, the name derives from *Smethefelde*, or 'Smooth field'. Bartholomew Fair was held here from 1125 until 1850, when it became the scene of such violence and debauchery that it was suppressed. It was the scene of many tournaments, one in 1357 being attended by the kings of both England and France, and was a place of public execution for over 400 years, until the permanent gallows was moved to Tyburn in the reign of Henry IV.

In 1381, Wat Tyler came to Smithfield with his rebels to meet Richard II. Here he was stabbed by the Lord Mayor Walworth, and later executed before St Bartholomew's Hospital.

Many supposed heretics and witches were also put to death at Smithfield, and in the uneasy swing of favour between the Protestant and Roman Catholic faiths in the sixteenth century, both churches claimed martyrs put to the fire in Smithfield.

The first Protestant martyr was John Rogers, vicar of nearby St Sepulchre's Church:

On the fourth of February in the year of our Lord 1555, being Monday in the morning, he was suddenly warned by the keeper of Newgate's wife to prepare himself for the fire, who being then sound asleep, could scarce be awaked . . . And so he was brought to Smithfield by Mr Chester and Mr Woodroofe, then sheriffs of London, there to be burnt; where he showed most constant patience, not using

many words, for he could not be permitted, but only
exhorting the people constantly to remain in that
faith and true doctrine which he before had taught,
and they had learned, and for the confirmation
whereof he was not only content patiently to suffer
and bear all such bitterness and cruelty as had been
showed him, but also most gladly to resign his life,
and to give his flesh to the consuming fire, for the
testimony of the same.

(Book of Martyrs, John Fox, 1563)

In the reign of Mary Tudor, no less than 200 Protestant
martyrs were burned – most of them at Smithfield.

As for the livestock market, it remained a place of
unutterable squalor until it was transferred, in 1855, to
the Metropolitan Cattle Market in Islington. In *Oliver
Twist*, Dickens records his observation of the market:
'The ground was covered nearly ankle-deep, with filth
and mire; a thick steam perpetually rising from the reek-
ing bodies of the cattle . . . the unwashed, unshaven,
squalid and dirty figures constantly running to and fro,
and bursting in and out of the throng, rendered it a stun-
ning and bewildering scene, which quite confounded the
senses.'

With the opening of the Central Markets in 1865, the
old Smithfield became waste ground and was subsequently
laid out as a public open space by the Corporation of
London in 1872.

Spanish Boot

These instruments were in general use in Europe during
the sixteenth and seventeenth centuries and, like all techniques of torture, were subject to individual variations of
design and use of materials. The basic principle was of
metal (occasionally wood) containers which encased the
victim's naked legs from ankle to knee. While he was
restrained long wedges of wood or metal were inserted
between the leg and the inside of the 'boot' and gradually

hammered down with a mallet, each blow driving the wedge deeper, compressing the flesh and crushing the bones. The Spanish Boot was used mainly as an inquisitorial torture, and it would be common for the prisoner to have the request for his confession repeated after each blow of the hammer, stopping only when he complied. So terrible was the effect that few suffered the Boot without being permanently crippled; however, as it was but one stage on the inexorable journey to scaffold or pyre, it was the short-term infliction of pain that motivated its use.

Although it was usually called the 'Spanish' Boot, this device was imported into Britain from the Continent and found special favour in Scotland, where it was often known as the 'bootikins'. Perhaps its most notorious use in that country was during the trial in 1590 of Dr John Fian (aka John Cunningham), a schoolmaster of Saltpans and the alleged leader of Scotland's North Berwick witches.

According to his accusers, Dr Fian was implicated in a conspiracy to take the life, by witchcraft, of King James VI of Scotland (later James I of England). The king took a personal interest in the trial, which charged that Fian entered into a pact with Satan to wreck the ship conveying James to Norway to visit his future queen – this was to be effected by throwing a dead cat into the sea; he also oversaw the process of torture to extract Fian's confession.

A contemporary pamphlet described 'the most severe and cruel pain in the world, called the Boots'; following three sessions with it Fian confessed. He was brought once more before King James to offer a personal admission of culpability and repentance, but Fian withdrew his confession and was 'convaied againe to the torment of the bootes, wherein hee continued a long time, and did abide so many blowes in them that his legges were crushed and beaten together as small as might bee; and the bones and flesh so bruised, that the bloud and marrow spouted forth in great abundance; whereby they were made

unserviceable for ever.' Finally, still protesting his innocence, John Fian was burned on Edinburgh's Castle Hill
in late January 1591.

James VI, however, had clearly blinded himself to the
political background to the North Berwick witches trial,

Imposing the torture of the Spanish boot

nd his own unpopularity among certain of his senior
ubjects. James had always been a gullible youth (he was
4 at the time of the trial), and the incident had persuaded
im so strongly that witchcraft was 'a most abominable
in' that he spent the next five years compiling his cele-
rated *Demonologie* (published in Scotland in 1597), a
anatical treatise demanding the discovery and per-
ecution of sorcerers. Following union in 1603, when
ames became king of Scotland and England, a new
dition of the *Demonologie* was issued, and in the follow-
ng year he persuaded Parliament to pass 'An Act against
onjuration, witchcraft, and dealing with evil and wicked
pirits'. This so-called 'Statute of 1604' made unrepented
orcery punishable by death, and those who were pre-
ared to see the error of their ways committed to periods
f public exposure in the Pillory 'by the space of six
ours, and there shall openly confess his or her error and
ffence'. Although by the end of his reign in 1625 James
ad become a sceptic and the Statute had fallen into
lisuse, it was enthusiastically revived during Cromwell's
ersecution of the Roman Catholics.

Brodequins

Scotland also made extensive use during the seventeenth
century of a variant of the Boot, called the Brodequins.
Short planks of wood bound tight with cords, one each
side of the prisoner's lower legs, replaced the iron cylinder
of the Boot. Wedges were then hammered between the
boards and the victim's legs, causing the cords to tighten
and cut into the flesh and the pressure of the boards to
crush the bones.

Spanish Chair

An instrument of torture in common use by the agents of
the Spanish Inquisition, consisting of an armchair
fashioned from iron in which the victim was confined by
metal bands round his neck and arms. Attached to the
bottom front of the chair were metal 'stocks' into which

the ankles were immovably clamped. When the prisoner
had thus been rendered completely helpless a brazier of
red-hot coals was placed close to his feet so that they
slowly roasted; in order to extend the agony and prevent
too hasty burning, the feet were frequently basted with
oil.

Spanish Donkey
(see **Wooden Horse 2**)

Spanish Inquisition
(see **Inquisition**)

Spider
(see **Pincers**)

Spiked Collar
(see **Collars**)

Squassation
This form of torture – suspension from a pulley – under-
pinned the whole of the torture regime of the Inquisition,
and the technique almost certainly informed the later
designs of such mechanical 'stretchers' as the **rack** and
the Austrian Ladder.

From the illustration opposite we can see that a prisoner
due for what was termed 'painful questioning' was often
stripped of all but an undergarment and his hands bound
tightly behind his back. When his ankles had been similarly fastened, a heavy rope (or sometimes a chain) was
passed through the prisoner's arms and secured to his
wrist fetters. The other end of the rope was passed up
and through a pulley attached to the roof-beam and down
again within the executioner's reach. When all was in

The prisoner prepared for squassation

readiness for the inquisition, the wretched prisoner was
unceremoniously hauled up into the air to about a man's
height from the floor. Already the pain caused by having
his shoulders wrenched backwards against the full weight
of the body would have been intense. But the torture had
hardly begun. Now was the time gradually to add the iron
weights to the weight of the body, suspending them from
his ankles like some grotesque pendulums. By this stage
the executioner and his assistants would be getting into
their stride, and with much merriment would begin to
indulge their natural talent for inflicting suffering by
adding small refinements. This skill might reveal itself by
the use of red-hot **pincers** to nip the victim's naked flesh,

or of rakes, like razor-sharp wool-combs, to tear his skin
into tatters; the less imaginative might simply engage in
a modest **flagellation**.

But however cruel these needless tortures might have
been, there was worse to come – much worse: a special
finale that could have been dreamed of only by a madman.
Now the executioners exerted all their strength to raise
the man and his encumbrances high up to the ceiling of
the chamber. They let go of the rope and the prisoner
plummeted rapidly towards the stone floor; but only for
a few feet, before the rope was gripped tight again and
the body jerked and twisted in unimaginable agony just
above the ground, the bones jarred, the joints dislocated,
the nerve fibres torn to useless shreds by the sudden
shock. This could be repeated many times before the arms
were finally torn loose, and often was; it could prove
fatal, and often was.

More frequently, however, there were 'degrees' of this
torture to fit the severity of the alleged offence, and
although it was impossible to impose the rules uniformly,
most experts agree that there were five distinct stages in
the torture of suspension. First it might only have been
necessary to threaten torture in order to get the desired
response; failing this, the second 'encouragement' was
leading the prisoner to the torture chamber to become
acquainted with what was in store – possibly he might be
stripped and bound to emphasise the urgency of his co-
operation. The third degree was to hoist the prisoner up
and leave him for a while to meditate on the immediate
pain; if a confession or information was not forthcoming
he would pass into the next stage of the ordeal, the
weights; this could be aggravated by swinging the victim
about on the rope to exert more pressure on the joints.
But if all else failed, the fifth degree of torture was
reached and the body was suddenly dropped.

Stocks

Although similar in principle to the **pillory** in that both are designed to display offenders for the scorn and amusement of the community, it is possible that some form of stocks is of even greater antiquity than the pillory.

There is, for example, no shortage of direct references to the stocks in both the Old and New Testaments of the Bible, and according to the sixteenth chapter of Acts, Paul and Silas were taken up by the Romans and 'when they had laid many stripes upon them they cast them into prison, charging the jailer to keep them safely. Who, having received such a charge, thrust them into the inner prison and made their feet fast in the stocks.' Perhaps the gaoler should have known better than to think that his stocks could hold such an illustrious pair of prisoners, for no sooner had they been constrained than Paul and Silas 'prayed and sang praises unto God . . . And suddenly there was a great earthquake, so that the foundations of the prison were shaken: and immediately all the doors were opened and every one's bands were loose'. In all, the most impressive prison break in classical history!

In England, the Saxon word *stocc* was current in 862, and referred to a wooden pole apparatus in which felons' ankles could be put between two heavy logs set to raise and lower between uprights. It was not until some centuries later that the stocks developed into a board structure with a single hole cut in it to trap one ankle; they further evolved into the more familiar apparatus with holes for both wrists and both ankles. According to Burford (*In the Clink*), the earliest contemporary illustration of the stocks can be found in a twelfth-century Psalter in the library at Trinity College, Cambridge.

Predictably, regional fads and fashions have left a legacy of different designs; those illustrated originated in fifteenth-century Germany, where stocks were the punishment for a range of sexual misdemeanours such as adultery and procuring, and for idlers and vagabonds.

Although the stocks are more familiar in the setting of a village green or market square, they were also as

An elaborate variation of the pulley torture

frequently to be found *inside* the prisons of the Middle
Ages as they were when Paul and Silas gave the Romans
a surprise. It was always useful to be able to isolate and

This and following page: two variants of stocks design

confine prisoners, but most accounts seem agreed that the stocks were used as a form of torture to further increase the discomfort of incarceration. During the English persecution of John Wycliffe's followers, the Lollards, in the

Lollards in the stocks

fifteenth century, George King, John Wade, Thomas Leyes and William Andrews were confined in stocks in the Lollard's Tower where they sickened and died.

There is some controversy over the exact location of the Lollard's Tower, because although there was a prison with this name at Lambeth Palace it postdated the deaths of King, Wade, Leyes and Andrews. In his *Prisons and Punishments of London*, Richard Byrne suggests the explanation that the authentic Lollard's Tower was close by the old St Paul's cathedral where it is known that 'heretics' were tortured and killed. The cathedral was destroyed by the Great Fire of London at about the time the Lambeth tower became a prison in the seventeenth century. 'Perhaps,' Byrne advances, 'the title was unwittingly transferred by later generations.'

The stocks remained in general use until the middle of the nineteenth century, though probably their last use was in 1872. Pettifer quotes Walter Money's account of the incident from his *Popular History of Newbury*:

Previous to the destruction of the old Guildhall [Newbury] in 1828, the whipping post and pillory – one above the other – were placed close to the south side of the building, and the stocks were at the opposite end. The latter were stowed away in the Town Hall cellars, where they had lain forgotten for years. But in 1872 [11 June] these favourite instruments of punishment devised by the ingenuity of our forefathers, were once more brought into requisition when one Mark Tuck, an incorrigible bacchanalian, was sentenced to four hours incarceration in the stocks for insobriety and creating a disturbance at the Parish Church. It being a pouring wet day the stocks were not set up in the Market Place, but placed in the Shambles, while a constable was stationed close by to see that the prisoner was not molested by vengeful missiles or other indignities. Still the punishment was sufficiently severe, for Mark was surrounded the whole time by a crowd of jeering juveniles, to whom the process was a novelty. Mark is reported to have borne up fairly well, fervently ejaculating every time the quarter-hour of the church clock chimed: 'Thank God, another quarter gone', at the same time marking it in the accumulated dust of years that still lay thickly upon the stocks. At length the period of incarceration was at an end, and on being released and feeling his feet once more, the victim of this degrading punishment bounded into the police station, almost overturning an old woman in his haste to escape from the sarcastic onlookers.

Mark Tuck was lucky in having the full protection of the law, but in earlier days when the crowd was allowed to hurl more than abuse at their captive victim, the stocks, like the pillory, claimed many fatalities.

The following quaint story tells of a rather different kind of fatality, though where it and the illustration originated I have been unable to discover:

The circumstances to which we refer occurred some time ago in Staffordshire. A tramp named William Pitcairn, weary and footsore, rested at a small roadside house. Some young men who happened to be there treated him to several pints of ale. Poor Pitcairn, it appeared, had not broken his fast for several hours, and as a natural consequence he became half stupefied with the beer. While in this state his tormentors led him to the stocks in which they firmly fixed his feet. This done they hung his faithful dog on one of the supports, and left both dog and master to their fate. In the morning poor Pitcairn was found dead by some of the neighbours. A coroner's jury sat on the matter and returned a verdict that he 'Died from want and exposure'. The inhuman wretches who had placed the tramp in the stocks escaped with a mere nominal punishment.

Chinese stocks

Stoning to Death

As a convenient implement of *ad hoc* assassination, a lump of stone probably featured throughout the unwritten criminal history of early primitive man. However, it was left to the Jews to formalise stoning to death and adopt it as a method of judicial execution – mainly for heresy, blasphemy and idolatory, but also for a number of sexual offences such as adultery. There are several Old Testament references to stoning, for example in Deuteronomy (xvii, 2–5) there is written the warning:

> If there be found among you, within any of the gates which the Lord thy God giveth thee, man or woman, that hath wrought wickedness in the sight of the

Lord thy God, in transgressing his covenant, and hath gone and served other gods and worshipped them, either the sun, or moon, or any of the host of heaven which I have not commanded, and it be told thee, and thou hast heard it, and inquired diligently, and behold, it be true, and the thing certain, that such abomination is wrought in Israel, then shalt thou bring forth that man or woman which have committed that wicked thing unto thy gates, even that man or woman, and shalt stone them with stones till they die.

In the year 35, the Jews created the first Christian martyr (or 'protomartyr') when they stoned to death Saint Stephen outside the main gate of the temple at Jerusalem. Stephen had been condemned by members of the Sanhedrin – the Jewish High Court of Justice comprising seventy priests and elders which had also condemned Christ to death – for bearing witness before them that Christ was the Messiah and that he had risen from the dead. According to Acts (viii, 54–59):

When they had heard these things they were cut to the heart, and they gnashed on him with their teeth. But he, being full of the Holy Ghost, looked up steadfastly into heaven and saw the glory of God and Jesus standing on the right side of God, and said: 'Behold, I see the heavens opened, and the Son of Man standing on the right hand of God.' Then they cried out with a loud voice, and stopped their ears, and ran upon him with one accord, and cast him out of the city and stoned him; and the witnesses lay down their clothes at a young man's feet, whose name was Saul. And they stoned Stephen, [who] called upon God, saying: 'Lord Jesus receive my spirit.'

The persecution of the Christians was enthusiastically adopted by the Romans and by the Alexandrians who, in a purge carried out in the final year of Emperor Philip's reign (249), stoned to death a whole hagiography of future martyr saints. The first victim of the mob's rage was a venerable old man named Metras, whom the heathens had tried to compel to utter blasphemies against his God; when he refused, they beat him and thrust splinters of reed into his eyes. Then they stoned him to death. The next person to be seized was a woman called Quinta, whom they led to the temple to force her to worship an idol. She addressed the false god with such words of scorn and so angered the people that they dragged her by her heels over the cobbles, scourged and then stoned her . . .

During their persecutions of each other the different Christian factions employed stoning as a punishment for what was perceived to be 'heresy'. During the persecution of the Protestants at Piedmont in the seventeenth century, Henry Moore records the death of a young woman named Judith Mandon who had refused to adopt the Roman Catholic faith. Although in this instance wood was thrown, this form of execution was normally carried out with stones:

> [She] was fastened to a stake and sticks thrown at her from a distance in the very same manner as in that barbarous custom formerly practised on Shrove Tuesday of throwing at cocks. By this inhuman proceeding her limbs were beat and mangled in a most terrible manner, and at last one of the bludgeons dashed out her brains.

Although in most developed nations stoning to death was replaced by more 'civilised' methods of punishment there are, in the approach to the 21st century, still countries where stoning remains on the statute. Confined mainly to the Arab nations, stoning is the most protracted and potentially painful means of administering the death sentence in the world today. Indeed, according to Article 119 of the Islamic Penal Code of Iran, that is exactly what it should be: '. . . the stones should not be too large so that the person dies on being hit by one or two of them; nor should they be so small that they could not be defined as stones.' The following graphic description of a modern stoning is taken from the 1989 edition of Amnesty International's *When the State Kills*:

> The lorry deposited a large number of stones and pebbles beside the waste ground, and then two women were led to the spot wearing white and with sacks over their heads . . . [they] were enveloped in a shower of stones and transformed into two red sacks . . . The wounded women fell to the ground and Revolutionary Guards smashed their heads in with a shovel to make sure they were dead.

On 26 November 1991, Farhama Hyat was repeatedly raped by an armed gang who had broken into her home in Karachi, Pakistan. During the attack Ms Hyat was told that she was being punished for her friendship with the leader of the Pakistani opposition party, Ms Benazir Bhutto. It was alleged that the gang were operating on instructions given by Irfanullah Khan Marwat, son-in-law of President Ishaq Khan. Ms Bhutto was, understandably, the first to condemn the appalling crime, and she demanded that the culprits should be stoned to death (in Muslim law, *sansar*). It should be added that when she was in power as Pakistan's Prime Minister, Benazir Bhutto asked the President to commute the sentences of all those under threat of execution in the country (then about two thousand) – which he did. This seems a clear case of the popular contention that it is the duty of the opposition party to oppose!

Surgeons' Hall
(see **Dissection**)

Swimming

As a means of determining innocence or guilt, Swimming a suspect has a pedigree dating back to the third millennium before Christ, when the Babylonian king Hammurabi decreed that if a man charged his fellow with sorcery then the accused must jump into a river to prove, by floating, that he was innocent. However, if the man drowned, he was guilty and his possessions fell forfeit to his accuser. On the other hand, if the accusation proved false then the accuser forfeited not only his property but also his life.

In the eleventh century Edward the Confessor, King of England, established *Iudicum aquae* – trial by water – as a test for all crimes, but reversed the judgement so that a suspect who *sank* was innocent. Further refinements were tying the victim's left thumb to their right toe (and sometimes the right thumb to the left toe as well); and if there was a danger of a suspect being washed downstream by the current, or of an innocent person remaining on the bottom, a rope was passed under the arms and held by inquisitors on either bank of the river or pond.

Although it was officially abolished in the reign of Henry III, Swimming persisted in common use until the late nineteenth century, mainly as a trial by ordeal for those suspected of witchcraft. However, it was in the seventeenth century that Swimming had its heyday, and the method was enthusiastically championed by Matthew Hopkins, Witch Finder-General of England, in his *Discoverie of Witches* (1647). The following account of the ordeal derives from a pamphlet of 1613, *Witches Apprehended, Examined and Executed*, describing the Swimming of one Mary Sutton:

> . . . His friend understanding this, advised him to take them up to his mill dam, having just shut up the mill gates that the water might be at its highest, and then binding their arms across, stripping them into their smocks, and leaving their legs at liberty, throw them into the water. Lest they should not be

The Swimming of Mary Sutton in 1612

witches, and so that their lives might not be in danger of drowning, let there be a rope tied around their middles so long that it might reach from one side of the dam to the other, where on each side let a man stand, that if she chance to sink they may draw her up. Then, if she swim, take her up and cause some women to search her, upon which, if they find any extraordinary marks upon her [see **Pricking**] let her a second time be bound, and have her right thumb bound to her left toe and her left thumb to her right toe, and your men with the same rope to preserve her, and be thrown into the water when if she swim you may count on it that she is a witch . . . At which his men presently bound her to their master's horse, and brought her home to his house, and shutting up his mill gates did as the gentleman had advised him. When being thrown in the first time she sank some two feet in the water with a fall, but rose again and floated on the water like a plank. Then he commanded her to be taken out and had women search her, who found under her left thigh a kind of teat, which she confessed her familiars, cats, moles, etc. used to suck. Then was she a second time bound, her thumbs and toes across, and she sank not at all, but sitting on the water turned about like a wheel. Notwithstanding Master Engers' men standing either side of the dam with the rope tossing her up and down to make her sink, but could not.

Despite isolated supporters, trial by Swimming was never popular on the Continent, and in many places it was actively forbidden. It is likely that the **ducking stool** developed out of Swimming.

T

Thousand Cuts
(see **Death by the Thousand Cuts**)

Thumbscrews
Invariably used in order to extract either information or
a confession, the origin of the screw was a simple but
excruciatingly painful torture called 'thumb-tying' where
the digits were subjected to pressure by being tightly
bound with strong thin cord. The later, mechanical device
was capable of exerting greater force.

Like the **rack**, thumbscrews are an eternal symbol of
the torture chamber, and for those in any doubt of the
agony which this modest mechanism is capable of inflicting, just remember the last time you hit your thumb with
a hammer while tapping in a nail. Like most torture
instruments, the design of thumbscrews was subject to the
whims and fashions of their makers; they could be single
or double, simple or ornate, but there was just one guiding
principle behind all of them:

> First the thumbscrews nipped the flesh, then, after
> a turn or so, the blood commenced to flow, and the
> flesh of the victim began to ooze from between the
> teeth of the iniquitous machine. Then a horrible
> blood-curdling scrunch would announce the fact that
> the screw was biting its way through the bone. Twist,
> twist, twist, until finally the teeth of the thumbscrew
> meet.
>
> (*Famous Crimes Past and Present*)

The last person to be so tortured in Britain (so it is
claimed) was William Carstares. Carstares was implicated

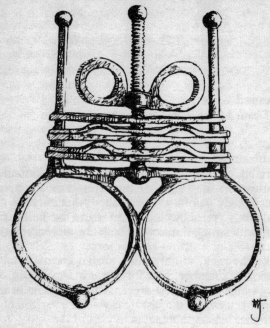

Complex handcuff and combination thumbscrew originating in Germany

in the notorious Rye House Plot of 1683 to murder King Charles II and his brother James as they passed near Rye House, Herefordshire, on their return from Newmarket. The conspiracy was the brainchild of Whig extremists and former supporters of Oliver Cromwell, and failed simply because the royal party left earlier than planned. Because the use of torture was already officially (though not un-officially) abolished under English law, Carstares was removed to Scotland where he was put to the torture in order to elicit the names of the Rye House plotters:

> Upon his refusing, they put his thumbs in the screws, and drew them so hard that as they put him to extreme torture, so they could not unscrew them till

the smith that made them was brought with his tools to take them off.

(*History of the Reformation*, Bishop Burnet, 1829)

During the persecutions of the so-called Covenanters, the Scottish Presbyterians, between the Restoration in 1660 and the revolution of 1688, the thumbscrews, also called thumbikins, acquired the deceptively jolly name of 'Pillie-Winkies'. Their use continued in Caledonia until the end of the seventeenth century, and the last recorded instance appears to have been in 1690, when Henry Nevil Payne suffered for two days in an attempt to extort him to give information about a suspected plot to restore King James to the throne.

Handscrews were an elaborate form of the thumbscrew which had the capacity to entrap all the fingers together.

Footscrew

Built rather like what bookbinders call a 'nipping press', footscrews, or 'foot presses', worked on the same

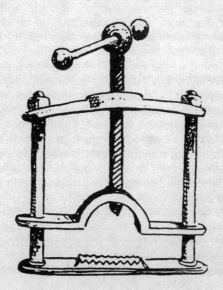

principle as thumbscrews. Often additional features such as a serrated base would be imaginatively added to ensure greater discomfort, and one variant had a vicious spike in the top plate which bored through the upper bone of the foot as the screw was turned.

Dice
The Dice was a form of foot compression in which the prisoner was first secured spreadeagled on the cell floor and two metal blocks, resembling dice but concave on one side, were bound firmly either side of the heel of the right foot. Turning a screw caused the ropes to tighten and the metal blocks to cut into and crush the foot.

Treadmill

The treadmill, eternal symbol of all that was wrong with the approach to early penal policy, was devised by the celebrated English civil engineer Sir William Cubitt. The principle of rotative power was already ancient, and driven by animals such as donkeys and cattle, and by wind and water, had been used for millennia to perform tasks such as raising water and grinding cereal grain. It was in the year 1818 that Sir William was invited to turn his estimable mind to the problem of providing some simple means of employing Britain's large, but mainly idle, prison population. He adapted the wheel (it was alternately called the 'treadwheel') to generate energy from upwards of ten prisoners at a time. The huge devices were in the shape of a cylindrical wheel laid on its side and turned by means of treading on steps around its periphery. Convicts stood side by side or in individual compartments along the wheel, and operated the machine with the same movement as climbing stairs.

The first treadmill was installed at Brixton Prison (then in the county of Surrey, now south-west London) at a cost of £6,913 3s 6d, and until the novelty wore off it was a popular attraction for members of the public to watch the convicts at work.

In their extensive study *Criminal Prisons of London* (1862), Henry Mayhew and John Binney gave the most exact contemporary description of the treadmill:

This invention was introduced at most of the prisons more than forty years ago, but the machine with few exceptions has never been applied, even to this day, to any useful purpose. The prisoners call the occupation 'grinding the wind', and that is really the only description applicable to it – the sole object of the labour of some 150 men, employed for eight hours per day, being simply to put in motion a big fan, or regulator, as it is called, which, impinging on the air as it revolves, serves to add to the severity of the work by increasing the resistance.

Each wheel contains twenty-four steps which are eight inches apart, so that the circumference of the cylinder is sixteen feet. The wheels revolve twice in one minute, and the mechanism is arranged to ring a bell at the end of every thirtieth revolution, and so announce that the appointed spell of work is finished. Every man put to labour at the wheel has to work for fifteen quarters of an hour every day.

Those who have never visited a correctional prison can have but a vague notion of the treadmill. The one we first inspected at Coldbath Fields was erected on the roof of the large, cuddy-like room where the men take their meals. The entire length of the apparatus was divided into twenty-four compartments, each something less than two feet wide and separated from each other by high wooden partitions.

When the prisoner has mounted to his place on the topmost step of the wheel he has the same appearance as if he were standing on the upper side of a huge garden-roller, and somewhat resembles the acrobat we have seen at a circus perched on the cask that he causes to revolve under his feet.

All the men work with their backs to the warder

supporting themselves by a hand-rail fixed to the
boards at the back of each compartment, and they
move their legs as if they were mounting a flight of
stairs; but with this difference, that instead of their
ascending, the steps pass from under them and, as
one of the officers remarked, it is this peculiarity
which causes the labour to be so tiring, owing to the
want of a firm tread. The sight of the prisoners on
the wheel suggested to us the idea of a number
of squirrels working outside rather than inside the
barrels of their cages.

In time this utterly pointless means of keeping prisoners
'busy' was given some purpose by attaching the wheel to
some grinding or pumping mechanism so that the energy
created at least had some beneficial effect. At Holloway
Prison, for example, the treadmill was used as a water-
pump filling roof-top storage tanks from a deep under-
ground well. Treadmills had mostly been abandoned by
the early twentieth century, and of the 39 still in operation
in 1895 only thirteen survived into the new century.

Trülle
(see **Whirligig**)

Trial by Battle

The Primrose and the Wretch
Abraham Thornton was a 25-year-old bricklayer, son of
a prosperous builder at Castle Bromwich. In August 1817,
he stood indicted at the Warwick Summer Assizes for the
rape and murder of Mary Ashford, held locally to be the
unsullied flower of country maidenhood.
    From the evidence, it appears that on 26 May 1817 –
it was a Whit Monday – Mary attended a special dance
held at Daniel Clarke's tavern, the Three Tuns (or Tyburn
House), in the hamlet of Tyburn. At seven o'clock in the

evening, she called on her friend Hannah Cox who, with her mother Mrs Butler, lived at Erdington. Here, Mary changed from her everyday clothes into the party finery which she had left with Mrs Butler earlier in the day; after which the two girls set off for the pub, arriving at around 7.40 p.m. just as the dancing had commenced. No sooner had Mary entered the room than she became the object of Abraham Thornton's lustful attentions, and despite an appearance described by one witness as 'brutal and repulsive', Mary responded to his flattery.

Hannah Cox left the festivities at around eleven o'clock with her fiancé Benjamin Carter, while her friend was still engaged with Thornton. The four met up again on the bridge by the tavern and together walked along the Chester Road towards Erdington. At one stage Ben Carter decided that he had not made merry enough, and returned to the Three Tuns. Further on, Mary announced that she intended spending the night at her grandfather's cottage which stood on the corner of Bell Lane (now Orphanage Road) and Chester Road, and so Hannah returned alone to her home in Erdington, leaving Thornton, she supposed, to escort Mary to her grandfather's. This was at midnight, and in fact Mary spent the next several hours in young Thornton's company before she went knocking on Hannah Cox's door at about four in the morning. Mary claimed that she had left her escort some hours before, and had been at her grandfather's house; she was on her way back to her uncle's at Langley Heath, and wanted to change into her everyday clothes before setting out. This done, Mary took leave of her friend and passed along the route home that took her through the secluded Bell Lane, where she was seen by, and greeted, several early-rising farm labourers. A little further on, Mary entered Penns Mill Lane (now Penns Lane), taking a short cut across the fields, in one of which there was a deep water-filled pit.

When George Jackson, a road mender, came upon a blood-stained bonnet and pair of shoes by the pit near Penns Mill Lane later that morning, he immediately raised the alarm; soon a crowd had gathered to witness the dragging of the pit, and the consequent discovery of the battered body of Mary Ashford.

A contemporary account describes the state of the ground immediately surrounding the scene of the murder which gave eloquent clues to the girl's last tragic struggle:

> The circumstances proved in evidence were that the footsteps of a man and a woman were traced from the path through a harrowed field, through which [Mary's] way lay home to Langley. The marks were at first regular, but afterwards exhibited proofs of the persons whose footfalls they represented running and struggling; and at length they led to a spot where a distinct impression of a human figure and a large quantity of coagulated blood were discovered, and on this spot the marks of a man's knees and toes were also distinguishable. From thence the man's footprints only were seen, and accompanying blood marks were distinctly traced for a considerable space towards the pit; and it appeared plainly as if a man had walked along the footway carrying a body, from which the blood dropped. At the edge of the pit, the shoes, bonnet, and bundle of the deceased were found; but only one footstep could be seen there, and that was a man's. It was deeply impressed, and seemed to be that of a man who thrust one foot forward to heave something into the pit.

The finger of suspicion was at once pointed at young Abraham Thornton – partly by dint of his reputation, and partly by his very obviously lecherous approaches of the previous evening. Mr Bedford, a magistrate of Birches Green thus sent the landlord of the Three Tuns, Daniel Clarke, to fetch Thornton in for questioning. During this interrogation, the youth admitted his nocturnal involvement with Mary, but swore that it was by her total consent.

Most of the subsequent legal investigation was con-

cerned with the verification of alibis – notably Thornton's
– which proved no easy matter in the year 1817, when
clocks were scarce, and ones that kept good time rarer.

The trial took place in the County Hall at Warwick
on 8 August, before Mr Justice Holroyd. Mr Nathaniel
Gooding Clarke KC presented the case for the Crown,
and Messrs William Reader and Henry Revell Reynold
conducted Thornton's defence:

> The prisoner declined to say anything in his defence,
> stating that he would leave everything to his counsel,
> who called several witnesses to the fact of his having
> arrived home at an hour which rendered it very
> improbable, if not impossible, that he could have
> committed the murder, and have traversed the dis-
> tance from the fatal spot to the places in which he
> was seen, in the very short time that appeared to
> have elapsed; but it was acknowledged that there
> was a considerable variation in the different village
> clocks; and the case was involved in so much diffi-
> culty, from the nature of the defence, although the
> case for the prosecution seemed unanswerable, that
> the judge's charge to the jury occupied no less than
> two hours. 'It were better,' he said, in conclusion,
> 'that the murderer, with all the weight of his crime
> upon his head, should escape punishment, than that
> another person should suffer death without being
> guilty'; and this consideration weighed so powerfully
> with the jury that, to the surprise of all who had
> taken an interest in this awful case, they returned a
> verdict of not guilty, which the prisoner received
> with a smile of approbation.

Next morning Abraham Thornton, free again, returned
to Castle Bromwich. However, such was the public,
official, and newspaper outrage at the verdict, that it was
but weeks before a means was found to take Abraham
Thornton once again before a court. This was achieved
by means of the rarely invoked law allowing the next of

kin, or 'heir-at-law', of the deceased to issue a private
writ of appeal; in this case it was taken out in the name
of William Ashford, Mary's elder brother, and served by
the Sheriff of Warwick.

On 5 November 1817, Thornton was escorted by Mr
Tatnall, Keeper of Warwick Gaol, to appear at West
minster Hall, London, before the Court of the King's
Bench. And here legal history was to be made.

Not to be outwitted, Thornton's advisers had also been
doing a little homework with the ancient law books, and
came up with the archaic right of the appellee (Thornton)
to challenge William Ashford (the appellant) to Trial by
Battle – a process forgotten since the time of Charles I.
It was clear that, in any form of physical combat, the
frail, slow-witted Ashford would be no match for the
burly, aggressive Thornton. After seemingly endless legal
wrangling – throughout which time Thornton was held in
the Marshalsea Prison – the Lord Chief Justice decided
that Abraham Thornton *was* entitled to his 'trial by
battel', and that as the appellant had refused to accept
the challenge, the appellee must be set free.

Free he may have been, but such was the loathing in
which he was held in his native county, that Abraham
Thornton emigrated to America. His notional 'adversary'
William Ashford, died in 1867 in Birmingham.

Mary Ashford's body was buried in Sutton Coldfield
churchyard on 1 June 1817, beneath the inscription:

> As a warning to Female Virtue and a
> humble monument to Female Chastity
> this stone marks the grave of
> MARY ASHFORD
> who in the 20th year of her age
> having incautiously repaired to a scene of
> amusement
> without proper protection
> was brutally violated and murdered
> on the 27th May, 1817
> Lovely and chaste as the primrose pale
> Rifled on virgin sweetness by the gale

Mary! the wretch who thee remorseless slew
Avenging wrath, which sleeps not, will pursue.
For though the deed of blood be veiled in night
Will not the judge of all the earth do right?
Fair Blighted flower! The muse that weeps
thy doom
Rears o'er thy sleeping from this warning tomb.

The procedure for Trial by Battle as claimed in the Thornton case is as follows:

When the privilege of Trial by Battle was claimed by the appellee, the judges had to consider whether, in the circumstances, he was entitled to the exercise of such a privilege; and his claim thereto having been admitted, they fixed a day and place for the combat, which was conducted with much solemnity.

A piece of ground was set out, sixty feet square, enclosed with lists, and on one side a court was erected for the judges of the Court of Common Pleas, who attended there in their scarlet robes; and also a bar for the learned serjents-at-law. When the Court was assembled proclamation was made for the parties, who were accordingly introduced into the area by proper officers, each armed with a baton, or staff, of an ell long, tipped with horn, and bearing a four-cornered leather target for defence. The combatants were bare-headed and bare-footed, the appellee with his head shaved, the appellant not, but both were dressed alike. The appellee pleaded not guilty and threw down his glove, and declared that he would defend the same by his body; the appellant took up the glove, and replied that he was ready to make good the appeal body for body. And thereupon the appellee, taking the Bible in his right hand, and in his left the right hand of his antagonist, swore this oath: 'Hear this, O man whom I hold by the hand, who callest thyself [name], by the name of baptism, that I who call myself [name], by the name of baptism, did not feloniously murder thy [father], [name], by name, nor am any way guilty of the said felony. So help me God.'

To this the appellant replied, holding the Bible and his antagonist's hand, in the same way: 'Hear this, O Man whom I hold by the hand, who callest thyself [name], by the name of baptism, that thou art perjured, because that thou feloniously did murder my [father], [name], by name. So help me God and the saints; and this I will prove against thee by my body, as this Court shall award.'

Next, an oath against sorcery and enchantment was taken by both the combatants in this, or a similar, form: 'Hear this, ye justices, that I have this day neither ate, drank nor have upon me either bone, stone or grass; nor any enchantment, sorcery or witchcraft, whereby the law of God may be abased, or the law of the devil exalted. So help me God and His saints.'

The battle was thus begun, and the combatants were bound to fight till the stars appeared in the evening. If the appellee was so far vanquished that he could not or would not fight any longer, he was adjudged to be hanged immediately; and then, as well as if he were killed in battle, Providence was deemed to have determined in favour of the truth, and his blood was declared attainted. But if he killed the appellant, or could maintain the fight from sunrising till the stars appeared in the evening, he was acquitted. So also, if the appellant became recreant and pronounced the word 'Craven', he lost his *liberam legem*, and became infamous; and the appellee recovered his damages, and was for ever quit, not only of the appeal, but of all indictments for the same offence. There were cases where the appellant might be counter-pleaded, and oust the appellee from his trial by battle – these were vehement presumption or sufficient proof that the appeal was true, or where the appellant was under fourteen or above sixty years of age, or was a woman or a priest, or a peer or, lastly, a citizen of London, because the peaceful habits of the citizens were supposed to make them unfit for combat.

Needless to say, this remnant of barbarity was

eventually abolished by an Act of Parliament, the introduction of which was attributable to the Thornton case,
which removed it from the statute.

VW

Venomous Gloves

I am indebted to Scott's *History of Torture* for this uniquely bizarre entry. Scott acknowledges James Greenwood's *Curiosities of Savage Life* (1863) as his source, though as yet I have not been able to trace a copy of this original.

A curious form of torture, according to Greenwood, was adopted as an initiatory rite by the Mandrucu tribe of Amazonian Indians. To look at, the instruments employed in this particular ordeal appeared remarkably innocent. They consisted of two cylindrical cases fashioned out of palm-tree bark, measuring about a foot in length, and stopped at one end. They were for all the world like a pair of huge and crudely made gloves, and it was as gloves they were used. The initiate thrust his hands into the cases and, followed by a procession of onlookers, which in fact amounted to all the available members of the tribe, started upon a tour of the village or camp, stopping at the door of every wigwam to execute a sort of dance. These 'gloves' were, however, by no means as innocent as they seemed, and the dance their wearer performed was more real than mimic. For each gauntlet contained a collection of ants and other insects, all selected for their venomous, biting capacities. And what with the heat generated within and the blazing sun playing without the bark gloves, the wretched hands seem literally a furnace.

Violin
(see **Halters**)

Vlad the Impaler
(see **Impaling**)

Wheels
There are a surprising number of variations on the theme of punishment and execution by means of wheels, the most frequently encountered being 'breaking'. In its simplest form, the prisoner was bound spreadeagled on a large cart wheel, and his arms, legs and body

systematically smashed with iron bars or clubs.* The second basic technique was to use a smaller wheel to break the body of a prostrate victim. Other variants included binding the prisoner around the circumference of a cart's wheel like a human tyre and setting the vehicle slowly in motion, gradually crushing the life out of him.

The notorious Wheel and Bed was a sophistication of the Middle Ages. The prisoner was strapped to a ladder-like bed where the 'rungs' were raised and sharpened along their upper edge, and a weighted wheel then rolled up and down his body. Breaking on the wheel was

* Sometimes the wheel was replaced by two beams of wood in the figure of a St Andrew's cross – see **Breaking on the Cross**.

common throughout Europe and survived to the end of
the eighteenth century.

Wheel and bed

Various wheel tortures were known in the ancient world,
and later became firm favourites of the Romans who used
them in their ceaseless persecution of the early Christians.
Exclusive to the Romans was joining together two wheels
with flat planks of timber to form a cylinder. The engine
was rolled to the top of a slope, and, to make it heavier,
was filled with rocks. The victim was tied to the cylinder
so that he was bent backwards around the circumference;
as the drum was pushed down the slope, gradually picking
up speed, it crushed and mutilated the body in a most
hideous manner.

Another ingenious Roman wheel was a sort of hybrid
rack. The wheel itself was mounted on a shaft with handles either side for the purpose of turning it; around the
edge of the wheel were numerous vicious curved spikes.
It was around this edge and on top of the spikes the
prisoner was tightly bound. A rope was attached to his
feet and passed through a ring secured to the bed of the

Roman cylinder

Wheel and rack

wheel frame; this rope was held taut by several men while two others operated the handles that turned the wheel. The result was that the victim's body was torn to shreds by the spikes as well as being stretched by the rope. Finally the body would become so traumatised that the effort of pulling would tear it in two.

In the museum at the Bastille in Paris a very elaborate wheel torture is preserved. The wheel is mounted vertically on a shaft which is raised some eighteen inches off the ground. Close to the base of the supports were several rows of sharp metal spikes the position of which could be adjusted by the executioner so that when a prisoner was bound naked around the rim of the wheel and the wheel slowly rotated, it dragged his body across the spikes. At first the points just scratched the body, but as they were gradually moved in towards the wheel they inflicted greater and greater damage until they had ripped through to the bones and into the organs of the rapidly expiring victim. In a different version the effect is reversed, and the cruel spikes are embedded around the wheel itself and the prisoner bound to a plank beneath it. When the wheel was turned the teeth tore his flesh to shreds and disembowelled him.

Probably the best-known victim of the Wheel was St Catherine of Alexandria in the fourth century. According to her legend, Catherine was born into a patrician family in Alexandria. A vision of the Virgin and Child converted her to Christianity, and Catherine became so fearless in her faith that when Maxentius began his persecution the eighteen-year-old ordered him to stop the tyrannies immediately. Maxentius, finding himself unable to defend his pagan gods against the girl's arguments, sent for fifty philosophers to do the job professionally. When they too failed to do more than strengthen Catherine's belief, all fifty were burned to death. Worse still, she had managed to convert Maxentius's wife, the senior officer of his army and several hundred soldiers. All were immediately slain and Catherine was sentenced to die on the spiked wheel. No sooner had she been bound to the monstrous machine

*The Infernal Punishments of the Seven Deadly Sins: the prideful
are broken on the wheel*

than the ropes miraculously loosened and the wheel was
rent asunder, scattering spikes in all directions and killing
a number of bystanders. In the end Catherine was
beheaded, and it is said that instead of blood, a milk-
white liquid flowed from her veins. Catherine became a
very popular saint in Europe and it was her voice which
spoke to Joan of Arc. The pyrotechnic called a 'Catherine
Wheel' is a reference to her martyrdom.

Whipping
(see **Flagellation**)

Whipping at the Cart's Tail
(see **Flagellation**)

Whirligig
In his *Punishments of Former Days*, Pettifer repeats a description of a rare type of pillory called a whirligig, first noted by C. W. Hatfield, the Doncaster historian. It was, apparently, 'a round wooden cage, turning on a pivot'. The culprit, guilty usually of some fairly modest offence, was placed in the cage and spun round, which caused extreme disorientation and nausea. Pettifer concludes: 'Whether this really happened . . . or whether Hatfield dreamed of it after an evening on a roundabout at the Doncaster Fair cannot now be decided.' In fact this design of rotating pillory was common on the mainland of Europe, certainly during the late eighteenth century, and was a cage in which prisoners stood to be mocked. It was usually attached to the front of some public building such as the town hall. The citizens of Rothenburg called their device the Fool's Cell, and the example in the city of Berne in Switzerland was known as the trülle (see **Pillory**).

A 'Whirlgig' [*sic*] was described as being in use in the American army in 1788, and it was said that 'lunacy and imbecility' often followed excessive punishment.

Wild Animals
(see **Roman Circus**)

Witch Trials
Although there is evidence of strict laws governing the practice of witchcraft in England from early Anglo-Saxon times, the concept of its evil was based on the purely

practical expedient of punishing crimes against man and against his property. However, the spread of the Church of Rome throughout western Europe ensured that witchcraft would eventually be seen as a heresy and an offence against God, and the suppression of heretics – real or imagined – became a crusade (see **Inquisition**). The Spanish Inquisition was established in Castile with royal assent in 1478, with Thomas de Torquemada as Grand Inquisitor. Aimed especially at the Jews and the Moors, its initial mandate was the eradication of all heretical beliefs and practices. By a Bull of Pope Sixtus V in 1585, the Inquisition was enabled to eradicate all forms of sorcery. In 1486 Jakob Sprenger and Heinrich Kramer composed the terrifying treatise on 'Witchcraft, Its Discovery, Treatment and Cure' called the *Malleus Maleficarum* (see **Inquisition**), a practical handbook on each step in the denunciation, trial and execution of 'heretics'. It is impossible to compute the numbers of the Spanish Inquisition victims, but in 1481 it is said that 3,000 were burned in Andalucia alone, and 17,000 others tortured.

Two Dominican monks burned at the stake for witchcraft by order of the Inquisition, Geneva, 1549

A Day in the Life. . . .
Translation of a report made by the overseer of a torturer
responsible for 'questioning' a suspected witch at Pross-
neck, Germany, in 1629.

1. The hangman bound her hands, cut off her hair and placed the woman on a ladder. He poured alcohol on her head and set it afire in order to burn the hair to the roots.

2. He placed strips of sulphur under her arms and around her back and set fire to them also.

3. He tied her hands behind her back and hoisted her to the ceiling by a pulley; she was left hanging there for about three or four hours while the executioner was away at breakfast.

5. On his return he threw alcohol over the woman's back and set fire to it; he attached heavy weights to her body and drew her up again to the ceiling. After that the hangman put her back on the ladder and placed a very rough plank full of sharp points against her body. Having thus arranged her, he jerked her up again to the ceiling.

6. Afterwards he squeezed her thumbs and big toes in a vice, and trussed up her arms with a stick; in this position he kept her hanging for about a quarter of an hour, until she fainted away several times. Then he squeezed the calves and the legs in the vice, always alternating the torture with questioning.

7. The hangman then whipped the woman with a raw-hide whip which caused the blood to flow out over her shift. Once again he placed her thumbs and big toes in the vice and left her thus in agony on the torture stool from ten in the morning till one o'clock

after noon while the court officials and the executioner took sustenance.

8. In the afternoon a functionary arrived who disapproved of this harsh procedure. But they whipped the suspect again in a frightful manner to conclude the first day of torture.

The next day they started all over again, but without quite such savagery as the previous day.

The Witch Hunts in Britain

At first the insular nature of Britain protected it in large measure from the worst excesses of the Inquisition; although 'sorcery' was still legislated against, penalties were mild – one has only to recall the penalty meted out to one William Byg who, for using a crystal ball, was sentenced merely to appear in public with a notice on his head inscribed '*Ecce sortilegus*' ('behold the fortune-teller'), and compare it with the many thousands of 'sorcerers' across the channel in France who had already been put to the fire.

Witchcraft first became a heinous crime in England under a 1563 statute of Queen Elizabeth I, arising in part from political insecurity and in part from pressure from the clergy. This Act of Elizabeth made the invocation of spirits 'whereby any persons shall be killed or destroyed, or wasted, consumed or lamed in his or her body or matter' an offence punishable by death. The steady growth of superstition during the Queen's reign is amply exhibited by the spectacular nature of some of the contemporary trials – at Chelmsford in 1566, the first major witch hunt in England; at St Osyth in 1582; and the extraordinary trial of the Warboys Witches at which, in 1593, three completely innocent people were executed as result of the caprice of five children.

In 1604 James I increased the severity of the punishments for all kinds of witchcraft, and the eastern counties trembled before the name of Matthew Hopkins, self-styled

Father Urbain Grandier publicly executed for allegedly signing a pact with the Devil; Loudun, 1634

Witch Finder-General of England, responsible for the executions of more than a hundred so-called 'witches' and the imprisonment and torture of countless others. Hopkins masterminded the lurid trials of the Manningtree

¶ The Apprehension and confession

of three notorious Witches.

Arreigned and by Iustice condemned and

executed at *Chelmes-forde*, in the Countye of
Essex, the 5. day of Iulye, last past.

1 5 8 9.

¶ With the manner of their diuelish practices and keeping of their
spirits, whose fourmes are heerein truelye
proportioned.

IOAN PRENTIS
& hir Bid

IACK

GILL

witches in 1645, and the Bury St Edmunds witches in the same year.

Earlier, a number of notable local witch hunts had resulted in the executions of the witches of Northamptonshire on 22 July 1612, and the deaths of many of the Lancashire witches tried in August of the same year.

Of the many pamphlets, broadsides and chapbooks recounting the trials and executions of the witches in England, the most remarkable – for its style, its accuracy and detail, and its retention of atmosphere – is *The Wonderful Discovery of Witches in the County of Lancaster*, written by Thomas Potts, clerk to the Lancaster court, and published in London in 1613. The book is uncommonly long and recounts many instances of 'bewitching to death' or murder by witchcraft. In all, ten of the 'witches' were hanged, and the one called Old Demdike died in gaol before trial.

The last witch to hang in England was Alice Molland at Exeter in 1684, though with the restoration of the Stuart line in 1660 there were few executions, and most indictments for witchcraft were charged only with the more serious crimes of murder and destruction. The last recorded witch trial was in 1712 when Jane Wenham was convicted at the Hertford Assizes but not executed.

Wooden Horse (1)

According to Swain this was the instrument responsible for spreading the terror of the **Inquisition** to the Netherlands, at that time a Spanish dominion. It is described by Ernestus Eremundus Frisius in his *History of the Low Country Disturbances*:

> There is a wooden bench, which they call the Wooden Horse, made hollow like a trough, so as to contain a man lying on his back at full length, about the middle of which there is a round bar laid across upon which the back of the victim is placed so that he lies upon the bar instead of being let into the

bottom of the trough, with his feet much higher than his head. As he is lying in this posture his arms, thighs and shins are tied round with small cords or strings which, being drawn with screws at proper distances from each other, cut into the very bones so as to be no longer discerned. Besides this the torturer throws over his mouth and nostrils a thin cloth so that he is scarcely able to breathe through them. Meanwhile a small stream of water like a thread – not drop by drop – falls from on high upon the mouth of the person lying in this miserable condition, and so easily does the thin cloth sink to the bottom of his throat, that there is no possibility of breathing, his mouth being stopped with water and his nostrils with the cloth, so that the poor wretch is in the same agony as persons ready to die and breathing their last. When this cloth is drawn out of his throat, as it often is in order that he may answer questions, it is all wet with water and blood, and is like pulling his bowels through his mouth.

It is surprising to find this combination of water torture and the rack being called a Wooden Horse, and were it not attested by Swain might be thought an error. Scott* also cautions against this same confusion in relating the ordeal of William Lithgow, a Scot who, in 1620, was tortured as a spy by the Spanish at Malaga. In this case the rack was of an unusual upright triangular form, but the water torture similar:

Then the tormenter having charged the first passage above my body . . . he went to an earthen jar standing full of water a little beneath my head; from whence, carrying a pot full of water, in the bottom whereof there was an incised hole which he stopped with his thumb until it came to my mouth, when he

* The Total Discourse of the Rare Adventures and painefull peregrinations . . . , William Lithgow, 1640.

did release it and pour it in my belly (the measure being a Spanish *sombre* which is an English pottle [about half a gallon]. The first and second of these treatments I gladly received, such was the scorching drought of my tormenting pain and that I had not drunk for three days before. But afterwards, at the third charge . . . Oh strangling tortures!

Wooden Horse (2)

This military punishment was carried out on an apparatus more closely resembling a horse, and was current in England and in America when that country was a British colony. The body of the 'horse' was constructed from planks of wood nailed together at an angle to form a sharp ridge representing the animal's back. This was raised to a height of six or seven feet on four 'legs', and to complete

Spanish Donkey

the irony a modelled head and a tail were often attached. The victim was mounted astride the ridge, his hands tied behind his back and heavy weights suspended from each ankle. In this painful position a prisoner would remain for many hours, experiencing such agony that it was eventually outlawed as a punishment in England, 'Riding the wooden horse having been found to injure the men materially, and sometimes to rupture them'.

A similar arrangement was known as the Spanish Donkey, and consisted of a single vertical plank of wood, sharpened at its top edge and held secure by heavy crosspieces at its base. The naked victim was made to straddle the Donkey, and increasingly heavy weights attached to his feet; it is recorded that many of its victims were almost literally cut in two by the Donkey.

INDEX

On the following pages are details of some other books available in the True Crime series

THE BUTCHERS

by Brian Lane

Which is the most effective way to dispose of a corpse? Eat it? Dip it in acid? Feed it to pigs? Turn it into sausages? Or put it in the furnace?

These are among the tried and tested methods of the thirty cold-blooded killers in *The Butchers*, from Dennis Nilsen to Marcel Petiot and Albert Fish, who compounded their original crimes of murder with deliberate and macabre mutilations.

However meticulous and ingenious, none of them got away, but only painstaking investigation and forensics led to the final unmasking of the sadists and psychotics who sought such bloody concealment of their crimes.

ISBN 0 86369 600 7

PRECIOUS VICTIMS

by Don W. Weber and Charles Bosworth Jr

Who would believe a mother could murder her own baby? It seemed the least likely explanation to the Jersey County police when they heard Paula Sims' story of a masked kidnapper in June 1986. But then, in April 1989, her second newborn daughter suffered an identical fate. This time the police would not stop searching until they had discovered the whole, horrifying truth.

Written by the lawyer who won the case, and the reporter who covered it from beginning to end, *Precious Victims* is a riveting journey into the twisted heart of a family with a dark and murderous secret.

ISBN 0 86369 598 1

DAMSEL OF DEATH

by Sue Russell

On Death Row in Florida is the rarest of criminals – a female serial killer.

Arrested in January 1991, Aileen Wuornos confessed to murdering seven men. Abandoned by her mother and abused by her grandfather, at eleven she had prostituted herself; at fourteen she became pregnant; and by thirty-three she had begun to kill. In this gripping true story, British journalist Sue Russell slices through the horror of America's underbelly to find out what made the quiet little girl from Michigan grow up into a multiple killer.

ISBN 0 86369 608 2

THE RED RIPPER

by Peter Conradi

He was a soft-spoken grandfather. The 'perfect' family man. A former Russian literature teacher. And a serial killer.

Beneath Andrei Chikatilo's model-citizen exterior lurked the warped mind of one of the most prolific killers of all time. At his 1992 trial, watched in his cage by the world's media, Chikatilo was convicted of murdering a horrifying total of 52 women and children over twelve years.

Peter Conradi, an English journalist based in Moscow, has interviewed key figures – from the police who finally caught Chikatilo (six years after an initial arrest in 1984) to the psychiatrist who helped track him down – to lay bare a damaged mind in a damaged society.

ISBN 0 86369 618 X

A QUESTION OF EVIDENCE

by Christopher Berry-Dee
with Robin Odell

When Brighton nine-year-olds Karen Hadaway and Nicola Fellows were sexually assaulted, strangled and found in a park near their homes, local man Russell Bishop became the sole suspect and the story was meant to be over. Even though Bishop was found not guilty, the police decided the case should be closed . . .

But this was no ordinary murder investigation. Blighted by a string of police and forensic misjudgements that raise many chilling and still unanswered questions, the case is a damning indictment of the English judicial system. This startling and disturbing account by renowned investigative writers Christopher Berry-Dee and Robin Odell is the first serious attempt to answer the grim question – 'Who killed the Babes in the Wood?'

'A well-researched, highly persuasive argument . . . an admirable lack of hysteria'
Time Out

ISBN 0 86369 636 8

THE SERIAL KILLERS

by Colin Wilson and Donald Seaman

White. Twenty-eight years old. High IQ. And a law student. Yuppie success story?

No, portrait of a serial killer. Ted Bundy, one of the most notorious serial killers of recent years, confessed to killing 23 women. But he was no aberration. Statistics show that most serial killers are young, white, intelligent males. Triggered by either sexual fantasies or a need to inflict pain and fear, their sadistic addiction to frenzied killing is the most horrifying of all crimes. And serial killers are increasing at an alarming rate.

But with the formation of the world's first National Centre for the Analysis of Violent Crime in Virginia, made famous in the hugely popular *The Silence of the Lambs*, the methods of tracking down these killers have been revolutionised.

Using their privileged access to the centre's sophisticated techniques of pyschological profiling, Colin Wilson and Donald Seaman have produced the most comprehensive study to date of this terrifying modern phenomenon. *The Serial Killers* is the definitive study of the psychology of the criminal mind.

ISBN 0 86369 615 5

THE LONG DROP

by Christopher Berry-Dee
and Robin Odell

Late in the evening of 26 September 1927, PC George Gutteridge, the village policeman of Stapleford Abbots in Essex, attempted to stop a speeding car. Instead, he was murdered, both of his eyes shot out in a horrific attack.

In April 1928 Frederick Guy Browne and William Henry Kennedy were tried for the murder and hanged. It seemed an open and shut case. Or was it?

According to Kennedy's solicitor (Christopher Berry-Dee's grandfather), Browne was never at the scene of the crime, and the police knew it. A detailed analysis of the trial and hitherto unrevealed evidence shows that the basis on which Kennedy was convicted was dubious in the extreme and obtained by questionable tactics, and that Browne's conviction and execution was a tragic miscarriage of justice in which the police colluded. Like Derek Bentley, the subject of the authors' much-acclaimed book *Dad, Help Me Please*, Browne was the victim of a judicial system determined that someone should hang for the killing of one of their own.

In the light of recent events, *The Long Drop* is a timely reminder that police injustice has always been with us, and a powerful argument against the reintroduction of the death penalty.

ISBN 0 86369 603 1

DYING TO GET MARRIED
The Courtship and Murder of Julie Miller Bulloch

by Ellen Harris

At 30, Julie Miller was a successful executive who dreamed of a white knight who would come and bring romance to her well-ordered life. Then, after placing an ad in a St Louis personal column, Julie met Dennis Bulloch. Movie-star handsome, an MBA, a member of the young Republicans, he seemed to be the perfect husband.

But underneath the perfect façade was a violent, disturbed man. A compulsive womaniser and social climber, Bulloch married Julie for her money and connections. Just ten weeks after their wedding, Julie's burnt body was discovered after a fire in the garage. Naked, she had been bound to a rocking chair with more than 76 feet of tape.

The shocking true story of Julie Miller Bulloch's desperate search for love and her tragic death is the story of an American dream that turned into a brutal nightmare.

ISBN 0 86369 638 4

HANGMAN
From Ketch to Pierrepoint –
300 Years of Execution

by Brian Bailey

'Capital punishment achieved nothing except revenge,' wrote Albert Pierrepoint, the man who hanged Ruth Ellis in 1955. Yet for well over 300 years, the chilling figure of the hangman has fascinated and revolted by turns. Even the sinister shapes of the gallows and the noose fade in the shadow of the men who carried out the ultimate penalty.

Here is the full, grim story of these men, from the infamous Jack Ketch to William Marwood (inventor of the 'long drop') and Albert Pierrepoint, the last state executioner. The earliest hangmen, many recruited from the same prisons as their victims, established a brutal and brutalising tradition which culminated in the sophisticated professionalism of the nineteenth and twentieth centuries – a tradition which came to an end in Britain only a quarter of a century ago.

ISBN 0 86369 623 6